CARTEL CRIMINALITY

Cartel Criminality
The Mythology and Pathology of Business Collusion

CHRISTOPHER HARDING

JENNIFER EDWARDS

Aberystwyth University, UK

ASHGATE

Published by
Ashgate Publishing Limited
Wey Court East
Union Road
Farnham
Surrey, GU9 7PT
England

Ashgate Publishing Company
110 Cherry Street
Suite 3-1
Burlington, VT 05401-3818
USA

www.ashgate.com

British Library Cataloguing in Publication Data
A catalogue record for this book is available from the British Library.

The Library of Congress has cataloged the printed edition as follows:
Harding, Christopher, author.
  Cartel criminality : the mythology and pathology of business collusion / By Christopher Harding and Jennifer Edwards.
     pages cm
  Includes bibliographical references and index.
  ISBN 978-1-4094-2529-8 (hardback) -- ISBN 978-1-4094-2530-4 (ebook) -- ISBN 978-1-4724-0312-4 (epub) 1. Antitrust law--Criminal provisions. 2. Cartels. 3. Commercial crimes. 4. Restraint of trade. I. Edwards, Jennifer, (Research assistant), author. II. Title.
  K3854.H37 2015
  364.16'8--dc23

2015025269

ISBN: 9781409425298 (hbk)
ISBN: 9781409425304 (ebk – PDF)
ISBN: 9781472403124 (ebk – ePUB)

MIX
Paper from
responsible sources
FSC
www.fsc.org FSC® C013985

Printed in the United Kingdom by Henry Ling Limited,
at the Dorset Press, Dorchester, DT1 1HD

Contents

List of Tables

List of Figures

Preface

This work sets out ambitiously to be a first dedicated criminology of business cartels. The topic – that of now widely condemned and intensively regulated business strategies such as price fixing, market sharing and bid rigging – has become the subject of an increasingly voluminous critical literature, which is for the most part to be found in the academic domains of law and economics. But as the policy and practice of regulation has moved into a higher gear and enforcement has become more repressive, with an increasing resort to criminal law and quasi-criminal sanctions, the time is ripe for a detailed criminological investigation of the phenomenon of cartelisation and its legal control. In so far as there has been a significant programme of criminalisation of business cartels, this incursion of criminal law into the sphere of business activity deserves critical attention and assessment, not least for what it reveals about the nature of contemporary governance and the interface of the political, the economic and the legal in global society. The justification for such a policy of enforcement and an account of its operation is an important matter, since this is a major public intervention, involving significant resources and consequences. The focus of this criminological enquiry has been the working and impact of the legal sanctions that have been deployed more and more extensively and in an increasingly determined fashion over the last 30 or so years. Much of the material drawn upon in the following report of this research has been assembled as part of a research project carried out by CH and JE at Aberystwyth University, and funded by a grant from the Leverhulme Trust: 'Explaining and Understanding Business Cartel Collusion'.

The research has been undertaken in a certain empirical manner, in the sense of examining the actual record of enforcement in relation to major international business cartels since the start of the 1980s. The method has been described as 'biographical', since the analysis and argument have been based on narratives of enforcement, which have been used to present an historical account of the prehistory, the actual operation of cartels and anti-cartel legal enforcement, and then cartelist 'after-life'. The centrepiece of the discussion set out here is a selection of 'cartel biographies', which seek to draw out the salient features of cartel activity and its legal regulation. The reader of the book will be presented first with a theoretical and methodological discussion of the topic and the approach being taken in the research, then with a set of narratives, and finally with some concluding analysis and argument derived from those narratives. Without wishing to spoil too much the reader's anticipation of those conclusions, there is a clear message which emerges from a reading of those narratives – that global and international cartel regulation is a complex and imperfectly understood matter, an uneasy amalgam of strong rhetoric and uncertain outcome, bedevilled by inarticulate ambition, dauntingly complicated issues of agency and, above all, diverse cultures of both business activity and legal enforcement. Anti-cartel enforcement has become big global business, but its motivation, operation and outcomes, despite the assured tone adopted by many regulators, economists, lawyers and politicians, remain hard to pin down. In this sense, a criminological investigation and its conclusions appear more unsettling than many of the assumptions and arguments of lawyers and economists, the two groups of experts who have to date arguably been driving the policy and regulatory agenda.

As already indicated, the underlying research here has most recently been based on the project based at Aberystwyth and funded by the Leverhulme Trust, with CH as the principal investigator and JE as the project researcher and co-author. For CH the subject and the research project have a prehistory which could be turned into another narrative in its own right. As with any story-telling, the problem is to know where to begin. Perhaps, once upon a time in the early 1970s, cartel regulation was not exactly a new subject as such (as will be evident from some of the discussion in this book), but at that time its European and criminal law dimensions, now so significant and manifest, were barely contemplated. The seminal *Quinine* and *Dysestuffs* Cases had only just happened when CH and fellow postgraduate student William Allan met on Waterloo station half way through the Christmas vacation to exchange the one copy of Arved Deringer's 1968 book *The Competition Law of the EEC* (referred to in Chapter 3) then available in the University of Exeter library. Well, that was the way the subject was studied in those days. Some, in fact many, years later, the same two were together again, talking about business cartels, CH by then Professor of Law at Aberystwyth University and Bill with much experience of competition law practice working for Linklaters, and embarking upon a term of office with the UK Competition Appeal Tribunal. Walking up and down in Bill's garden, CH asked whether Bill thought there was any evidence that large firms responded positively to anti-cartel sanctions and reformed their way of doing business as a result. Bill's remarks were typically insightful, but served only to reinforce CH's view of the complexity and obscurity of the subject. And in such a way the Leverhulme project and its underlying criminological approach began to materialise and take on this present shape.

More recently, CH and JE have benefited from a number of expert encounters and discussions. CH should acknowledge an ongoing debt to his former collaborator and co-author Julian Joshua, who, as a veteran cartel-buster and sharp legal adviser, provided invaluable lessons about what theorising could draw upon from the practice of enforcement. Along the way, a number of colleagues and friends have shown an interest, asked valuable questions and passed perceptive comment. The following deserve special mention for giving their time and providing insight, shrewd observation and critical feedback, although without wishing to attribute any complicity in the present authors' final analysis and conclusions (in other words, do not hold them responsible for anything which follows here which may appear outrageous or daft rather than wise): Bill Allan (as above), Caron Beaton-

Wells, Scott Crosby, Jeffrey Fear, Vanessa Franssen, Richard Havell, Michael O'Kane, Andreas Stephan, Melanie Williams and Wouter Wils.

Having become narratologists as well as legal scholars and criminologists, the present authors are well aware that they are here presenting just one story, one account of the subject, among a number of possible narratives. But that, after all, is how we all see life around us. They are also aware that this is a story which, for the present, ends at a point in 2015. Even this book and its writers will have an after-life, and that might include a continuation of the story or the telling of further related tales. One thing is certain, and that is that the subject is not over and completed, a matter just for history, at the present time, and that the literature will continue. The aim here is to provide a helpful staging-post in that journey of research and discussion.

Christopher Harding,
Jennifer Edwards,
Aberystwyth, February 2015.

A Note on Reading the Text

In presenting the discussion in this book a device of layout has been used to supplement some of the detail of the subject without intruding too much on the flow and readability of the main discussion and argument, by inserting incidentally some further information and discussion at an appropriate point in a box. In effect, the reader may treat the boxed discussion rather like a detailed footnote reference of the kind which provides something further and supplementary in the form of comment, argument or additional information aside the main text. As such, the reader may decide to skip the content of the box, or reserve it for later reading and reference, so enabling the main part of the book to be read in different ways, or at a different pace at different times, depending on the reader's time and level of interest.

An Alphabet Glossary

The Alphabet Glossary is intended as a guide to terminology and names for those approaching the subject for the first time or less familiar with the commonly used vocabulary.

A is for ANTITRUST. An American (US) term to describe the area of law and policy concerned with anti-competitive business behaviour.

B is for BOSCH. Carl Bosch was a German industrial chemist, Nobel laureate, entrepreneur and early cartel designer, associated with the BASF company and the emergence of IG Farben. There is a Carl Bosch museum in Heidelberg.

C is for CARTEL. The term used to describe a business arrangement in which, typically, competing suppliers agree to restrict competition between themselves.

D is for DUISBERG. Friedrich Carl Duisberg was also a German industrial chemist and entrepreneur, and pioneer cartelist, associated with the Bayer company and a leader of IG Farben.

E is for EUROPEAN COMMISSION. The Commission is a leading EU institution and has developed a major role in the formulation and enforcement of competition policy and become a significant prosecutor of major business cartels.

F is for FINANCIAL PENALTY. This is the sanction (a 'fine') typically applied to corporate cartel offenders in anti-cartel enforcement.

G is for GAMING. A view of cartel activity and its legal control as a kind of game. Economists employ **GAME THEORY** to analyse cartel behaviour and the ability of cartelists to exploit regulatory methods such as Leniency programmes is sometimes referred to as leniency gaming.

H is for HOECHST. Hoechst AG was a German chemicals company with a long-term involvement in cartel activity and since 1999 part of the Aventis company. Notorious as the subject of periodic penalty payments imposed by the EC Commission for non-compliance in a cartel investigation.

I is for IMMUNITY. A term often applied to the legal immunity from sanctions awarded to the first provider of crucial evidence under a leniency programme.

J is for JULIAN JOSHUA. A British lawyer who spent many years as a cartel investigator for the EC/EU Commission, and co-author of a leading work on anti-cartel enforcement, *Regulating Cartels in Europe*.

K is for KROES. Neelie Kroes was a Dutch politician, then EU Commissioner for Competition from 2004 until 2009, and noted for an energeti, 'zero tolerance' approach and rhetoric in relation to anti-cartel enforcement (for instance her speech in Brasilia in 2009).

L is for LENIENCY PROGRAMME. A 'carrot and stick' enforcement device pioneered by the US Department of Justice and now employed by competition authorities globally, offering legal immunity to an insider cartelist who is first to provide crucial evidence of a cartel's activity.

M is for MARINE HOSE CARTEL. An international cartel busted by the Department of Justice in 2007 and giving rise to a number of legal issues, notably the first convictions under the UK Enterprise Act 2002 for the British cartel offence, as part of a deal with the US authorities.

N is for NONCOMPEARANCE. Resistance to and defiance of the rules against cartels and in relation to the possible imposition of sanctions, a major challenge for anti-cartel enforcement and the work of competition authorities.

O is for OPTIMAL SANCTION or PENALTY. A concept employed by economists to indicate in economic terms the most effective deterrent penalty which will serve to dissuade illegal cartel activity by removing the prospect of illegal gain.

P is for PRISON TERM. Imprisonment is advocated by many regulators and academic commentators as a sanction to be applied to individuals involved in cartel activity, as a deterrent and effective component ('stick') of leniency programmes.

Q is for QUININE CARTEL. The Quinine Cartel was a long-established international cartel, notorious for the first-ever imposition of fines on companies by the EC Commission in 1969 for involvement in a cartel.

R is for ROCKEFELLER. John D. Rockefeller was a leading American business magnate and philanthropist, notable for his role in establishing Standard Oil as an early American monopolist organisation and example of an anti-competitive trust arrangement.

S is for SHERMAN ACT. Iconic US legislation of 1890, enacted to regulate trusts and other anti-competitive activities and notable for its use of the legal concept of conspiracy. It provides a leading model of dogmatic condemnation and the use of criminal law for purposes of enforcement.

T is for TREBLE DAMAGES. Part of the Sherman Act strategy to deal severely with anti-competitive behaviour, enabling injured parties to claim compensation, which is multiplied by three times the actual assessed amount of injury.

U is for USUAL SUSPECT. A term which may be used to describe an offender with a known record of offending behaviour, and so may be applied to repeat offenders or recidivists in a criminal law context. A number of well-known companies would qualify as usual suspects in relation to cartel activity.

V is for VITAMINS CARTELS. A number of significant cartels in the vitamins market dealt with by competition authorities in the 1990s, discussed in a paper 'The Great Global Vitamins Cartels' by John M. Connor.

W is for WOOD PULP CARTEL. A major alleged cartel in the wood pulp market, dealt with by the EC Commission in the 1980s and leading to a notable ruling by the European Court of Justice, which rejected the use of circumstantial market evidence to establish cartel collusion, arguably then a trigger for the development of such enforcement methods as dawn raids and leniency programmes.

X is for E(X)ECUTIVE. A term applied to describe an individual employed at a high managerial level in a company who may be implicated in the operation of cartel strategies on behalf of the company.

Y is for YOKOHAMA. A Japanese company involved in the Marine Hose Cartel, and the whistle-blower (immunity applicant) in relation to that cartel.

Z is for ZERO TOLERANCE. Tough talking on the part of governments and law enforcement agencies that certain illegal conduct will be vigorously prosecuted and sanctioned, characteristic of the tone of the rhetoric of competition authorities in relation to cartel activities since the 1990s.

Glossary of Explanatory and Analytical Concepts and Metaphors

ACTOR SENSITIVITY. The way in which, or degree to which, individual or corporate actors may be susceptible to legal sanctions and may be affected by such sanctions. > **CULTURE OF RECEPTION** – the context in which such sensitivity occurs and develops.

AGENCY (INDIVIDUAL, COLLECTIVE, CORPORATE). The capacity for action on the part of individual, collective or corporate entities as a basis for assessing that action.

BUST (> CARTEL CRACKING). The legal identification and investigation of a cartel which effectively brings to an end its operation ('cracking' is the preferred term of some economists).

CARTEL BIOGRAPHY (or NARRATIVE). A narrative account based on factual evidence of the antecedent circumstances ('pre-history'), and actual operation of a business cartel, and the consequent history of its human and corporate participants ('after-life').

CARTEL AS A BOX. An explanatory device, as used by Harding and Joshua (2010), to model the necessary external elements of any cartel arrangement (duration, market and geographical scope, and membership).

CARTEL CIRCLES AND ORBITING. An explanatory tool used by Harding and Edwards (2012) to model the internal elements of participation in and membership of a cartel.

CARTEL DELINQUENCY (> TYPOLOGY OF INFRINGEMENTS > SPECTRUM OF DELINQUENCY > SPIRAL OF DELINQUENCY > DELINQUENCY RANKING). The normatively prescribed activity involved in a cartel arrangement, judged according to its mode of conduct and/or its harmful consequences (see also **Offences of conduct and outcome**).

CARTELIST PROFILING. Criminological analysis based on an examination of the roles of particular individuals and companies in a cartel operation as a way of identifying levels and types of delinquent business behaviour.

COSYING (> 'BETTER TOGETHER'). Regular joint participation by two or more businesses in the same cartels over time and/or in related markets (regular co-conspiracy).

DANCING GIANT. A metaphor originally applied by Barham and Heimer in 1998 to describe the multinational company Asea Brown Boveri (ABB), as a 'globally connected corporation' (see Chapter 5), and more widely applicable (in later chapters) to large transnational companies with complex corporate structures and operating in a number of different markets.

DENOUEMENT ANALYSIS. A method of analysis based upon a certain narrative reading of particular outcomes (denouements) and using the latter to explain action and motivation.

ENFORCEMENT IMPERATIVE. The preferences, interests and goals of enforcement authorities and agents as a major determinant of efforts of legal control.

ENFORCEMENT or LENIENCY GAMING. A strategic response by the subjects of legal enforcement which exploits in a self-interested way the business and other opportunities presented by such enforcement.

ENFORCEMENT PROCLIVITY. The preferred strategies, methods and procedures of particular enforcement agencies.

GARDEN STATE. The description of an economic market in contrast to a state of nature, chaos or 'anarchy', whereby 'gardeners', usually public regulators, develop and impose order.

IMPACT REPORT. An assessment of the effect of sanctions according to certain objectives and criteria.

INFERNO. How the prospect of imprisonment (and other associated penal consequences) may be viewed by individual business actors. A metaphor employed by those, especially American commentators, wishing to assert the deterrent effect of criminal law sanctions.

MARKET DIVERSION. A strategic response by the subjects of legal enforcement involving an evasive relocation to different markets or geographical areas.

MAVERICK. An idiosyncratic and unpredictable actor highly motivated by individualised self-interest.

NORMATIVE ESCALATION (> SPIRAL OF ENFORCEMENT). The development of an increasing number of levels and amount of normative control and regulation, generating its own dynamic and leading to an upward spiral of enforcement activity.

OFFENCES OF CONDUCT AND OUTCOME. A categorisation of delinquency according to either its method of accomplishment (conduct) or its effects and impact (outcome).

RECIDIVISM. Repetition of offending behaviour, usually sequentially (in criminological literature) or perhaps contemporaneously (in the context of cartels and organised delinquent activity).

SANCTION ACCUMULATION. The 'whole panoply (or full amour) of sanctions'. The accumulation or multiplication of legal and other sanctions in relation to the same category of conduct, either across a number of jurisdictions or taking into account multiple victims ('spectrum of victimhood') of the conduct, possibly raising concerns about unjustifiable 'double counting' of offences for purposes of penalty ('double jeopardy', or *ne bis in idem*).

USUAL SUSPECT. A company that regularly engages in cartel conduct over time and in different markets. The term may be used to describe a repeat offender or recidivist.

PART I
Theory and Method: Probing the Pathology and Mythology of Business Collusion

The first three chapters of the book provide an overview and discussion of what might be described as a criminology of business collusion and cartel activity. In effect, this is the theory and method of the subject as a criminological study. Chapter 1 supplies some orientation, or mapping out of the subject in disciplinary terms, in order to locate the role of criminological enquiry into this subject within the broader field of legal, social scientific and historical discussion. It also raises an argument and critical line of enquiry, casting the subject as a pathology (the presentation of cartelisation as a disorder) and a mythology (that presentation as an ideology). Chapter 2 examines cartelisation as a business activity and strategy and in doing so engages in an ontology of the subject (in what sense cartels may be said to exist), then a phenomenological enquiry (how to understand the actuality of the practice), and finally an examination of the agency of the subject (identifying the relevant actors). Chapter 3 then addresses the judgmental and evaluative view of cartelisation and cartel actors, by unpacking the normative perspective on the subject and exploring and explaining the basis for regulation and legal control, and the emerging sense during the twentieth century of cartel delinquency. Put another way, the third chapter follows the route leading to pathology and mythology.

Chapter 1

Orientation

People ask: 'What, or who, is a cartel?' The best answer is: 'It is something that is in the eye of the beholder'. In a material-world sense, the term describes a kind of economic or business activity – an arrangement, between suppliers of a particular commodity or service who might normally be expected to compete with each other to ply their trade and thrive in business, not to do so. Instead they agree to charge the same price and apply similar conditions of supply, and how much they will supply, or protect each other's share of trade by allocating potential markets or the award of lucrative contracts. In short, they govern, regulate and take charge of their own market. And of course this will have certain economic or other consequences, and this last issue will always be up for discussion.

That, in broad summary, is what business cartels are all about.[1]

The emergence of the subject and the field of study

Anti-competitive business cartels, engaging in practices such as price fixing, market sharing, bid rigging and restrictions on output, are now subject to strong official censure and rigorous legal control in a large number of jurisdictions across the world. The long-standing condemnation under the US Sherman Act of 1890 has been taken up (although in a rather different form) during the last 30 years or more in the European Community/European Union and in European national jurisdictions in particular, but also in a range of countries outside North America and Europe. Legal control has not only extended geographically but has intensified, as a number of jurisdictions have moved beyond administrative regulation and penalties to embrace enforcement through civil liability and (most significantly in terms of policy and rhetoric) the methods of criminal law.[2] Indeed, it is possible to talk of a major transformation of the subject, from its historical location in the domain of economics and competition law, into a new field of criminal law, criminal justice and criminology. In the European context there has occurred a notable shift in the modalities of enforcement, strategies of prosecution and defence, and perceptions of the subject matter. In practice, criminal justice has come to predominate (even in the 'non-criminal law' EU), models of criminalisation have been actively debated, and it may be fair to say that 'cartel criminality' has come of age.

---

1   Research presentation, 2009.

2   For an overview, see Christopher Harding and Julian Joshua, *Regulating Cartels in Europe* (2nd edn, Oxford University Press, 2010).

The outcome is the emergence of an impressive and substantial infrastructure of legal control and a veritable anti-cartel regulation industry,[3] comprising an increasing number of enforcement bodies (usually competition authorities but also criminal enforcement agencies such as the US Department of Justice), courts, sectors of the legal profession, and a variety of experts, ranging from economists to game theorists and investigators of deterrent effect. The cartels themselves (especially at the international level) represent big business and large (illicit) profits, but equally the activity of legal control has become big business, based upon a huge public investment in human and material resources. It is therefore timely to consider critically this development of legal control and assess its achievement to date and its future prospects. But such an exercise requires also an understanding of the reasons and need for such regulation, based on a clear appreciation of the nature and extent of the economic and social malaise (or 'evil', to adopt some of the regulatory vocabulary) which is its subject. What, more exactly, are such business cartels, why do they come into existence and persist, why are they regarded as being so bad, and what are the objectives within this increasingly complex and multi-level phenomenon of legal control? To pose such fundamental questions is to set a research agenda for a pathology, aetiology and criminology of business cartels – to probe more accurately their nature, operation, endurance and perceived delinquency, so as to assess the working and achievement of this now significant project of regulation located at the 'sharp end' of global competition governance.[4]

The enquiry underlying this research and reported in the following account has been structured around 'five big questions' concerning cartels and the development of anti-cartel regulation, and which lead to the heart of the discussion of cartel criminality.

First, there is a question of *identity and definition*. What is a cartel? Interestingly, the word 'cartel' is not a well-developed term of legal art and rarely has a precise legal definition. There is an agreed rough notion of what comprises a cartel, but on closer examination there are difficult issues of identity and more precise definition concerning the scope of the organisation commonly termed the cartel, regarding its spatial and temporal dimensions and its constituent parts or membership. These uncertainties bedevil the process of legal control and disturb

---

3   A term used by Harding in 'The Anti-Cartel Enforcement Industry', chapter 16 in Caron Beaton-Wells and Ariel Ezrachi (eds), *Criminalising Cartels: A Critical Interdisciplinary Study of an International Regulatory Movement* (Hart Publishing, 2011).

4   'Competition governance' – understood here as public and governmental policy, management and legal regulation of economic competition – is an important context and frame of discussion for this study, which comprises essentially a critical examination of the use of criminal law and criminal sanctions as a component of such governance. 'Sharp end' is used as a convenient shorthand term to describe methods of regulation and legal control which are more incursive, confrontational and hard-hitting.

the underlying philosophy of regulation.[5] This problem of the ontology of cartels will be considered more fully in Chapter 2.

Secondly, the *moral and political basis for strong censure* remains uncertain and a matter of uneasy consensus. What is so bad about cartel activity so as to justify criminalisation? Despite a strong official rhetoric, the basis for strong condemnation remains unclear and contestable, and an effective and credible system of legal control requires a firmer foundation, and indeed legitimacy. The normative basis for the present system of regulation of cartel activity and the resort to certain types of legal sanction will be discussed further in Chapter 3.

Thirdly, a fuller understanding of the *motivation behind cartels* is necessary. Why do companies, and the individuals working for companies, enter into such prohibited activity in the first place, and often persist in such conduct in the face of strong potential sanctions? This is the real criminology of cartels, seeking to explain and understand delinquent motive, recidivist tendency and the questionable impact of deterrent strategies.

Fourthly, there is a problem of *coherence in the whole project of legal control*. What are the regulatory aims, and are these aims sensibly ordered and prioritised, and compatible with each other? To what extent is any proclaimed objective of eradicating cartels feasible; how do penal, compensatory and preventive strategies relate to each other; does it make sense to hurl so many sanctions at cartels and cartelists; to what extent is this a matter of managing public and private power relations? These are crucial questions, still awaiting clearer answers.

Finally, there is the question of *outcome*: how to understand the impact and likely consequences of the emergence of this impressive 'enforcement industry'. This is to probe the political economy of anti-cartel enforcement, to focus on the regulation rather than the perceived ill, and from this perspective to enquire about the origins, interests and future directions of this enforcement enterprise and profession.

These last three questions of cartelist motivation, and the coherence and outcome of efforts of legal control may be addressed via an examination of the application and impact of the relevant legal procedures and sanctions, and those of a criminal law and penal nature in particular. The investigation of the working and impact of such procedures and sanctions has formed the core of present research and is reported on and discussed in much of the rest of the book.

These big questions may be borne in mind as an *aide-mémoire* of the objectives of this critical discussion. At the same time, the questions may be set in an increasingly interesting cultural context, which in itself provides an illuminating lens through which to view the growth of an international regulatory movement.[6] As the process of legal control and criminalisation moves forward,

---

5 For some earlier consideration of these problems, see the discussion in chapter 6 of Harding and Joshua, *Regulating Cartels in Europe*, note 2 above.

6 The term used by Beaton-Wells and Ezrachi in the subtitle of their edited collection, *Criminalising Cartels*, note 3 above.

it is clearly becoming fractured, despite an apparent official consensus. Not only may the policy underlying criminalisation be contested (for instance by businesses and defence lawyers), but in reality, and certainly at ground level, the project of legal control is one of uneven energy, resources and commitment. For instance, there may be impressive new legislation, but then enforcement proves slow or tentative, or judges and lawyers may not share the degree of enthusiasm displayed by regulators. Or some jurisdictions may actually vote against criminalisation. At least, that is an impression of what is happening outside the US, leading to a feeling that the US and other parts of the world may not be singing from exactly the same hymn sheet after all. Such a fractured culture of enforcement tells an interesting story of governance in itself.

One further point about the nature of the subject under discussion here can usefully be emphasised at this early stage. The regulation of business cartels is a matter of significance, although it has yet to engage very much of the wider interest and concern of the general public or be taken up as a hot political issue. Indeed it is an interesting part of the story to be told here that there has been a conscious effort to depict a matter of material importance but mainly mundane aspect as something for all to be worried and excited about, and hence the metaphors of villainy and disease. But, despite the still largely low profile, the real, underlying nature of the subject has be acknowledged as economically significant (the value of trade affected), socially significant (as a matter of organisation and dealing with others), and politically significant (as a matter of contemporary governance through regulation and the emerging culture of a 'regulatory society').[7] And in essence, the subject is as much about regulation and governance as about trade, economics and competition. Yes, it is about an area of business practice and a matter of economics, about cartels per se. But equally it is about the development of a regulatory industry which has become as significant as the traditional kind of industry that is now being regulated. Should it be asked bluntly, what is the value of the research and discussion which feeds into this particular book, then a blunt answer may be given in the following terms.

> Orthodox policy and conventional wisdom argue that the operation of business cartels results in considerable economic damage, adversely affecting desirable conditions of competition and harming the interests of other traders, consumers and the functioning of a healthy open market. Cartels enable certain traders to make an illegitimate supra-competitive gain at the expense ultimately of a

---

7   On the role of regulation in contemporary governance, see the discussion by David Levi-Faur, 'Regulatory Capitalism and the Reassertion of the Public Interest', 27 (2009) *Policy and Society* 181. He argues: 'Neoliberalism has not led to the retreat of the state but instead to the restructuring of the state. This has led to new forms of governance where regulation represents the expanding part of the state, and where the various modes of governance compete and are sometimes synthesized into global forms of regulation' (at p. 181).

large number of citizen-consumers around the world (in other words, most of us lose out unfairly). There is therefore a strong public interest in controlling and eliminating such practices. Competition authorities have been given that task as part of their role, and given increasing resources and are publicly funded to do so. Their investigations and handling of individual cartel cases is time-consuming and expensive, and if that task is not carried out effectively, that may be an extra cost and loss, ultimately borne by the citizen-consumer. There is thus a strong public interest in monitoring the effectiveness of the project of legal control and in particular of the strategies employed for that purpose. The costly move towards a more incursive, hard-hitting and penal approach requires a careful monitoring and evaluation and it is important to be able to assess the impact of the range of sanctions now being employed against business cartels. In other words, if those strategies do not succeed, most of us lose out twice over.

Ownership of the subject: The province of discussion determined

The subject of business cartels and the regulation of that particular form of anti-competitive activity has undergone a major change in its categorisation, treatment and discussion over the last 50 years. Whether such cartels themselves – as they exist and operate in the material world – have undergone such change during that time and over time and place more generally is another matter, but something which will be addressed this study. But the major and continuing shift in the view of such business activity, and the way in which it is understood and interpreted and so dealt with in terms of economic policy and legal control will serve as a starting point and trigger for the discussion which follows. For undoubtedly there has been a sea-change and one of global dimension. In the middle of the twentieth century, with the exception of the United States, business cartel activity was a matter of relatively low public concern and located within a fairly new and emergent field of action described by Europeans as competition policy and law. It was largely a question of 'commercial' or 'business law', to be regulated, if at all, through private claims in contract and tort, or, if some public intervention was deemed appropriate, through administrative procedures of control.[8] By the turn of the twenty-first century the general perception and feeling was very different. There had evolved by then a strong official and governmental rhetoric of condemnation of 'hard core cartels',[9] operating as 'egregious' violations of policy and law, metaphorically like a 'cancer on the open market',[10] cartelists should be seen as 'well-dressed thieves

---

8   See for instance, Valentine Korah, *Monopolies and Restrictive Practices* (Penguin Books, 1968).

9   The term 'hard core' seems to have been first used in this context by the OECD in the later 1990s, and quickly gained wider currency.

10   Mario Monti, 'Fighting Cartels – Why and How?', Opening Address at the Third Nordic Competition Policy Conference, 11 September 2000, Stockholm.

in suits',[11] competition authorities were being established in countries around the world to deal in particular with this threat to market and consumer interests, the investigation and sanctioning of business cartels had become a major regulatory enterprise, employing increasingly sophisticated and canny methods of collecting evidence, culminating in a penalisation and criminalisation of the conduct involved in the cartel operations.[12] The road to criminalisation, to this apogee of law enforcement, provides an instructive site for the study of and reflection on present approaches to governance and regulation across the world. How has this transformation come about, how should it be understood, and what lessons may be drawn from a critical study of these developments?

The focus of the research and discussion reported here is very much the working of these present strategies of legal control of business cartels, and a consideration of how the procedures and sanctions used for that purpose can be measured and evaluated. In broad terms the study is a social scientific investigation and discussion; more specifically, in so far as there is a particular focus on the deployment of penal sanctions to deal with perceived delinquent conduct, it may be characterised as a criminological study. But as such it needs to draw upon other fields of knowledge and enquiry – more obviously, for example, the economics of cartelisation, or the history of economic policy and the governance of trade, or the jurisprudence of legal control, or organisation theory as applicable to the relation between firms and individuals – to carry out the main criminological task. It would thus be useful at this stage to say something more about the epistemology and disciplinary ownership of the subject.

It was remarked above that already there has been a notable shift in the legal *locus* of competition governance in relation to cartels, broadly from the domain of private law (contract, tort) to that of public law (administrative review and criminal law), although there also remains a significant collateral use of private law in the active encouragement of claims for damages on the part of injured private parties. In truth, antitrust or competition law may be understood as an amalgam of private domain business law, public intervention through administrative processes of review, and public intervention in the form of penal and criminal law. But the latter aspect is on the whole more recent – as will become clear in later discussion, the use of penal and criminal law processes has, for most of the world, been something that has happened in the last quarter-century.[13] Go back some time, and competition law and criminal law would not have been seen as obvious bed-fellows. In that sense, cartel criminalisation and even penalisation is a relatively new and untested project, and certainly it has not attracted so very much attention

---

11   A term apparently first used by Department of Justice Attorney General Joel I. Klein, 14 October 1999, Fordham Corporate Law Institute Annual Conference.

12   For an overview, see Harding and Joshua, *Regulating Cartels in Europe*, note 2 above.

13   Ibid.

in the field of criminology.[14] Indeed, the present work might rather ambitiously assert itself as a pioneering 'criminology of cartels'. But as a criminology of the subject, the study will have preoccupations and perspectives and ask questions in a different way from the earlier work of economists and competition lawyers, which has hitherto tended to dominate the discourse. And given that this is an enquiry which is concerned not only with cartels but also the regulation of cartels, it is important to have a good sense of the range of disciplinary perspectives on the subject and their respective value in understanding and explaining such cartel activity and its regulation and control. Moreover, it is important to emphasise at the beginning that the theoretical foundation and methodological approach of this study is determinedly interdisciplinary and catholic[15] in its departure from the traditionally more confined and specialist epistemology[16] of cartel discourse.

The epistemology of cartel discourse

Which groups of experts have shown or should show an interest in the operation of business cartels and its regulation? The history of cartel discourse is an interesting and revealing subject in its own right, and much could be said on the matter, but for present purposes an overview must suffice.

Economics

It is tempting to use a headline description such as 'from economics to culture' but that would risk a simplification. However, economics (predictably enough – cartels are most obviously economic and business phenomena) may be listed first, beginning with some reference, for instance, to Adam Smith's depiction of business behaviour as including a natural tendency for business actors to band together, cartel-like, in their own interests.[17] Cartelisation, as it became a significant and more obvious feature of more sophisticated industrialised economies from the later nineteenth century, attracted a growing amount of

---

14   With a few exceptions – for instance, Katherine M. Jamieson, *The Organization of Corporate Crime: Dynamics of Antitrust Violation* (Sage Publications, 1994).

15   Used here in the broad sense of all-embracing of a variety and range of approaches and discourses.

16   Used here in the sense of working out valid fields of knowledge and understanding. For an earlier, brief attempt at epistemological classification of this area of discussion, see Harding and Joshua, *Regulating Cartels in Europe*, note 2 above, pp. 374–82, which enumerates: the economist's tale, the prosecutor's tale, the defence lawyer's tale, the game theorist's tale, and the penologist's tale.

17   Smith's classic assertion ('people in the same trade seldom meet together ... But the conversation ends in a conspiracy against the public, or in some contrivance to raise prices' – *The Wealth of Nations* (1776), Book I, chapter X) will be revisited further below. See also Appendix Two to Chapter 3.

attention on the part of economists, spawning for instance an impressive and scientific literature in Germany alone some 100 years ago (*das Kartellproblem*).[18] Economists have maintained a close interest in the enduring anti-competitive strategies of business groupings which became almost universally described as 'cartels', with attention being paid to the questions of how and why they come about, endure or break up, and their economic consequences. At an earlier stage such investigation could more easily be carried out in relation to actual cartels as they operated or were known to have operated, when (again North America excepted) they were not deemed clearly illegal and there was a ready openness about what was happening.[19] But as the policy and legal condemnation hardened, from about the 1970s, continuing cartels needed to hide away and could not be directly observed so easily. Much of the work of economists then turned from the empirical to the abstract and speculative, employing econometric modelling based on rational business actor assumptions and game theorising.[20] Nonetheless, this kind of research and commentary has remained influential – policy-makers and lawyers, for example, appear to have been easily persuaded by arguments about so-called optimal sanctions worked out in this way.[21] This mainstream 'predictive' approach to the subject of cartels in economics literature is based upon a view of the firm or business as an essentially economic and rational actor. On the other hand the work of behavioural economists,[22] economic and business historians,[23] and business psychologists[24] probe the social, human and 'irrational' motivation of business activity, arguably providing a richer and more convincing account of cartel activity (see further the discussion of methodology in Chapter 4).

---

18   See David J. Gerber, *Law and Competition in Twentieth Century Europe: Protecting Prometheus* (Oxford University Press, 1998, 2001), especially chapter 4.

19   As can be seen in some of the mid-twentieth century literature; see, for instance, George W. Stocking and Myron W. Watkins, *Cartels in Action: Case Studies in International Business Diplomacy* (The Twentieth Century World Fund, 1946) – a survey 'of concrete experience with international business diplomacy' (at p. ix). The use of the term 'diplomacy' is telling in this regard. See also the discussion in Chapter 4.

20   For a concise and critical summary of this approach, see Maurice E. Stucke, 'Am I a Price Fixer? A Behavioural Economics Analysis of Cartels', chapter 12 in Beaton-Wells and Ezrachi (eds), *Criminalising Cartels*, note 3 above, at p. 263 *et seq*.

21   As is evident for example in many policy statements emanating from the OECD, and speeches and writing by a number of US Department of Justice officials.

22   For example, Stucke, 'Am I a Price Fixer?', note 20 above; and also, Stucke, 'Behavioral Economists at the Gate: Antitrust in the Twenty-First Century', 38 (2007) *Loyola University Chicago Law Journal* 513.

23   For example, Jeffrey Fear, 'Cartels and Competition: Neither Markets nor Hierarchies', Harvard University Working Papers, October 2006.

24   For example, David Tuckett, *Minding the Markets* (Palgrave Macmillan, 2011). As Tuckett argues critically: 'the economist's world is one without ambiguity, uncertainty, emotional memory, and the experience of anxiety' (at p. 24).

Economic analysis and the economic context are crucial to the subject. Business cartels are arrangements for conducting trade and business, their *raison d'être* and consequences are economic in character and they are understood via economic analysis and argument. Moreover, the subject has to be seen through the lens of economic policy, which is dynamic and changes over time. While the basic strategies of cartelists – such as fixing prices or sharing markets – may remain fairly constant over time, the policy context in which cartelists operate changes through time and space. It is axiomatic (although it might seem to be largely forgotten or ignored in some discussion) that businesses involved in cartel activity inhabited a very different world of policy and regulation in 1910 compared to 2010. Early twentieth-century cartelists in Europe would have had a very different sense of their own behaviour and of the reaction of others compared to contemporary cartelists of today, and certainly nothing approaching a secretive, clandestine and delinquent mind set. Nor is this just a matter of history, but rather a question of embedded culture or (if this is not too fanciful) corporate DNA.

In this regard, the more empirical work and behaviourist studies of business and cultural historians and business psychology is equally as important and deserving of attention as the game theorising and predictive modelling favoured by many economists. After all, companies and individuals working for them are real life actors occupying their own particular time and space and not abstracted and predetermined calculating agents. This observation will have an important bearing on the theoretical position being adopted in this study, which proceeds from an *idiosyncratic rather than a generic* understanding of business action. It should be borne in mind that cartelist action and decision-making is essentially a way of dealing with uncertainty in the world of trade and business and here it is worth quoting the insight presented by psychoanalyst David Tuckett:

> logico-deductive-based thinking and prediction of the kind enshrined in probability theories (and then modelled by economists as rational decision-making and optimisation under constraints) may be worth using but may also be of limited value and perhaps not even rational at all. Trying to work out what to do when the relationship of past and present to future is uncertain is not the same as dice-throwing or playing roulette.[25]

This led Tuckett to identify a risk in what he identifies as the prevailing 'normative'[26] discipline of economics arising from a 'suppressed premise in economic thinking – namely the practice of treating all kinds of markets for all kinds of objects as essentially the same'.[27] Similarly for the present subject: treating all cartelists as the same, whatever the market, whatever the context of

---

25   Ibid., at p. xvi.

26   Not normative in the juridical sense (as used below) but rather in the sense of modelled.

27   Tuckett, *Minding the Markets*, note 24 above, at p. xvi.

economic policy, and whatever the provenance of business and legal culture, may not lead to the best understanding of what is happening.

Law

Historically, the other substantial body of literature on cartels has comprised legal commentary and analysis, as competition law has emerged as a substantial field of policy, legal practice and legal discussion. In contrast to the work of many economists the legal discussion has, as might be expected, a significant normative aspect, with an underlying assumption that the activity in question is not only problematic but, increasingly over time, also wrongful and ethically objectionable. The lawyer's view of the cartelist lacks ethical neutrality and there is a significant element of legal enforcement in this perspective. This is equally true of both 'prosecution' and 'defence lawyer' positions. The role of legal defence in anti-cartel enforcement has proven to be exceptionally productive, especially in a European context, bringing the subject into the realm of basic rights protection and argument,[28] but this is still very much within the frame of an ethically pejorative view of cartel activity. As enforcement has moved into higher gear, and employed penal and criminal law strategies, so the legal view of the subject has expanded and deepened, colouring the basic business activity with a greater normative complexity.

But once more, it is possible to identify differing legal perspectives and starting-points for argument. A more positivist approach would take the formal legal position as a given and tend to see *das Kartellproblem* as one of compliance and effective enforcement. A more critical legal perspective, however, would probe the instrumental role of legal rules and the legal process as just one expression of policy and values, and so emphasise for instance the need for due process in enforcement or the need for legitimacy in the use of criminal law and sanctions, and draw upon foundational principles (such as the protection of defence rights, or *ultima ratio* – criminal law as last resort) rather than substantive rules. Thus some legal discourse may be technical – how would the given rules apply to a certain situation?[29] Other legal discussion and analysis may be more jurisprudential and critical – is there a case for criminalisation/decriminalisation, or for alternative kinds of legal process? In the present study, the role of legal analysis will be critical and jurisprudential, probing the relationship between legal systems and underlying values.

---

28   See Harding and Joshua, *Regulating Cartels in Europe*, note 2 above, Chapter 7.

29   This, for example, may be seen as a standard (or conservative) approach of practitioner-oriented textbooks on competition law; contrast, e.g. Giorgio Monti, *EC Competition Law* (Cambridge University Press (Law in Context), 2007), as a more critical examination of how law may be used to give effect to economic policy, focusing on the system rather than precise rules.

There is another aspect of legal literature on the subject, which concerns the relationship between legal rules as used to manage and implement underlying competition policy and that policy as a matter of economic argument and thinking. This brings the subject into the disciplinary domain of 'law and economics', which often emerges as a site of engagement for lawyers grappling with economic argument.[30] One relevant tension which has emerged at this interface in the context of competition law and policy relates to the view that lawyers may try to contain economics too much within a legal framework, and assert an approach which is too rigid, rule-bound and simplistic, overriding economic complexity. Such for instance, was an earlier reaction to the efforts of the EC Commission to fashion rules of competition law,[31] and this tension is also evident in the distinction between 'rule of reason' and '*per se*' approaches to legal regulation.[32] But such criticism of legal dogmatism may also be bound up with a more political objection to public intervention in the market place, such as the Chicago School paradigm[33] associated with laissez-faire economic philosophy. Such 'law and economics' debates and tensions form a significant background to cartel regulation and in particular inform an understanding of regulatory culture, and important differences in such culture as between the US and Europe. In so far as the history of cartel regulation, and indeed also its present condition, may be presented as a narrative of clash of regulatory cultures, this field of theorising and discourse is also important in gaining an understanding of cartel activity.

Criminology

On one view, a criminological consideration of cartel activity only really becomes feasible when the latter is characterised as criminal in character, something which has happened only recently in most legal orders. But arguably, criminology should concern itself with conduct that is more broadly seen as delinquent or deviant, whatever its formal legal description, in order to avoid fruitless argument of definitional foreclosure. For instance, much cartel activity is penalised through systems of 'administrative offending' in a number of continental European jurisdictions, and in the EU – should that legal classification disqualify any criminological investigation? The term 'criminology' will be used in this study to describe research activity and knowledge in a broad sense, to encompass any social scientific investigation into and analysis of delinquent, prohibited or disapproved

---

30   As an interdisciplinary observation, legal scholars seem to be quite bold in this respect, even in the face of hostility or condescension in the other domain ('they can't do the math', or 'why do you worry about proportionality, we are only interested in efficiency').

31   For a useful summary of this point, see Monti, *EC Competition Law* (note 29 above), at pp. 79–82; 'it is trite to say that, historically, EC competition law has not been affected by economic paradigms to the degree that US antitrust has' (at p. 79).

32   See Monti, note 29 above, at pp. 29–31.

33   Ibid., at pp. 73–9.

behaviour. In that way, an earlier sociology or social anthropology of cartels[34] might now more readily be thought of as criminological. Certainly, as the condemnation of business cartels has hardened and legal control has become more invasive, confrontational and penal in character and method, criminological enquiry and assessment has appeared both appropriate and necessary, and the present research, with its focus on the impact of sanctions, is self-consciously criminological. Research which has been funded[35] to seek 'explanation and understanding' of the operation of business cartels must take up the classic concerns of criminological enquiry: the reasons for and causes of prohibited conduct, how that conduct actually takes place and endures, and the assessment of any measures of legal control or application of sanctions. Moreover, the justification of such study and research is not difficult, in that its results should inform and benefit the formulation of policy, design of measures of control and application of sanctions. Potentially there is much here that may be taken on board by policy-makers, lawyers and officials as they ponder the success or otherwise of regulatory efforts, and generally much that may be relevant to the evolution of competition governance. As stated above, the present research is part of an effort to inform and advise any policy project of criminalisation and penalisation and there is a public interest in this effort of theorisation, information finding and evaluation.

But there is also an important question of research positioning (something which is generally true of criminological research). This kind of enquiry may serve a number of interests and the researcher should be aware of this. In so far as it disseminates information and knowledge and enhances understanding it may help both the interests of law enforcement and of legal defence, those of official policy and self-centred business. But the research itself, in its design and objectives, may also, consciously or not, base itself on certain assumptions – for instance, that the policy underlying legal control is legitimate, and politically and ethically justified,[36] and this is an important consideration in a field such as competition governance, which proceeds from certain value judgments and political preferences in terms of economic policy (that competition is a good that needs to be promoted and protected in certain ways and with a certain degree of force). At issue here is the intellectual detachment and objectivity of the social scientific researcher, and that explains the tone of agnosticism and perhaps even scepticism suggested in the subtitle of the present work, 'pathology and mythology of antitrust collusion'. After all, even the Sherman Act in the United States, which has achieved a kind

---

34   For instance, John M. Conley and William M. O'Barr, 'Crime and Custom in Corporate Society: A Cultural Perspective on Corporate Misconduct', 60 (1997) *Law and Contemporary Problems* 5; and Debora Spar, *The Cooperative Edge: The Internal Politics of International Cartels* (Cornell University Press, 1994), as much as Jamieson, *The Organization of Corporate Crime*, note 14 above.

35   Leverhulme funding for the present researchers, 2012–14.

36   This may be described as criminological positivism, by analogy with legal positivism (above).

of constitutional and culturally iconic status,[37] has not been without its doubters and critics – take, for example, Oliver Wendell Holmes' description of the antitrust legislation as an 'imbecile statute' aimed 'at making everyone fight and forbidding anyone to be victorious'.[38]

Any criminological study of the subject therefore needs to consider carefully how it may be locating itself in this way. This is, in the first place, a question of *critical stance*, and hence the preferred 'agnostic' position being adopted here, which will view cartelisation as a problem rather than a matter of right or wrong, as in much of the legal literature, or as a matter of economic efficiency, as in much of the economic analysis. In this way, the present study signals a retreat from normative argument and a return to the tone of much of the earlier twentieth-century critical writing on cartels, particularly in Germany. A good part of what follows here may be described as descriptive and empirical, although that will be accompanied by analysis along a number of lines (see further below).[39] It is, secondly, also a question of *disciplinary perspective*. A criminological approach will clearly in a broad sense be social scientific, but that is not to say that other disciplinary approaches should not be drawn upon, and indeed will be drawn upon. In particular, this research has been undertaken with a keen sense of the *history* of the subject and how this has contributed to present-day outcomes and uncertainties. Linked to the history, there is also an important *geography* of cartel activity, which will also be stressed in the following account, especially in so far as it deals with the regulation of cartels in an international dimension. Moreover, shifting for the moment to questions of method rather than substance, there is much that can be drawn from the field of *narratology*, in analysing the subject as a number of different narratives or stories – or, it might be said, different histories, biographies and even autobiographies. A certain narrative method has been adopted here, and more will be said about this in due course.[40] Perhaps, to aid clear explanation of the approach being adopted, this interdisciplinary fusion may be collected together under a particular expository label: cultural anthropology.[41]

---

37   Harold H. Greene: 'The Sherman Act is similar in the economics sphere to the Bill of Rights in the personal sphere' (1983). Greene was a judge in the District Court for the District of Columbia. See Trudy E. Bell, 'The Decision to Divest: Incredible or Inevitable?' IEEE SPECTRUM, November 1985, p. 48.

38   See Appendix Two to Chapter 3.

39   See below in this chapter, at p. 22.

40   See Chapter 4.

41   In linking together closely the narrative method and the disciplinary field of cultural anthropology, the study here draws inspiration from the work of Mieke Bal and the idea of the 'travelling concept' between disciplines. For background, see Mieke Bal, *Narratology: Introduction to the Theory of Narrative* (3rd edn, University of Toronto Press, 2009), and *Travelling Concepts in the Humanities: A Rough Guide* (University of Toronto Press, 2002).

Cultural anthropology

The emphasis here on cultural anthropology as a field of discussion springs from
the fact that the study of business cartels is very much the study of groups and
organisations and their interaction with each other as well as with their individual
human components. The cartel itself is of course a kind of group, and the
corporate members of cartels, as companies or business firms, may also be seen
as groups; both cartels and corporate actors may also be analysed as complex and
sophisticated organisations.[42] Moreover, the regulation of cartels has developed
in a number of different legal systems, sometimes in significantly different ways,
and the present 'globalised', supranational and international dimension of the
subject has led to the involvement of intergovernmental organisations, as another
kind of group activity. Viewed in this way, cartel activity as a field of study,
may be presented as the jostling of a large number of groups and organisations:
business actors, and official bodies, both national and supranational, of different
descriptions. These groups, with their varying provenance, will have their own and
sometimes distinctive cultures – and the term 'culture' is used here to encompass
value systems, attitudes, normative codes, patterns and modes of operation
and behaviour, and outlooks or world-view. Understanding cartels, companies,
regulatory authorities, policy and rule-making elites and their interaction with
each other is a matter of understanding and penetrating their respective cultures.

An empirical investigation of business cartels, especially across national legal
systems and in the context of global or transnational trading, quickly suggests
the importance of considering both business and regulatory culture in achieving
an understanding of cartel activity and behaviour. As stated already, this study
is as much about regulatory activity ('the anti-cartel enforcement industry') as
business activity, and cultures of both will therefore form a significant element
of this account and analysis of the subject. For instance, the now well-known
and well-observed differences of approach and in legal models as between the
US and Europe in relation to competition regulation,[43] may be better understood
through the lens of both business and legal culture in those two parts of the
world, and appreciating the different historical, economic and political context
of, respectively, the adoption of the Sherman Act in the US and the development
of competition policy and law in European countries and in the European Union.
Equally, it is a pertinent to ask as part of this research whether anti-cartel sanctions
are received and experienced differently by companies in different parts of the
world – for instance, North America, Europe or East Asia – and, if so, how far that
different outcome may be understood as a matter of the business and legal culture

---

42   For a background discussion of crime and organisation, see Christopher Harding,
Criminal Enterprise: Individuals, Organisations and Criminal Responsibility (Willan
Publishing, 2007).

43   For an overview of these differences, see Harding and Joshua, *Regulating Cartels
in Europe*, note 2 above, chapter 2.

which has historically prevailed in those different regions. Thus, a main research question underlying this study concerns the impact of legal sanctions in this context, and then testing the role of such 'cultural' differences in understanding and explaining that impact.

Such a line of enquiry is closely related to the narrative method which has been used here to provide an account of the subject and deploy the data and evidence which have been collected through an examination of actual cases of anti-cartel enforcement, as 'cartel biographies', comprising the factual prehistory of each case, the legal record of investigation and enforcement, and the factual afterlife of the individual and corporate cartelists. An important informing aspect of such biographical accounts will naturally be the provenance of such cases, or, it might be said, the cultural location of the principal actors – the individuals, corporations and enforcement agencies. Thus the criminology of cartels might also be seen as a cultural anthropology of cartels, and a study not only of economic processes and legal rules, but importantly of the main human, corporate and official actors, through the construction of narratives of their involvement in cartel stories or biographies.

Critical theme: A pathology and mythology of antitrust collusion

The subtitle of this book, 'The mythology and pathology of business collusion', is intended to encapsulate one of the main lines of critical interest in the subject of business cartels: why these forms of business strategy and organisation are seen as a matter of concern, as a significant problem to be addressed, and how this concern has resulted in the last one hundred years in an impressive structure of regulation and legal control, and a revealing example of public intervention in the market place and competition governance. In contemporary (early twenty-first century) official policy, business cartels, or at least 'hard core' cartels, are seen as a form of economic (and perhaps even political) disease or disorder, and in that sense it is appropriate to talk in terms of a pathology which can explain and describe the nature of that disorder. In so far as it is regarded as imperative to deal with this disorder there emerges an ideology of legal control and a justification of policy, which may then be described as a mythology of the subject, in the sense of a sacred narrative, which is used to underpin the official response and effort of regulation. The pathology and mythology are closely related, the former informs and promotes the latter, and together they represent a statement of the problem and its proposed solution.

Yet it should be remembered that neither pathology nor mythology are infallible scientific processes: both diagnosis and remedy or cure, as in the case of disease, may be based on imperfect knowledge and understanding and contestable assumptions. This then becomes the starting point for critical evaluation of cartel control – an examination of both diagnosis and cure and also an appreciation that any judgment regarding the impact of sanctions, as part of the cure, should entail some exploration of how the problem has been diagnosed in the first place. In its contemporary usage the term 'myth' is also strongly suggestive of a contestable account – an imaginative or fictional depiction or explanation of natural phenomena – which merges into the practice of folklore[44] and attempts to understand the real world through simplified metaphorical narratives and explanation.

The 'pathology' of the subject will be discussed in more detail in Chapter 3. Its 'mythology' will appear as part of the various narratives or biographies which will be presented later in the book, and might even be extracted from those narratives as one in its own right, the story of the development of regulatory systems and the ideology used to justify that development.[45] In telling that story, some reference could be made to representations and images of the subject matter, which are part and parcel of the underlying ideology of legal enforcement, and which have a mythological quality in its traditional sense, as imaginative or fictional depictions of real life phenomena. Such a mythology has been presented, for instance, in pictorial-metaphorical representations of cartelisation and the threat that it poses to society. A notable example of this kind of mythic representation is the use of the snake or octopus monster depiction of the early American trusts such as Standard Oil as dangerous and predatory creatures intent on gaining a stranglehold on society; see, for instance, 'The Infant Hercules and the Standard Oil Serpents', by Frank A. Nankivell in 1906,[46] 'Standard Oil as an Octopus', by Udo Keppler in 1904,[47] and the earlier depiction of a monster by W. Rogers in 1888, 'The Trustworthy Beast'.[48] The serpent representation has provided a potent mythical image of cartel activity – the serpent or snake-like animal drawn from Christian mythology (for instance Milton's *Paradise Lost*), as a devious and untrustworthy (an ironic play on words in the American context) creature, capable of wrapping itself around and strangling (or in the case of the octopus attaching itself to and capturing) innocent victims. Such potent and persuasive mythical representations may be explored through the biographical narratives of cartels which follow later in the book.

---

44   Compare the contemporary use of the term 'urban myth' or 'legend', sometimes used as a modern version of folklore.

45   For a short attempt to tell that particular story, see Christopher Harding, 'The Anti-Cartel Enforcement Industry', chapter 16 in Beaton-Wells and Ezrachi (eds), *Criminalising Cartels*, note 3 above, section III, under the heading 'The War Against Cartels'; and also the narrative account presented in chapter 5 of Harding and Joshua, *Regulating Cartels in Europe*, note 2 above.

46   Used as a cover illustration for *Puck*, volume 59, no. 1525, 23 May 1906, showing Theodore Roosevelt as the infant Hercules fighting large snakes with the heads of Nelson W. Aldrich and John D. Rockefeller.

47   This shows a huge octopus (Standard Oil) wrapping its tentacles around the Capitol building and average Americans, and setting its sight on the White House.

48   W. Rogers, for *Harper's Weekly*, 1888: showing Uncle Sam looking suspiciously at a monster, standing next to Andrew Carnegie; the monster has six heads, labelled respectively as coal, steel, sugar, oil, lumber and salt trusts.

Returning to the role of myth as means of conveying 'sacred text', ideology or dogma, it may be useful just to register the argument that some of the anti-cartel rhetoric presented in legal texts and official enforcement agency statements embody a dogma of competition governance that is used to justify regulation and a certain style of legal control. Reference may be made, for instance, to the quasi-constitutional status of the language of Section 1 of the Sherman Act,[49] or of Article 101 of the Treaty on the Functioning of the European Union (TFEU) in its commitment to Single Market ideology. Equally, contemporary competition policy and enforcement argument and assertion may be seen as 'mythical' statements regarding cartel activity which almost invite some critical probing as present-day 'urban myths' or 'legends', such as the following 'truths to be tested', that:

- Cartel activity is irredeemably bad.
- Cartel activity removes competition.
- The cost of cartel activity and its regulation can be calculated.
- Companies and their executives are rational actors who will be dissuaded by optimal sanctions.
- Cartelists are well-dressed thieves in suits.
- Anti-cartel enforcement is a war zone and a fight to the end.

A number of these assertions can be seen, in a very dogmatic form, in a 'classic' statement, delivered very much like a sermon from the pulpit or speech at a political rally, on the part of Joel I. Klein, as Assistant Attorney General in the Department of Justice:

> The *War* against International Cartels: *Lessons from the Battlefront* –
> Let me start with *the obvious*: cartel behavior (price-fixing, market allocation and bid-rigging) is *bad* for consumers, *bad* for business and *bad* for efficient markets generally. And let me *be very clear*: these cartels are the equivalent of *theft by well-dressed thieves* and they deserve *unequivocal public condemnation*.[50] [emphasis added]

The above assertions may be conveniently retained as hypotheses to be tested in the discussion below.

---

49   Harold H. Greene, note 37 above.

50   Joel I. Klein, 'The War against International Cartels: Lessons from the Battlefront', *Fordham Corporate Law Institute*, 26th Annual Conference, International Antitrust Law and Policy, 14 October 1999, New York.

Probing the mystery of the cartelist mind: Cartel narratives and the biographical method

A major contemporary problem – for policy-makers, enforcement agencies, lawyers and researchers – resides in the difficulty in penetrating the motivations for and the dynamic of collusive cartel business behaviour which (like much other criminal activity) may be highly secretive and skilfully hidden. Thus explaining both the original motivation of cartelists and the endurance and persistence of cartels in the face of heavier sanctions is largely at present a matter of speculation, based on either sociological or legal guesswork or abstract econometric modelling.[51] Then, assessing the achievement of cartel regulation and the deterrent and other impacts of measures of legal control is still very much a matter of approaching the 'mystery' of the cartelist's mind. There are a few anecdotal accounts provided autobiographically by convicted cartelists,[52] and while some of these may be potentially revealing,[53] they remain small in number and historically random.

What is being described as the 'biographical method' undertaken here in researching the impact of sanctions employed in the legal control of business cartels may appear as something of a novelty in the context of social scientific deterrence research. Whereas much deterrence research is of a predictive nature, speculating on the likely outcome of sanctions, the biographical method is retrospective and historical, drawing upon the record of actual case histories, events and their context to evaluate what appears already to have been the outcome of particular policies and measures. This approach exploits a by now significant body of evidence of legal action taken against cartels in a number of jurisdictions over 30 or more years, and particularly that involving 'usual suspects' or repeat offender participants in these investigated and sanctioned cartels. The main research evidence therefore comprises case studies of actual significant delinquent corporate actors, based upon reliable data drawn from legal proceedings: verifiable historical material rather than predictive analysis.

A number of advantages may be seen in this approach. First, it allows for a longer-term historical analysis which may take into account the possible impact of both particular corporate cultures and histories and also the role of human individuals working for companies, as factors in the formation of corporate policy and attitudes. Secondly, such a study can provide data on corporate and individual contributions to delinquent activity in the cartel context, and help in disentangling relations between companies and individual employees, managers and top executives. In particular, this may help in probing the possibility that

---

51   See the further discussion in Chapter 3, pp. 67–70.

52   For instance, those provided by Mark Whitacre, Alfred Taubman, and Keith Packer; see Chapters 5, 7 and 8.

53   In particular, Michael O'Kane's interview of Bryan Allison (Marine Hose Cartel), in *The Antitrust Bulletin* in 2011: Michael O'Kane, 'Does Prison Work for Cartelists? The View from Behind Bars', 56 (2011) *The Antitrust Bulletin* 483.

some companies may be 'corporate good citizens' struggling to manage 'rogue executives'. Thirdly, this kind of study can take into account the impact and influence of corporate restructuring over time and shifting corporate identities (a notable feature of a number of large international cartel cases, the legal processing of which may extend over 10 years or so). Fourthly, it enables cross-jurisdictional and international comparisons, also important for large cartel cases, so taking into account any variable national or market-based cultures of corporate behaviour, and differences regarding legal processes of investigation, use of evidence, enforcement and application of sanctions. Fifthly, it provides a picture of evolving relationships between three crucial actors, especially in the context of the exploitation of leniency programmes: (a) the companies involved in cartels; (b) the regulatory agencies charged with enforcement; and (c) law firms and legal experts advising the companies. And finally, in the case of recidivist firms, it may provide some insight into behaviour and attitudes following earlier instances of sanctioning, and also some information on the 'after-life' of individuals involved in such legal proceedings and subject to personalised sanctions.

Sample and method

This biographical method as used in this research has been based upon the collection and ordering of data relating to legal investigations, prosecutions, sanctions and appeals, taken together with relevant informative circumstantial data, such as the nature and conditions over time of markets, the history of corporate structures, the development of legal regulation, and biographical details of individuals. The biographies are then presented as longitudinal narrative accounts of corporate participation in cartels (i.e. narratives of particular cartel activities and their legal prosecution), in a format which can facilitate analysis of key points relevant to the assessment of the impact of legal action.

The sample comprises a large number of major international cartel cases (i.e. activity extending across two or more countries) investigated, prosecuted and subject to legal determination and sanctions, over the period 1980–2010, focusing upon the more significant jurisdictions in this context: the United States, the European Community/European Union and EU Member States, and some other countries relevant to international cartel activity, such as Canada, Australia, Korea and Japan. 1980 has been chosen as the start-point for the real take-off in international anti-cartel enforcement. Prior to that date, especially in the European context, such enforcement was much more tentative and haphazard, and may be fairly regarded as being in a stage of infancy. Across the selected jurisdictions, the resort to criminalisation both in terms of legislation and actual enforcement, has been variable, enabling further comparisons. Different jurisdictions may be variously classified in enforcement terms, for instance as 'active criminal law enforcement', 'passive criminal law enforcement', or 'strong administrative sanctions'. A comparative history of enforcement in these terms across jurisdictions is instructive.

Main lines of analysis

Analysis of this biographical data (see Chapters 6 to 8) has then been organised around some main questions and features of the cases involved which were perceived as relevant in explaining and assessing the impact of anti-cartel measures.

a. The character of the market: the economic sector and nature of the product or service, whether it is 'upstream' or 'downstream' in the economic process, and any relevant special historical circumstances associated with such markets.

b. The nature of the cartel activity in terms of anti-competitive strategies employed: whether one or more of the classic 'hard core' methods of collusion (price fixing, market sharing, limitation of production, and bid rigging) or other forms of communication or information sharing among competitors.

c. The corporate identity: the companies involved in cartel activity over time, taking into account any corporate restructuring and any evidence of their normative position as embedded in company policy (e.g. awareness of legal and regulatory structures, policy towards legal compliance).

d. The geographical location and national and cultural identity of companies: 'nationality', or conversely a 'transnational' identity, as a factor which might determine economic and business behaviour and the normative culture underlying corporate and individual behaviour (e.g. 'Rhineland capitalism' (more cooperative) compared to 'Atlantic capitalism' (more competitive)).

e. The jurisdictions involved and their approach to the legal control of cartels, including enforcement and legal cultures: legal differences and the temporal dimension of legislation and enforcement practice in relation to cartels, and any correlation between type of legal order (e.g. common law or other) and patterns or preferences in approaches to legal control (e.g. use of criminal law, administrative regulation, civil proceedings).

f. Kinds of sanction employed in dealing with convicted companies and individuals, and their selection and accumulation: prohibitive determinations, financial penalties, compensation, criminal law sanctions targeted at individuals, disqualification, adverse publicity.

g. Recidivist status – evidence of subsequent cartel activity or its absence in further legal proceedings, and the extent to which it involves the same corporate or individual identities.

h. Further legal proceedings, and the extent to which it involves the same corporate or individual identities.

i. The role of individuals (analysis of cartel decision-making within corporate structures and the role of individuals within corporate culture) and the use of sanctions against individuals, including the afterlife of convicted cartelists.

Alternatively, these categories of information may be organised into four main clusters:

Market and cartel strategy and (b)	Corporate identity and location (c) and (d)
Jurisdiction, method of legal control and types of sanction (e) and (f)	Normative character: offender status and agency (g) and (h)

Biography as story telling: Whose narrative?

In one sense this approach is based upon a surer and less contestable body of data, especially in so far as it draws upon an official record of legal process, which comprises in itself a careful and rigorous testing and presentation of evidence. But in another sense, it is a research strategy which is nonetheless vulnerable to contestable evaluations of the past, in the same way as any other historical account. Biographies, however objective in their conception and plan, remain stories or narratives, dependent on interpretation of the past through the present lens of the historian/researcher narrator, and on the combined contemporary narratives of those who play a part in the ongoing cartel stories, and these latter narratives will draw upon their own 'internal' interpretations of and perspectives on the same events.

The researcher therefore needs to bear in mind his or her own position and purposes as the end-narrator and also the respective positions and perspectives of the various narrators within the narration. A moment's reflection will reveal the possibility of very differing stories, as presented for instance by prosecuting officials, defendant corporations, advising lawyers and courts as official arbiters of these perhaps inconsistent or competing accounts. The research has therefore to navigate some tricky waters in which different narratives jostle with each other for a commanding version of the same events, and consider how these may be used to provide a single convincing meta-narrative.[54]

---

54 For further discussion of such narratological problems and challenges, see Francesca Polletta, 'Contending Stories: Narrative in Social Movements', 21 (1998) *Qualitative Sociology* 419; Christopher Harding, 'Vingt Ans Après: Rainbow Warrior, Legal Ordering, and Legal Complexity', 10 (2006) *Singapore Yearbook of International Law* 99; *Cambridge Introduction to Narrative* (ed. D. Herman, Cambridge University Press, 1997); Hermione Lee, *Biography: A Very Short Introduction* (Oxford University Press, 2009), chapter 1 'The Biography Channel' and chapter 8 'Telling the Story'.

There is, finally, one narrative which is naturally problematical within any biography and that is the account from within the subject – the subjective view of the person who is the object of study (or, it might be said, the autobiography within the biography). In the present case, this is the cartelist's own story (for instance, of motivation and intention and expectation), and in contemporary terms, this is a narrative version which may be significantly foreclosed by the operation of legal process. The risk here is that approaching the subject as one of policy and legal and criminal regulation may serve to foreclose and inhibit the inside narrative of the 'offender' by privileging that of governance and the legal system – as presented by policy-makers, lawyers, regulators and economists. Criminal law in particular, by outlawing the subject of legal control, serves to drive the outlaw-offender into a narrative wilderness, in which the latter's own telling of motives and events is inhibited by powerful forces of preferred external regulatory and professional narrative,[55] and these latter accounts are deemed more accessible, reliable and credible. The social scientific researcher, also in search of accessible, reliable and convincing data, may then reinforce such privileging of the official's and the lawman's account, leaving the inside view incomplete, remote and speculative – a 'wild' space which is not easy to approach, penetrate or cohabit (*ex post facto* 'apologia' accounts by former cartelists are as problematical as the rhetoric of crusading policy-makers and officials). The risk, then to be guarded against in the following discussion, is that cartel autobiography, like much criminal autobiography, might remain a narrative hole in the middle of the subject and a kind of research wilderness.[56]

---

55   An important example of such narrative foreclosure in the present context would be the preference in the US criminal justice system for guilty plea settlement of criminal cases, which in effect is an instruction to the defending party – 'Do a deal with us, and then say no more – do not try to justify yourself, explain why you became involved, or tell the world any more about this, and so allow our story, even if you feel that it is not the full and most accurate story, to prevail and go down in history'.

56   There is another element of this problem of attempting to gain access to the internal version of the matter in the criminal or law-breaker's own mind: the psychological and cognitive issue of knowing or understanding the 'mens rea', either on the part of external observers or the subject him or herself. For an interesting study of the problem of gaining access to the criminal mind, which compares nineteenth-century legal and fictional attempts to do so, see Lisa Rodensky, *The Crime in Mind: Criminal Responsibility and the Victorian Novel* (Oxford University Press, 2003).

Chapter 2

The Phenomenon of Cartelisation

We have a strong general idea of what constitutes an anti-competitive business
cartel, but how easily can we recognise or identify a cartel or a participating cartelist
when we look for them?[1]

Ontology and phenomenology

It may be useful to frame the discussion in this chapter as an ontology and
phenomenology of the subject, in the sense of broadly referring to first the existence
of cartels and secondly the experience of cartelisation. Both frames of discussion
enable the exploration of some challenging questions concerning the regulation
and legal control of business cartel activity and this way of viewing the subject
should also be related to what has been said already in the first chapter concerning
different epistemological narratives within this field. Issues of both existence,
identity and definition on the one hand, and the material experience of the activity
in question on the other hand can depend to some extent on the disciplinary frame of
reference, whether for instance the analysis is carried out by lawyers, economists,
sociologists, historians or others. Thus typically a lawyer's definition of a business
cartel may be different from that of an economist, stressing the normative
characteristics of such activity, differing from the economist's preoccupation with
its quantitative character. Also a lawyer's location of the experience of cartelisation
within a certain formal legal process can be distinguishable from an economist's
reading of what is happening in a market context. This discussion will therefore
strive to distinguish both ontological and phenomenological frames of discussion
and differing epistemological modes of analysis.

Ontology: The existence, identity and definition of cartels

At first sight and from some definitions business cartel activity might appear
straightforward: a group of suppliers in a particular market arranging their business
together in typical anti-competitive ways. But on closer consideration, and
especially in the context of legal control, matters of definition and identification
are complex and difficult. Indeed, it is possible to engage is some ontological
teasing and even question whether cartels have any real world existence, but (to
recall the observation at the start of the first chapter) just exist in the eye of the
beholder as a matter of social, economic and legal construction, and in particular

---

1   Christopher Harding, lecture presentation 2014.

an *ex post facto* construction within a process of legal control. On such a view cartels have meaning in the world of discourse, as a way of describing certain activities and human and corporate interaction, but do not have an independent material existence, not even the formal and legally constituted existence of entities such as companies.[2] Certainly, like a conspiracy, a cartel is not a legal person, but is really just a descriptive device and shorthand definition of certain activities and behaviour.

To illustrate this point, which will lead the discussion here shortly into a kind of ontological puzzle, it may be suggested that the term 'cartel' may be used to describe three different although related situations:

- An arrangement between two or more business actors, although described differently across jurisdictions (for instance, as a conspiracy under the USA Sherman Act of 1890, or as an 'agreement' or 'concerted practice' in the wording of Article 101 of the Treaty on the Functioning of the European Union (TFEU)) – i.e. an instrument of collusion.
- The grouping of colluding competitors, the two or more parties, whether corporate or human individuals, as they come together for their anti-competitive purpose.
- The infrastructure of anti-competitive activity, as a continuing series of meetings, communications, discussions, implementing actions (what in EU enforcement language has been described as a 'single continuing infringement').

The above may then be described respectively as *instrumental*, *personal*, and *organisational* senses of the word 'cartel', and in everyday language each of those situations might reasonably described as a cartel. If it is said, for instance, that the EU Commission has taken legal action against a cement cartel, the latter term describing the object of such action may refer at one and the same time to the arrangement (agreement or concerted practice) of the participating companies, these parties as a group acting with a common purpose, and also the ongoing joint practical and decisional actions of that group.

Each of the above senses of the word 'cartel' might reasonably be employed for legal purposes (so as to identify the object of legal control or regulation) or criminological purposes (so as to specify the nature of certain conduct as delinquent or criminal). But the failure to indicate or agree upon which sense or meaning is being employed can lead to problems. For this is not just a matter of philosophy or

---

2   But companies and other incorporated actors might also be the subject of ontological contestation: do such 'persons' exist only as legal constructions (i.e. because legal rules define their existence), or as real world autonomous actors, deriving existence from a material combination of human individuals and infrastructural processes and interactions. See Christopher Harding, *Criminal Enterprise: Individuals, organisations and criminal responsibility* (Willan Publishing, 2007).

existential enquiry and description, but is also a practical issue of how the relevant marketplace practices are understood and regulated. In any system of legal regulation, this is an important conceptual and practical question: what is a cartel, and who is a cartelist, and in the present factual circumstances can it be shown and proven that there are cartelists operating a cartel? It is perhaps no accident that there are few precise legal definitions of a cartel as such (Section 188 of the UK Enterprise Act uses the heading 'cartel offence', but does not define a cartel or use the word in the offence definition). Similarly, the European Commission will investigate a cartel, but issue formal decisions against and impose sanctions on individual corporate members of the cartel. Moreover, there are external and internal aspects of this ontological puzzle – how to recognise a cartel from the outside, with reference to its external boundaries; and how to recognise the crucial internal action and agency which supplies its substantively illegal character, a matter of participation and roles.

These are the existential and evidential problems of unlawful collusion, conspiracy and joint criminal enterprise, and these problems will bedevil both the practical legal prosecution of cartels and the analysis of historical cases of cartel activity provided by biographical data. Therefore, in attempting to navigate these practical and theoretical difficulties, a number of conceptual constructions may be put forward and used to provide a framework for clarifying the way in which historical data may be used for purposes of explanatory analysis and legal process: the cartel as a box, circles or rings of participation, and the cartel as an orbiting system.

The cartel as a box: Externalities

This is an explanatory device put forward by Harding and Joshua as a way of understanding the constant *external* features of a cartel as an organisational infrastructure and collectivity. Any cartel, whatever its factual or circumstantial content, will possess three essential dimensions: the temporal (beginning and end in time – duration); the spatial (where and what in terms of geography and market); and the personal (participation – who was involved). The cartel, as a three-dimensional box, will change size and shape, according to the facts of time, space and participation, but the three dimensions remain constant. This may be represented in Figure 2.1 (the cartel as a box, in abstract) and in Figure 2.2 (the cartel as a box applied to the Animal Feeds Phosphates Cartel).

In the context of criminal law, when it is sought to impose liability in relation to the business collusion described as a cartel, it is suggested that the box device serves to encapsulate the external features or *actus reus* of the offending conduct, clarifying what a prosecuting authority must show by way of evidence in that respect.

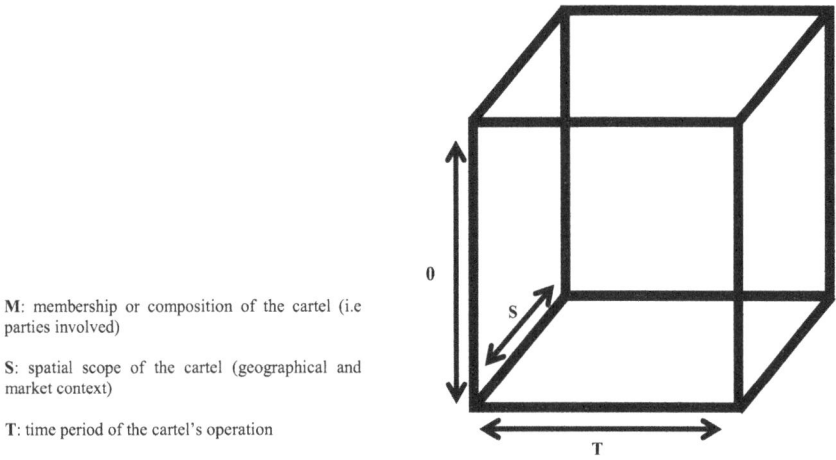

M: membership or composition of the cartel (i.e parties involved)

S: spatial scope of the cartel (geographical and market context)

T: time period of the cartel's operation

Figure 2.1   The cartel as a box (Harding and Joshua, 2010)

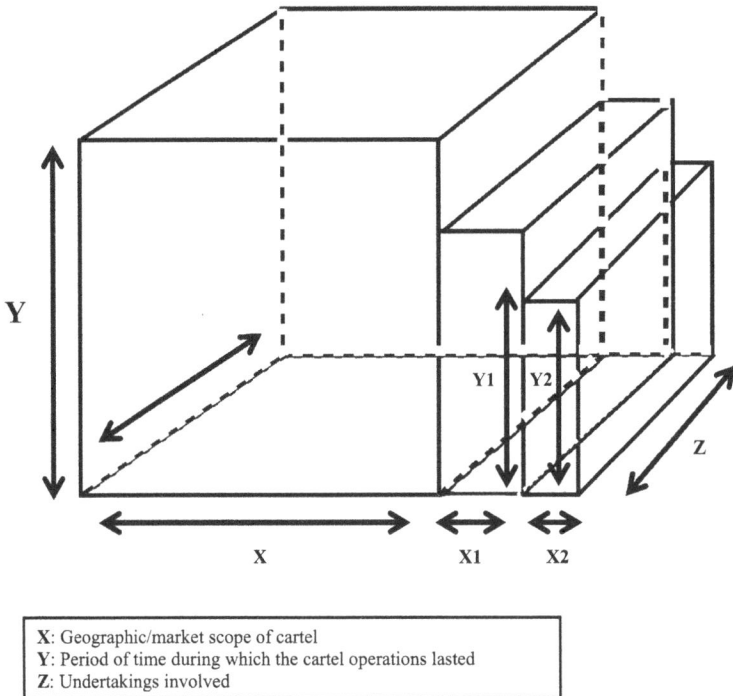

X: Geographic/market scope of cartel
Y: Period of time during which the cartel operations lasted
Z: Undertakings involved

**Figure 2.2   The cartel as a box – Animal Feeds Phosphates Cartel
(Karayanidi)**

The cartel as a concentric circle: Role and participation

An understanding of the *internal* cartel elements of participation and role is facilitated by the model of the *circles or rings* of involvement (such elements as core/peripheral participation, substantive/facilitative role, leader/follower involvement and status). So, for example, a cartel member company or trader may be more or less committed, either as a permanent and long-term member throughout the duration of the cartel, or an occasional, shorter-term, 'visiting' member of the grouping. Cartel members may have differing functions and roles. Typically, most will be competing traders or suppliers, restricting their 'normal' competition with each other through involvement in a cartel, and in that sense their participation is as substantive members. But some companies or individuals may be involved in a purely facilitative or organisational role, organising and overseeing the operation of the cartel, carrying out management and secretarial (but crucial) functions. Individual executives or employees may have different tasks, either agreeing on the main lines of policy ('governmental' directors) or fixing precise figures or quotas (implementation by marketing managers). Then, also, participants may perform different roles in relation to the policies and direction of the cartel, linked in some ways to their level of commitment. There may be natural leaders and followers, whose position will translate into a behavioural pattern of command or acquiescence, coercion or submission. The device of internal, segmented circles or rings may be used to convey and report upon such multifaceted involvement, and aid an understanding of internal cartel operation and responsibilities. This is represented in Figure 2.3 (circles of cartelist collusion).

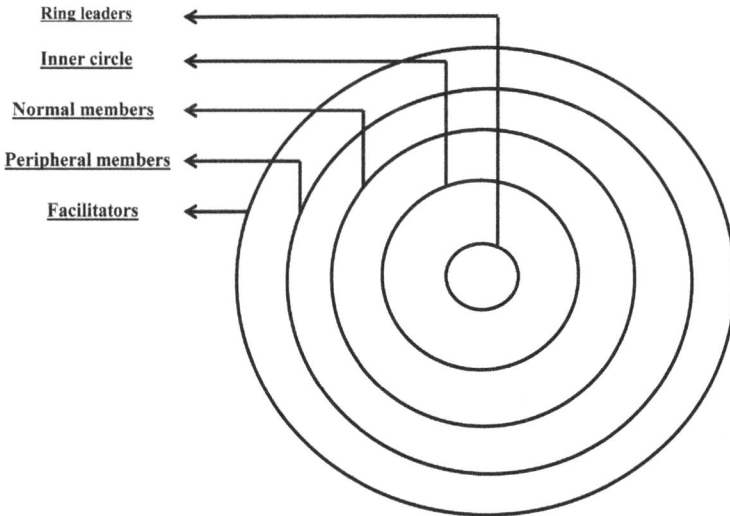

Figure 2.3   Circles of cartelist collusion
Source: Harding and Edwards, 2012

This model, again for legal and criminological purposes, enables a clear understanding of participation in a collective or joint activity (whether labelled conspiracy, concerted practice or joint criminal enterprise) by specifying and defining key individual roles in a collective context, and so clarifies the issues of agency and responsibility.

The cartel as an orbiting system: Individual variability

Furthermore, the *dynamic* quality of such internal participation and involvement may be represented through the idea of *the cartel as an orbiting system*, a model which enables a sense of centre or core and periphery, of entry and exit, and fluctuating movement to and from the centre, which may be characteristic of the actual operation and history of many cartels. Whereas the model of circles and rings risks a rather too static representation and understanding of cartel involvement, that of the cartel member as orbiting object takes into account the dynamic and perhaps fluctuating nature of participation over time, which may be an important consideration for purposes of judging individual legal liability and criminal delinquency

Figure 2.4, models the *Marine Hose Cartel* though its operation from 1986 to 1992. This time period was selected because it encompasses both periods of stability and instability within the cartel, and therefore provides a clear example of how the model works. The start/end point of the cartel is at the 12 o'clock point, with the ensuing years elapsing anticlockwise from there. Each of the coloured dots represents a member of the cartel, as shown in the key that follows.

In the diagrams above, the six members of the cartel – Parker ITR, Trelleborg, Dunlop, Yokohama, Manuli and Bridgestone – are all moving in the 'inner circle' stratum as time moves forward. Between the years of 1986 and early 1992, the cartel was stable. Meetings were attended by all of the companies involved, and all remained closely involved with the running of the cartel.

In mid to late 1992, however, Manuli left the cartel as shown in the next diagram by the orbit of the mauve dot outside the concentric rings that demarcate the cartel's extent of operation, while their former collaborators continued as before. In this way, Manuli's participation and liability is clearly distinguished.

These boxing and circling models can be used therefore in discussion and argument about cartels, but it should be stressed that they have a value especially for legal and criminological discussion, in aiding and informing an ontological understanding of cartel activity. For purposes of any kind of legal process such modelling serves to identify the subject-matter of that process, or at least the external dimensions and internal elements of participation of that subject-matter. The mental dimension of cartel activity – individual and corporate motive, intention and design – is even more elusive given the complexity of agency and difficulties of evidence, so that (in criminal law terminology) even if the *actus reus* may be clarified, the *mens rea* remains a matter of some obscurity or even mystery (as discussed at the end of Chapter 1 above). It is then not surprising

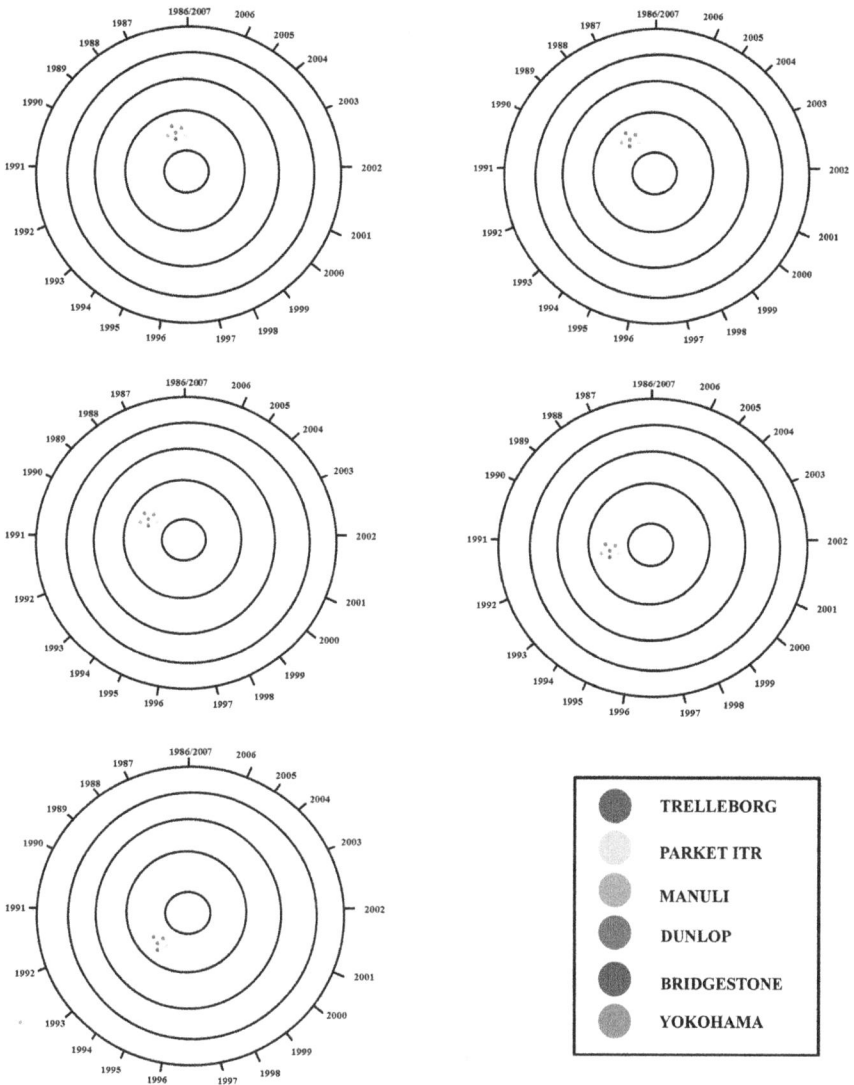

Figure 2.4   The Marine Hose Cartel as an orbiting system
Source: Harding and Edwards, 2012

to learn of the earlier attempt by European Commission enforcers to evade the problem by arguing in the seminal *Wood Pulp* proceedings that anti-competitive intention and design could be deduced from (and so proven by) market outcomes and circumstances (see the further discussion of the Wood Pulp Cartel proceedings in Chapter 3).

In short, cartel ontology is difficult and problematic: in what sense, more exactly, does a cartel exist? It is important to appreciate that cartels arise from a complex situation, comprising elements of geography, market behaviour and market analysis, organisation, business culture, and collective and individual determination and decision-making. The question of agency – the relationship and interaction between human individual and corporate actors within the scope of cartel arrangements – will be returned to later in this chapter, but first it will be useful to say something more about the nature of cartel activity in itself.

Phenomenology: The experience of cartelisation

The phenomenological question concerns the way in which cartels are used in economic markets and the reasons and motivation for business cartelisation. Viewed as a business strategy, it is not difficult to provide a general description of the action taken within supplier and producer cartels, as an agreement or understanding to limit or remove competition between themselves, for their own economic advantage and security. Such anti-competitive strategies may take a number of forms, but there are some recognised enduring, and almost universal and typical actions, now usually listed and classified as the 'hard core' activities of fixing prices and other conditions of supply, sharing markets, limiting production, and rigging bids. In this respect, it might be thought that cartels, in different places and at different times have a standard and universal character and mode of operation and on that view would not be a difficult subject for regulation. But it is worth probing further this apparent simplicity. Sure enough, there are some basic universal forms. But, as indicated already, the analysis of this kind of activity and its practical dimensions are complex, and also the context of the operation of these same basic strategies varies in time and space, and this will affect the way in which they are viewed.

How to describe the activity

It is important to note in the first place that the way in which this kind of activity has been described and defined has changed over time – the actual vocabulary of the subject has not been constant, as may be appreciated by an examination of the term 'cartel'. The use of the word in this sense is relatively modern,[3] deriving

---

3   See in particular the discussion of the etymology of the term in Christopher Harding and Julian Joshua, *Regulating Cartels in Europe* (2nd edn, Oxford University Press, 2010), at pp. 11–16.

from the earlier usage (Italian 'cartello', French 'cartel') referring to a cooperative arrangement between hostile parties, particularly for the exchange of prisoners or even a ship used for such exchange, connoting the idea of a *truce* between rivals or disputants. Its application in the context of business activity seems to have originated in Germany in the later nineteenth century. Reputedly, the first recorded use of the German term 'Kartell' was in a debate in the Reichstag concerning practices in the rail industry, when one of the deputies, Richter, used the word for this purpose. From that time onwards there was within Germany a large debate and literature on what was neatly described in German as 'das Kartellproblem',[4] but the use of the term in its English version followed more gradually during the earlier twentieth century.[5] In American parlance, the terms 'trust', 'combination' and 'conspiracy' (as employed in the Sherman Act of 1890) were favoured. As an exercise in business history it is not easy to understand precisely the comparative use of vocabulary and concepts such as 'trust' (mainly American and referring more to monopolisation), 'association', 'Kartell', and 'Interressengemeinschaft' ('IG' – another German term, as in 'IG Farben').[6] But certainly the German use of the term and concept some one hundred years ago was seminal.

It is important, then, to disentangle the use of descriptive language, and the appearance of a new term in the later nineteenth century, from evidence of the practices described by that language and to examine the longer-term history of strategies which are now located under that heading of 'cartels'. Writing in 1933, Roman Piotrowski,[7] refers to the misleading assertion by the Austrian academic Friedrich Kleinwächter that the 'Kartell' was a phenomenon of modern economic life not previously treated in the economic literature.[8] But as Piotrowski points out, Kleinwächter himself did not intend to imply that there were not earlier analogies or antecedent forms, since he compares the modern Kartell favourably with the medieval guild as an instrument for dealing with 'anarchism in the economy' (*Anarchismus in der Volkswirtschaft*).

---

4   See Harding and Joshua, note 3 above, chapter 3; also David J. Gerber, *Law and Competition in Twentieth Century Europe: Protecting Prometheus* (Oxford University Press, 1998, 2001), chapter 4.

5   As Stocking and Watkins noted in 1945, 'The term cartel was virtually unknown to the American language a generation ago': George W. Stocking and Myron W. Watkins, *Cartels in Action: Case Studies in International Business Diplomacy* (The Twentieth Century World Fund, 1946), at p. 3.

6   For an overview of the development of business forms (legal and otherwise), concentration, corporate structures and 'big business', see John F. Wilson, *British Business History, 1720–1994* (Manchester University Press, 1995), chapters 3 and 4.

7   Roman Piotrowski, *Cartels and Trust: Their Origin and Historical Development from the Economic and Legal Aspects* (George Allen & Unwin, 1933), at p. 1.

8   Kleinwächter, *Die Kartelle* (Verlag der Wagner'schen Universitaets-Buchhandlung, Innsbruck, 1883), at p. iii.

Cartels since the dawn of history?

Herein lies a lesson of historical enquiry, since a number of writers have asserted
that cartels have existed and operated since 'antiquity': Kotsiris, for instance has
asserted that 'the antitrust idea is as old as civilisation, yet as contemporary as
the human spirit'.[9] But care should be taken to appreciate the historical context
and the language used to describe these situations. It is interesting for instance
to note how many cited examples of early historical 'cartels' actually refer to
abusive exploitation for private profit in the important grain market in those earlier
societies, which may be seen as a more specific and crucial issue distinct from
the general regulation of trading activity – problems in the grain trade rather than
proto-competition policy.[10] Nonetheless, the comparison with organisations such
as the guilds and other earlier forms of trading association in Europe mentioned
above is instructive. For some of these organisations had a role in not only
controlling trading activities, comparable to the modern cartel, but also one in
regulating and sanctioning unacceptable trading activity, in a manner comparable
to modern competition regulators such as the European Commission. An example
is cited by Patrick Landtschner, as depicted by a surviving fresco of the Wool
Guild of Florence:

> Many guilds had their own governmental structure, drew up statutes, and
> functioned as courts. This gave them varying degrees of civil or even penal
> jurisdiction over their members and their trade … A telling illustration of the
> guilds' claims to a stake in the provision of justice in the city is a decoration in
> the audience chamber of the wool guild's court in Florence: there, a fresco from
> c1340–5 depicts Brutus, the alleged founder of the Roman Republic, as a judge
> surrounded by the virtues of Prudence, Justice, Fortitude, and Temperance, who
> push back men wanting to threaten the judge.[11]

In some respects the role and competence of the Florentine Wool Guild anticipates
that of the original European Community, the Coal and Steel Community, which
served as an intergovernmental organisation to govern and regulate significant

---

9   Lambros E. Kotsiris, 'An Antitrust Case in Ancient Greek Law', 22 (1988)
International Law 451, at p. 451.

10   See, for instance, Kotsiris, note 9 above; Franklin D. Jones, 'Historical Development
of the Law of Business Competition', 35 (1926) *Yale Law Journal* 905. Examples are drawn
by a range of authors from earlier English common and statute law, and earlier still, Greece,
Mesopotamia, India, China and Old Testament Israel.

11   Patrick Lantschner, 'Justice Contested and Affirmed: Jurisdiction and Conflict
in Late Medieval Italian Cities', chapter 3 in Fernanda Pirie and Judith Scheele (eds),
Legalism: Community and Justice (Oxford University Press, 2014), at pp. 80–81. The
fresco is entitled *Brutus, the Good Judge, Supported by the Four Cardinal Virtues* (an
allegorical political fresco by a follower of Giotto, in the Audience Chamber of the Arte
della Lana, *c.*1340, west wall, Florence).

markets across a number of European countries, while itself in doing so making use of cartel-like control mechanisms such as market allocation and production quotas.[12] It is therefore possible to talk about a history of *cartel-like* strategies, but the role, provenance and membership of these organisations must be read in the particular historical context. The basic method may remain constant, but motivation and participation may be very contingent.

Evidence of cartel activity

Space does not allow for much further early historical investigation, and it may be well then to take the discussion forward with Adam Smith's much cited observation in his work *The Wealth of Nations*, that 'people in the same trade seldom meet together ... But the conversation ends in a conspiracy against the public, or in some contrivance to raise prices'.[13] This statement has been exploited by more recent commentators on cartel activity as an early perception of the inevitable tendency of business persons, as rational actors, to seek private profit at the expense of others, so justifying efforts at regulation of practices such as price fixing and market sharing. Once again, there is a lesson here in the interpretation of historical data, since care must be taken regarding the way in which to understand Smith's observation. In particular, there is the question to what extent Smith's intention was empirical or judgmental, the latter being suggested perhaps by the choice of words such as 'conspiracy' and 'contrivance'. Yet there is also an argument that Smith's method was akin to that of a twenty-first-century behavioural economist and that he had a more complex and nuanced view of the conduct of people in business. Referring to the problem identified by a number of Adam Smith scholars of an apparent contradiction as between such a statement as that above in *The Wealth of Nations* and what may be found in his earlier work of 1759, *Theory of Moral Sentiment*, Ashraf, Camerer and Loewenstein have argued that:

> Adam Smith's world is not inhabited by dispassionate rational purely self-interested agents, but rather by multi-dimensional and realistic human beings' who are 'driven by an internal struggle between their impulsive, fickle and indispensable passions, and their impartial spectator.[14]

On this reading, Smith's empirical analysis of business activity suggests both an inevitable tendency towards cartel activity but also a complex motivation, and may stand then as a springboard for some of the argument and discussion which

---

12 See Treaty of Paris, establishing the European Coal and Steel Community, 1951, especially Articles 57–64, regulating production and prices (in this respect, acting rather like an intergovernmental crisis cartel).

13 *The Wealth of Nations*, 1776, Book 1, chapter X.

14 Nava Ashraf, Colin F. Camerer and George Loewenstein, 'Adam Smith: Behavioral Economist', 19 (2005) *Journal of Economic Perspectives* 131, at p. 142.

follows in this study, that cartelisation is likely to happen at some times and in some circumstances and comes about for various reasons and not just as a matter of rational actor calculation. Consciousness and discussion of the pervasive nature of cartel activity appears to have increased during the course of the nineteenth century, leading to a fuller and richer reporting of its occurrence and character. From the second part of the nineteenth century and well into the twentieth century there is a growing body of detailed reportage and comment, comprising a substantial literature on the subject in Europe and North America. Moreover, while much of this conduct remained broadly speaking lawful (at least in Europe), there was little to hide, and information about what was actually happening in this way in markets was accessible and usable. Thus it is possible to draw upon a large body of material, whether it be turn of the century American 'muck-raking' in relation to powerful but much disliked trusts, or more scientific discussion of 'das Kartellproblem' in Germany. It is not difficult, therefore to construct a picture of participation in cartel arrangements and their market operation through much of this period, well into the second half of the twentieth century.

Cartels in action: In a state of nature and as a means of controlling the anarchy of the market

As Michael Nesmith commented, 'total control of the subway, total control of my life, total control of all variables … I'm sure that's what happiness means'[15] – and there is a sense in which cartel activity is largely in itself a matter of control and regulation and of ordering nature. In presenting sources of information regarding the operation of cartels it would be useful to distinguish two different contexts: first cartels as they have operated in a world which does not seek significantly and strongly to regulate their activity, and secondly cartels as they now operate in a world in which there is a serious and determined effort of such regulation. The first context may be thought of as cartels *in a state of nature* (markets largely unregulated by public interest intervention) or as a kind of Garden of Eden in which traders themselves act as gardeners seeking to tame nature (or the anarchic market, to use Kleinwächter's phrase) in their own interest. In the second context, the state of nature has become a kind of *garden state*, subject to an externally imposed order for the benefit of those who wish to use the garden, and the cartels have become unwelcome features of the garden, to be weeded out for the benefit of the garden's design. This is an important distinction, which can help in understanding different perceptions of cartels and in turn also different approaches to their regulation. In the first place, in the 'state of nature', there is of course a more benign perception, and thus a different business culture and different regulatory culture. Secondly, the cartels will operate differently in each context and those participating in such arrangements will behave differently – in the second context, once subject to hostile legal control, the business behaviour will naturally become less open,

---

15   Michael Nesmith, *Total Control* (from the album *The Newer Stuff* (Rhino, 1989)).

more defensive, more subversive and itself more hostile, as methods of regulation evolve from the more consensual to the more confrontational, from the more peaceful to the more belligerent. In that behavioural sense, twenty-first-century cartels have become different phenomena from their earlier twentieth-century forbears and must be described differently, even if their basic anti-competitive strategies have remained constant.

For those reasons, and in spite of the growing historical distance, there is a fuller, willing and perhaps then more reliable account of cartels and monopolies in action in the later nineteenth and earlier twentieth centuries. This account has been handed down in a number of written sources, both descriptive and analytical.[16] The descriptive literature has a varying provenance: sometimes neutral reportage of an academic research nature (such as Stocking and Watkins' and Hexner's mid-century monographs),[17] sometimes politically motivated and more like journalistic investigation (such as the 'muck-raking' antitrust writings, some of it very detailed such as Ida Tarbell's book[18] on Standard Oil), and sometimes as part of a legal record from those earlier cases and more tentative attempts at regulation. Many of these sources are now readily accessible, with perhaps only some language barriers to overcome, and anyone now seeking some idea of the internal experience and operation of cartels during that time may quickly acquire a detailed picture of such cartels in action. The above-mentioned works of Stocking and Watkin, and Hexner, for instance, provide detailed narratives of the operation of some major international cartels through the first half of the twentieth century. The overall picture, certainly outside the United States and leaving to one side the operation there of more blatantly monopolistic trusts, is one of corporate striving to deal with the anarchy of markets, to guard against and respond to risks and uncertainty. The attempts to do so fared better or worse over time and place, and cartel success and achievement was to be measured in those terms, where cartel stability was a good and cartel breakdown was a mark of failure. As Conley and O'Barr have argued: 'In the business world, price fixing is the ultimate form of control – control over the vicissitudes of the market. It is the economic equivalent of a sailor being able to control the wind'.[19] In a world in which traders fear unexpected severe economic downturn, cartel arrangements can provide considerable comfort and security.

Viewed in this way, it may be illuminating to compare also the character and motivation of the American 'trust builders' and the European 'cartel pioneers'

---

16   For an overview, see Harding and Joshua, note 3 above, and David J. Gerber, note 4 above.

17   Stocking and Watkins, note 5 above; Ervin Hexner, *International Cartels* (Pitman, 1946).

18   Ida Minerva Tarbell, *The History of the Standard Oil Company* (McClure, Phillips and Co., 1904).

19   J.M. Conley and W.M. O'Barr, 'Crime and Custom in Corporate Society: A Cultural Perspective on Corporate Misconduct', 60 (1997) *Law and Contemporary Problems* 5, at p. 13.

in the late nineteenth and early twentieth centuries. It would be fair to say that the American trusts, as typified by Rockefeller's 'Oil Trust' (eventually the Standard Oil Company) and Duke's 'Tobacco Trust' (the American Tobacco Company) were aggressive drives towards monopolisation, often led by powerful and dynamic entrepreneurs such as John D. Rockefeller, James Buchanan Duke, Andrew Carnegie and John Pierpont Morgan.[20] The same may have been true of some British attempts to emulate that strategy such as William Lever's short-lived 'Soap Trust' in 1906.[21] These trusts provoked quick concern and a popular hostility, accompanied by journalistic campaigning and caricature in the press (indeed the campaign mounted by the *Daily Mirror* and *Daily Mail* in Britain against the 'Soap Trust' was largely instrumental in bringing about its quick demise).[22] In the US the political outcome was the enactment of what was to prove seminal *anti-trust* legislation in the form of the Sherman Act in 1890. To gain, then, an understanding of the contemporary view at the time of anti-competitive strategies on that side of the Atlantic it should be understood as an antagonism towards the attitude and demeanour of those individual leaders of the movement, the latter nicely encapsulated in 'Buck' Duke's (possibly apocryphal) announcement to the Player brothers (British tobacco 'barons') on disembarking at Liverpool: 'hello Boys, I'm Duke from New York, come to buy your business'.[23]

In contrast, the German counterpart cartel pioneers of the early twentieth century appear to belong to a different breed. Two individuals stand out in this role: Carl Duisberg of Bayer AG and Carl Bosch of BASF, and later both of IG Farben. Both men had a similar background, as industrial chemists, and both rose through the ranks of their respective companies, but very much as corporate-minded actors and not as entrepreneurial barons of industry (indeed Bosch was awarded a Nobel Prize for Chemistry in 1931).[24] In their leading corporate roles, they were mainly

---

20   The careers and roles of such iconic American entrepreneurs are well documented. See also Alfred D. Chandler, *Scale and Scope: The Dynamics of Industrial Capitalism* (Harvard University Press, 1994).

21   Charles Wilson, *The History of Unilever* (Cassell, 1954), chapter 6, especially pp. 72–8.

22   Ibid. See in particular the cartoon in the *Daily Mirror*, 22 October 1906, 'The Greedy Soap Trust'.

23   The Anglo-American 'Tobacco War' was a very revealing episode, whereby James Buchanan Duke's monopolising ambition in Britain resulted in the defensive formation of the huge Imperial Tobacco Company and the Anglo-American accommodation in the form of the British–American Tobacco Company. See Howard Cox, 'The Anglo-American Tobacco war of 1901–02: A Clash of Business Cultures and Strategies', unpublished paper, Business History Conference, 21–23 March 2013, Columbus, Ohio.

24   Peter Hayes, 'Carl Bosch and Carl Krauch: Chemistry and the Political Economy of Germany, 1925–1945', 47 (1987) *The Journal of Economic History* 353. Hayes argues about Bosch: 'In his view the progress of mankind, like that of his firm, depended on the unfettered expression of individual talent, and that in turn on the fostering of free thought, free trade, and free enterprise' (at p. 356).

motivated by the need to manage problems of market volatility, which led both towards the federated cartel-like solution of the interessengemeinschaft, and hence IG Farben. As architects of IG Farben, they clashed regarding the more precise method, Bosch favouring complete merger while Duisberg argued for a looser structure under the umbrella of a holding company.[25] But the kind of cartelisation that they promoted was defensive and managerial, distinguishable from the more nakedly aggressive and monopolising ambition of the American entrepreneurs. Across the Atlantic there were two different goals of control: an American quest for individualistic power, and a German striving for order and predictability in an anarchic market place.

Cartels in action: In the garden state and as objects of legal control

In the history of business cartel regulation, it is clear that, outside North America and especially in Europe, there was a degree of toleration and sometimes enthusiasm and governmental support for such strategies.[26] American impatience and even incredulity is well summarised in the famous Roosevelt Letter[27] in 1944, which in some way foretold the change to come, from the Garden of Eden to the garden state, although again, how that change came about is not a straightforward story. Competition regulation, and the sharp end of that as the control of cartels, evolved variably in different jurisdictions – more quickly and fully in Britain and Germany for example, but much later elsewhere, both in Europe (for instance, in Italy or Spain) and other parts of the world. But by the close of the century there was an evident momentum in legal development, with competition regimes springing up worldwide, the adoption of standard models of regulation and a significant resort to criminalisation across a number of jurisdictions.

---

25   Peter Hayes, *Industry and Ideology: IG Farben in the Nazi Era* (2nd edn, Cambridge University Press, 2000), Part I.

26   See, for instance, Harding and Joshua, note 2 above, chapter 3; Gerber, note 4 above, chapter 4; David S. Landes, *The Unbound Prometheus: Technological Change and Industrial Development in Western Europe from 1750 to the Present* (Cambridge University Press, 1969).

27   'During the past half century the United States has developed a tradition in opposition to private monopolies. The Sherman and Clayton Acts have become as much a part of the American way of life as the due-process clause of the Constitution. By protecting the consumer against monopoly these statutes guarantee him the benefits of competition ... Unfortunately, a number of foreign countries, particularly in continental Europe, do not possess such a tradition against cartels. On the contrary, cartels have received encouragement from some of these governments ... Cartel practices which restrict the free flow of goods in foreign commerce will have to be curbed ...'. Letter from the President of the United States to the Secretary of state concerning cartel policies, 6 September 1944.

There are now fuller more recent accounts and analyses of these significant changes in policy and law,[28] and for present purposes space will allow for just the salient points in this narrative of legal development to be drawn out. The main narrative would seem to start with a historical transatlantic division of opinion, and then post-1945 a narrowing of the gap, leading to what now appears as a virtually global consensus on the matter and a move towards a uniform and connected international system of cartel regulation. However, even some two decades into the twenty-first century the overall picture is complex and care should be taken not to indulge in an easy 'Whig' historiography[29] of this subject. There are a number of possible readings of this narrative of change.

It might first of all be tempting to interpret these developments as 'tales of Yankee power' and the Roosevelt Letter as a statement of a doom foretold. In so far as the official political and legal stance on business cartels has hardened over time, shifting from a consensual and administrative regulation to a tougher resort to legal enforcement (civil claims, penalties and criminal law), this might appear as a triumph for American ideology, as embodied in the seminal Sherman Act legislation. And, indeed, there has been some American crusading activity since the 1990s, exemplified by the Department of Justice's (DoJ) strategy of urging other jurisdictions to engage in stronger enforcement, typically through the use of criminal law.[30] Although rather belatedly, it might appear that the DoJ has taken up the Roosevelt Letter as a Papal Bull and embarked upon a vigorous diplomacy of persuasion, announcing that 'from Hollywood to Hong Kong, criminal antitrust enforcement is coming to a city near you',[31] and with some success, for instance, the conversion of a leading British politician to the cause in the late 1990s.[32] More cynically, it might be argued that American enthusiasm was mainly self-interested: a concern about the harmful impact of international cartel action on the US markets and economy led the DoJ to target such cartels in its own enforcement, in which case criminalisation abroad would aid processes of mutual legal assistance and extradition and so have greater deterrent impact on foreign business persons tempted to use cartel strategies.[33] Overall, this version of events is one of American intentions, influence and legal models.

---

28   For an overview and references, see Harding and Joshua, note 2 above, chapters 4 and 5.

29   In the sense of interpreting events as part of an inevitable progressive historical movement, particularly towards the attainment of greater enlightenment and liberal goals.

30   See Christopher Harding, 'Business Collusion as a Criminological Phenomenon: Exploring the Global Criminalisation of Business Cartels', 14 (2006) *Critical Criminology* 181, at p. 194.

31   Scott D. Hammond, 'From Hollywood to Hong Kong: Criminal Antitrust Enforcement is Coming to a City near You', Department of Justice speech, Chicago, 2001.

32   Gordon Brown, as Chancellor of the Exchequer: Irwin Stelzer, 'Guess What? Gordon has Done Something Right', *The Spectator*, 5 December 2007.

33   Harding, note 30 above, at pp. 194–5.

But there is a risk of overstating the impact of the Sherman Act model and its vision of deep cartelist delinquency. In the first place, despite some assertion of an inexorable move towards criminalisation, there have been notable sites of resistance, especially in a number of jurisdictions where there has been a political and legal debate which has decided against that legal strategy.[34] Moreover, the adoption of civil proceedings against cartels, although encouraged by the European Commission, has been a slow and problematical process in the European context.[35] Then, despite the strong intergovernmental (for instance, the OECD and the EU), governmental and legislative rhetoric, in practice enforcement efforts and sentiment have not always matched that rhetoric, whether it be the failure in the event to bring criminal prosecutions or civil claims, or judicial reluctance to engage in tough sentencing (the 'inherited treasure sword' syndrome).[36] And finally, as a matter of international standardisation, it is not the model of the Sherman Act which has been adopted around the world by the new competition law regimes, but rather that of the EU.[37] The explanation does not reside in an easy assertion of American hegemony.

Contrariwise, it might be instructive to explore instead an hypothesis of European hegemony and the possibility of the EU and its policies as an important catalyst of legal change. Certainly, in a European context, it is impossible to disregard the impact of the European Common/Single Market project and its development of competition policy and law. The EU regime has emerged as one of the most significant worldwide in terms of competition law and cartel control, and that fact has to be linked to the underlying trade liberalisation agenda of the EC/EU. Single Market policies and rules, and their growing ascendancy in the past half century or more, have had a decisive effect on the view of cartelisation and the role of business cartels. The favourable view of cartels in the first half of the twentieth century was closely linked with broader economic policy aimed at the protection of national markets and national industry,[38] and this found its logical conclusion in the integration of 'private' cartel-like organisations (such as IG Farben in Germany) into the totalitarian machinery of state (as happened in Nazi Germany and Japan).[39] That sinister association between the private and corporate mechanisms of market control and authoritarian government inevitably coloured the political view of business cartels in the post-Second World War period (this much was evident in the text of the Roosevelt Letter). But more importantly still,

---

34   For example: Belgium, Sweden and Finland.

35   See, for instance, Wouter P.J. Wils, 'Is Criminalization of EU Competition Law the Answer?' 28 (2005) *World Competition* 148.

36   Harding, note 30 above, at pp. 192–4.

37   For example, the Singapore legislation of 2004 enacts a cartel prohibition in Section 34 which reproduces the language of Article 101 of the Treaty on the Function of the EU.

38   See, for instance, Gerber, note 4 above, chapter 4.

39   Hayes, note 25 above.

the growing ascendancy of market liberalisation policy and promotion of the latter by significant and powerful intergovernmental organisations and their agencies – notably the European Communities, EFTA, NAFTA, the OECD, the GATT and then the World Trade Organisation, and a number of specialised agencies of the UN – elevated the role of competition policy and cast the anti-competitive character of cartels in a different light. Thus, to take the EC rules on competition, as laid down in principle in Article 85 of the original EEC Treaty, as an example of the new orthodoxy: such activities as price fixing and market sharing, not only restrictive of competition in themselves, also had an impact on the flow of goods and services between the Member States, so undermining the functioning of the larger common market. What was the point of removing fiscal and other state-imposed barriers to trade within the new EEC market, if companies were still able to set up barriers by means of a market sharing arrangement? Cartels were straightaway a main enemy of this regional and supranational competition policy, and their classic strategies were listed in pride of place ('in particular') in the main prohibition of Article 85(1) (a)–(c) of the EEC Treaty (now Article 101 of the TFEU).

In a way related to the fostering of the 'open market', competition policy of the later twentieth century also evolved a more significant element of consumer protection in an increasingly consumer-oriented and consumer-aware society, in a move to ensure value-for-money, choice and fair treatment for the end-consumer as a market actor. Thus the object of legal protection had shifted somewhat. Whereas earlier German cartel control was preoccupied with the impact of cartels on the interests of other traders (excluded from or pressurised into cartel participation),[40] by the late twentieth-century consumer interests had come to the fore, as the latter became identified as primary victims of cartelisation, having to pay unjustifiable mark-ups for the goods and services they require. In this way, the identity of the cartelist shifted from that of the market controller to that of market thief and fraudster. This view of the cartelist as a cheat, duping the unwitting consumer, is encapsulated in the famous DoJ Vitamin Cartel videotape quotation from an actual cartel meeting, one cartelist saying to another: 'You're my friend. I wanna be closer to you than I am to any customer'.[41]

Thus it is shifts in economic policy, and in particular the development of competition policy within the context of the international trading system and a greater emphasis on trade liberalisation[42] and consumer protection, which has transformed the perception of cartel activity and thus the identity and

---

40   Gerber, note 4 above, chapter 4.

41   US Department of Justice, Vitamin Cartel investigation, transcript from the recording of a cartel meeting in Maui, Hawaii, 11 March 1994.

42   For an informative and accessible critique of the argument that trade liberalisation and its associated policies are both inevitable and desirable, see Richard Kozul-Wright and Paul Rayment, *The Resistible Rise of Market Fundamentalism: Rethinking Development Policy in an Unbalanced World* (Zed Books, 2007).

characterisation of the cartelist. It is not difficult to find examples of recent official statements which neatly summarise the contemporary economic objection to cartel behaviour and the reasons for what is now a widespread and categorical legal prohibition. For instance, the Irish Competition Authority's *Guideline on Cartels* stated at one point that:

> The total cost to consumers and the economy of cartels cannot be measured with any certainty but almost certainly amounts to hundreds of millions of pounds. A cartel which adds a few pence to the price of a product purchased by the vast majority of consumers would earn substantial profits at their customers' expense. In addition, cartels impose losses on society in terms of reduced efficiency, and lower output (known as dead-weight losses). Estimates suggest that such dead-weight losses can amount to 1–2% of total GDP which is a substantial cost.[43]

This may be a statement of objection in terms of pure economic and market analysis, but it a prevailing orthodox vision of how the contemporary world works, and the world in question is a globalised, interdependent world of open market, the garden state which is now being managed by both national governments and intergovernmental organisations such as the EU, OECD and WTO. This management is no longer the business of 'state of nature' gardeners such as Duisberg and Bosch, since controlling economic anarchy has become the responsibility of public authority, and indeed this is also an assumption of democratic governance – to have elected rather than self-appointed controllers. The key to understanding the shifting perception of cartels lies of course in shifting ideas regarding competition governance, and in that sense the cartel of now is a very different phenomenon from the cartel of 100 years ago.

But there is an additional element, which may be evident in a historical comparison between 'old school' cartelists in the mould of Duisberg and Bosch and their twenty-first-century counterparts – for instance, businessmen such as Alfred Taubman, Ian Norris or Peter Whittle (whose roles will be recounted in more detail later).[44] The early German pioneers were respected (and remain respected – there is a Carl Bosch Museum in Heidelberg, for instance) and could be quite open regarding their efforts of cartel diplomacy. The more recent activity of Taubman, Norris and Whittle to establish and manage cartel operations was by contrast secretive and in legal terms cast in a sinister and delinquent light, and each of the these men served prison terms as part of the panoply of sanctions applied in relation to their cartels. The lesson of this comparison is that the business cartel now is not only a matter of economic objection, but also of legal objection in so far as it exists and operates in defiance of legal prohibition and will therefore also

---

43   Irish Competition Authority, *Guideline on Cartels*, chapter 1.

44   The roles of Taubman (Art House Auctions Cartel) and Whittle (Marine Hose Cartel) are discussed in more detail in Chapter 5. Norris (Carbon Products Cartel) was involved in a US extradition saga – see Harding and Joshua, note 3 above, at pp. 295–6.

most probably comprise an infrastructure of subterfuge, secrecy and obstruction of justice. The present-day cartel is therefore a phenomenon of two significant aspects – something which is first of all the product of market circumstances and economic policy, and then secondly also something which is an outcome of law enforcement.[45] This phenomenological analysis of the cartel as an entity which is both objectionable in economic terms and delinquent in normative terms will form an important part of the argument in this work and will be taken up further in the discussion in the following chapter.

Agency: The puzzle of individual and organisational interaction

There is a third important problematic aspect of how to understand the subject-matter of business cartels and cartelisation, and this is something which the subject shares with other organisational phenomena in the contemporary world, such as states, religious organisations, tribal groups, non-state governmental actors, companies and other incorporated persons, and at the far end of this spectrum, joint criminal enterprise and organised crime groups.[46] This is the problem of the human individual and collective units and arises from the fact that in the contemporary world so much human action is organised and realised through collectivities and groups. Arising from this situation there are a number of difficult questions, both theoretical and practical, regarding the attribution and understanding of action within and by such collective actors, and the identity of the latter for moral and legal purposes. Put simply, this is a puzzle of action and agency: is the action in question that of the individuals or the group? This is not the place for detailed examination of the underlying organisation theory and the debate on the nature of collective identity and personality;[47] suffice it to say that a strategic choice is now available to policy makers, lawyers, criminologists and even economists – to target either human individuals or collective/corporate actors for purposes of discussion, policy application and legal enforcement.

Business cartels inhabit this area of discussion in a particular way, since they present the possibility of *three levels of agency* – that of the human individual, that of the corporate person or company, and that of the cartel as a kind of organisation. To illustrate this point as a matter of legal process, it may be noted that typically an investigation may be undertaken in relation to a cartel, and then decisions taken

---

45   Christopher Harding, 'A Pathology of Business Cartels: Original Sin or the Child of Regulation?' 1 (2010) *New Journal of European Criminal Law* 44.

46   See generally Harding, *Criminal Enterprise*, note 1 above.

47   For an informative and enlightening overview of what may be termed the organisation theory in relation to this topic, see William H. Starbuck, 'The Origins of Organization Theory', chapter 5 in Haridimos Tsoukas and Christian Knudsen (eds), *The Oxford Handbook of Organization Theory* (Oxford University Press, 2003); also, Harding, *Criminal Enterprise*, note 1 above, chapters 3, 4, and 5.

against and sanctions applied to both companies and the individuals working for them. In the domain of law, ethics and criminology, this may be a complex matter for analysis, to disentangle the allocation of responsibility for action and understand the interaction between individual and corporate or collective actors. This conundrum of agency is important, yet insufficiently recognised for what it is in the discussion of anti-cartel policy and action at the present time. At the very least for practical reasons, much may depend on the strategic choice (and recognising that there is such a choice) regarding who to deal with as a matter of regulation, and for purposes of the outcome of legal procedure and the application of sanctions.

Enough has been said above in this chapter to show that the operation of a business cartel is a complex and sometimes uncertainly defined structure of action and participation. Economically significant cartels will involve the action and interaction of both human and corporate persons and an infrastructure of organisation over time, and the whole bundle or package of cartel activity (the 'cartel as a whole', as a 'single continuing infringement',[48] or as a 'box') may be read and interpreted in a number of ways. Here are three possible readings of cartel action:

- The cartel acts *in itself*, as an organisation, or according to a certain legal description, as a 'joint criminal/illegal enterprise', or as a 'conspiracy'.
- The cartel acts as *a group of corporate actors* (companies or firms) and the locus of action is to be found in these entities acting collectively.
- The cartel acts *as a group of individuals*, acting for and in the name of companies, but themselves determining what may appear as the collective cartel activity of the companies.

Each of the above would be feasible interpretations of the phenomenon and could serve as a basis for cartel narrative or biography, and it is important that those who then present such narratives have a clear idea of the agency that they rely upon within their account.

Cartel agency

In fact, most narratives, and much of the policy and legal action, focus upon the corporate and human agency, and not that of the cartel. Indeed there is little contemporary sense of cartel agency or of the cartel as an autonomous actor. The cartel is much of the time a description which is employed by outsiders, especially economists and legal prosecutors, to conveniently summarise and identify the employment of anti-competitive strategies in 'packages' of action. Moreover, it is unlikely that companies or individuals who may be labelled as 'cartelists' self-

---

48 For further discussion of these concepts, see Harding and Joshua, note 3 above, at pp. 170–77.

consciously regard themselves or refer to themselves as such, saying to each other for instance: 'Well, let's start this sixth private and secret meeting of the Nuts and Bolts Cartel'. Contemporary cartels have no formal identity, let alone legal personality, and, as has been noted, the extent and nature of their operation and participation may be evidentially uncertain. Actual cartelists, from the evidence, refer to their interactions with each other in a more oblique fashion – 'you are my friend, I wanna be closer to you',[49] or 'this is a great initiative'.[50] In part, this murky self-identity derives from a furtive underground existence and the consequent tendency to used coded language. Indeed, this is now the common depiction of cartelist behaviour in the new genre of educational films favoured by regulators,[51] which depict a dialogue of ambiguity ('it is my job to know everything',[52] or 'your secret is safe with me')[53] or of legal and moral uncertainty ('it sounds like you've got yourself into a cartel, mate')[54].

By contrast, historically earlier cartels, able to operate openly and lawfully, did possess a clearer formal and even legal identity, for instance as trade associations,[55] holding companies, or *Interessengemeinschaften*. In this respect, the morphology of cartels, in its historical perspective, is instructive. Earlier cartels were able to adopt a more formal character in terms of structure, decision-making and hierarchy, and even in the adverse legal environment in the US it is interesting to observe how some of the early trusts acquired corporate forms (Standard Oil and American Tobacco were leading examples) and then how the defensive British arrangement, a kind of reactive cartel of British tobacco suppliers, quickly took on a clear corporate form as the Imperial Tobacco Company.[56] Similarly, the arrangement of the trade association, much favoured in continental European countries, possessed a clear formal public identity, and endured well into the 1960s and 1970s, becoming a first major target of EC competition enforcement.[57] Such early cartels, adopting various formal identities, could more readily be seen as autonomous agents, leading

---

49   Vitamin Cartel Miami transcript, note 41 above.

50   Decision of the Office of Fair Trading: Agreements between Hasbro, Argos and Littlewoods fixing the price of Hasbro Toys and Games, 19 February 2003, quoted from the evidence.

51   See *The Cartel Cinema*, Appendix Two to Chapter 4.

52   Ibid., *The Raid*.

53   Ibid., *The Raid*.

54   Ibid., *The Marker*.

55   On the historical background, see Hiroaki Yamazaki and Matao Miyamoto (eds), *Trade Associations in Business History: The International Conference on Business History 14* (University of Tokyo Press, 1988). Comparisons may also be drawn between the role of the medieval guilds and modern trading associations.

56   Imperial Tobacco, *The Imperial Story 1901–2001: Celebrating One Hundred Years* (Imperial Tobacco, 2001).

57   On the early EC enforcement of competition law, see Harding and Joshua, note 3 above, p. 112 *et seq.* and pp. 121–2. For a recent account of how trade associations may continue to operate in an anti-competitive way, see Jon Leibowitz. 'The Good, the Bad and

and directing the action of their participating members, manifestly in the case of holding companies, in a more 'federal' manner in the case of associations. The main characteristics of formal structure and enduring and continuous operation, combined with the capacity for autonomous and authoritative decision-making, bequeathed to these earlier cartels a real sense of agency.

This is not to say that agency is wholly outside the reach of contemporary cartels of the early twenty-first century – much depends on their individual circumstances and internal configuration. Arguably, there is a world of difference between the situation of the Art House Auctions Cartel (Sotheby's/Christie's) and that of the industry-wide cartelised context of the Soda Ash Cartel, both of which will be examined in biographical detail later.[58] The Art House Auctions Cartel was very much a frolic, a matter of personal enterprise on the part of four powerful individuals within the two organisations, very distinct from the main culture of those two corporate actors and quickly disowned by others within both Sotheby's and Christie's. On the other hand, the Soda Ash Cartel (Solvay and ICI) was a long pedigree arrangement located in an industrial sector historically prone to and habituated to cartelisation,[59] and best seen as part of a well-established family or tribal group of related cartels, where the cartel incentive may be seen as part of the corporate genetic code (or it might be said, corporate fingerprint or DNA). The Soda Ash Cartel provides a good example of a long-standing arrangement, from the 1930s through to the 1980s, with a changing morphology, from a formal agreement to secret informal arrangement in the early 1970s in response to changes in legal regulation.[60] These two examples will be compared in detail later, but they illustrate an important point about the diversity of cartel forms, cultures, modes of operation and participation, and historical context, on the basis of which it may be more meaningful to attribute some kind of agency to the Soda Ash Cartel than to the Art House Auctions exceptional adventure.

In the final analysis, it is this diversity of arrangement in practice which would probably serve to defeat any sensible attribution of agency to the business cartel in its contemporary role. In coming to any decisions about organisational forms, participation and questions of agency, it may be more helpful to consider categories such as 'conspiracy' and 'joint criminal enterprise' in this particular context. Conspiracy is a well-established concept in Anglo-American criminal law and joint criminal enterprise has been employed more recently, especially in international criminal law; both are devices which can be used to clarify issues of individual participation in collective activity, by eventually attributing individual responsibility by reference to that individual's role in the collective action.[61] This

---

the Ugly: Trade Associations and Antitrust', American Bar Association, Antitrust Spring Meeting, 30 March 2005, Washington DC.

58   See Chapter 5.
59   See Appendix One to this chapter.
60   See the account provided in Chapter 5.
61   See Harding, *Criminal Enterprise*, note 2 above, chapter 10.

approach can serve well in legal decision-making on cartels as such. It is no accident that the wording of the Sherman Act picks up on a favoured approach to criminalisation in US law, especially at the federal level, in casting delinquent conduct as an offence of conspiracy.[62] Moreover, business cartels, as discussed and analysed just here, can be nicely accommodated within the contemporary idea of joint criminal enterprise[63] (or joint illegal enterprise, if criminal law is not used for purposes of legal control). 'Joint enterprise', it may be argued, is one of the fairest and happiest general descriptions of cartel activity ...

Corporate and individual agency

A cartel, whatever its scope, form and period of operation, will in most cases comprise a number of corporate[64] and individual human actors, and then the crucial question of agency would be: who is driving the activity and organisation of the cartel (on that view, making the companies and individuals the subjects of action and the cartel the object of action)? The Sherman Act makes an easy ontological assumption that it is or may be both at the same time, grouping both individuals and companies together as co-conspirators, even if there is an objection that individuals employed by and acting for a company should not logically be regarded as a separate agent for purposes of establishing cartel action.[65] Other legal systems attempt to distinguish the corporate and individual roles within a cartel for purposes of allocating responsibility and liability to sanctions. For instance, the EU rules, as laid down in Article 101(1) of the TFEU, apply to 'undertakings' (in practice, companies) and UK law distinguishes between the civil liability of companies in relation to infringement of the Competition Act 1998 and the criminal liability of individuals in relation to the 'cartel offence' laid down in Section 188 of the Enterprise Act 2002.[66] To some extent, this remains an ontological and legal puzzle, turning on the question whether the company has a separate identity from its employees and executives in relation to the relevant cartel activity. This is a crucial question for discussion in the present work, since it bears upon the

---

62   See, for background, George P. Fletcher, *Basic Concepts of Criminal Law* (Oxford University Press, 1998), chapter 11.

63   See Harding, *Criminal Enterprise*, note 2 above, chapter 10.

64   Since the present discussion has as its focus the more economically significant cartels, often international in scope, it will proceed on the assumption of corporate membership. In practice, of course, there are smaller-scale, more local cartels which will comprise individuals rather than corporate actors as the business person participants.

65   There appears to have been little American agonising on this point, associated perhaps with the enthusiasm for casting some criminal liability as conspiracy, as an entrenched feature of American legal culture, whereas European legal analysis may more readily pick up on a 'double jeopardy' or recycling of criminal charges objection in this approach: that a number of violations and possible defendants are being derived from the same, single event and situation.

66   For further discussion, see Harding and Joshua, note 3 above, at p. 347 *et seq.*

moral, criminological and legal evaluation of the cartel action, and in turn affects any analysis of the appropriate form and strategy of legal control, the impact and effectiveness of any sanctions, and the question of sanctions accumulation (the application of a number of different sanctions to different actors in relation to the 'same' situation or conduct, as discussed further in Chapter 3).

It is argued here that this big question of agency – whether this is all a matter of companies, individuals, or both – should be addressed and answered by some empirical enquiry into how cartels have operated in practice, in order to understand the roles of and interaction between companies and individuals: hence, the biographical method. But even factual evidence may not always present a clear picture of separated corporate and individual conduct in individual cases, and equally important, it will be seen that such enquiry may not provide a consistent picture or pattern over time and space.

The task of disentangling corporate and individual agency has two important problematic aspects, the first ontological, and the second empirical. The ontological problem arises from the reality of any distinct and autonomous corporate identity, agency and action – often expressed in terms of the question and debate as to whether companies and other corporate persons have an independent existence in the material (or 'real') world (as advocated by 'realists')[67] or are no more than aggregations of individual humans dressed up as legal fictions (no 'ding an sich', just what the law says is there at any one point in time).[68] This ontological debate, which was engaged in fiercely by lawyers, philosophers and sociologists some 100 years ago,[69] remains largely unresolved, as may be seen for example in recent attempts to deal with the issue of 'corporate homicide',[70] or from a certain retreat in international criminal law from 'abstract entity responsibility' towards human individual responsibility.[71] Sure enough, companies have legal personality and

---

67 For instance, the German theorist Otto Von Gierke and the British writer A.V. Dicey. As the latter argued: 'It is a fact which has received far too little notice from English lawyers, that, whenever men act in concert for a common purpose, they tend to create a body which, from no fiction of law, but from the very nature of things, differs from the individuals of whom it is constituted' (A.V. Dicey, *Law and Public Opinion in England* (2nd edn, 1914)).

68 Lord Hoffmann: 'a reference to the company as such might suggest that there is something out there called the company of which one can meaningfully say that it can or cannot do something. There is in fact no such thing as the company as such, no ding an sich, only the applicable rules' (*Meridian Global Funds Management Asia Ltd v Securities Commission* [1995] 2 AC 500, at p. 506).

69 Brian R. Cheffins, 'Corporations', chapter 23 in Peter Cane and Mark Tushnett (eds), *The Oxford Handbook of Legal Studies* (Oxford University Press, 2003).

70 Celia Wells, *Corporations and Criminal Responsibility* (2nd edn, Oxford University Press, 2001), chapter 4; Wells, 'Corporate Crime: Opening the Eyes of the sentry', 30 (2010) *Legal Studies* 370.

71 The approach advocated at the Nuremberg war crimes trials by the International Criminal Tribunal in its judgment: such crimes are committed by human individuals, not

may be subject to a range of legal liabilities – indeed in the context of cartel action, as will be seen below, companies remain the primary targets and recipients of sanctions. But even in the face of this political and legal practice, there are still those who would maintain that a company does not have a mind or will of its own, and that there is 'no soul to damn, no body to kick',[72] so that a company cannot be imprisoned or subject to capital punishment (although that remains open to question). In the end, political and legal practice simply prevails over most sceptical theorising (especially in US law). For the most part, companies involved in cartels will be accorded agency for purposes of legal process, and the main question is whether they are then the only parties with agency, and whether to apply concurrent or alternative liability on individuals.

That last observation then relates to the empirical question, which is really the search for evidence regarding individual participation, and its extent and significance. In one sense, of course, there will always be individual participation of some kind since companies in the material world will act through representative individuals. The relevant question is whether any individual action and role is of such a nature as may stand alongside or supplant any company action for purposes of moral and legal responsibility. As specific examples, this might then appear as the question whether a company executive will be treated as a co-conspirator with his or her company for purposes of Sherman Act liability, or whether an individual would be distinctly and criminally liable for the cartel offence under the UK Enterprise Act. In both cases any individual liability would *be based on* the assumption that such a person had a significant role in the operation of the cartel, and would *depend on* their action and conduct coming within the legal definition of the infringement or offence and also in more practical terms on a decision regarding the value and feasibility of investigating and prosecuting such individuals.

In less legalistic terms, much of this may depend on an assessment of the individual's role vis-à-vis the company. It may be asked, for instance, whether the individual was required or forced to act in that way by the company (or others in the company), whether the act was a knowing and willing application of corporate policy and strategy, whether the individual action was carried out without the company's knowledge or that of others in the company, or whether it was done more furtively in the knowledge that it was contrary to company or management policy. Various configurations can be visualised – for instance, the 'good citizen' company and 'rogue' executive (Art House Auctions), the reverse of that (the favoured scenario of competition compliance cinema, typically depicting executives with a conscience deciding to blow the whistle), or both being rather unthinkingly or uncritically complicit within a long-established cartel culture in

---

abstract entities.

72   A quotation attributed to Edward, First Baron Thurlow as Lord Chancellor. See John Coffee Jnr, '"No Soul to Damn; No Body to Kick": An Unscandalized Inquiry into the Problem of Corporate Punishment', 79 (1981) *Michigan Law Review* 386.

that industrial sector (Marine Hose Cartel).[73] At that stage of enquiry, much will depend on the available evidence in each case and how it may be read.

Shifting identity: That obscure object of regulation

The lesson to be drawn from the discussion in this chapter is to avoid easy generalisation and reduction, and to recognise shifts in the form, role, shape and perception of business cartels over time and space. Sure enough, the basic business strategies employed by suppliers, in fixing prices, sharing markets and the like, may be constant over time. But historical, economic, political and legal context is important and determines the perception and description, and so ultimately the identity and definition of these arrangements. Manipulating the supply of grain 2,000 years ago, reacting to sudden market downturn in an age of protected national markets, and furtively managing the price and availability of important components in the contemporary open and globalised market are all very different matters. Rockefeller's Oil Trust, Duisberg and Bosch's pioneering cartel work, and the late twentieth-century subterfuge and manipulation of the market in pre-insulated pipes should each be compared carefully, as should the temptation to engage in sweeping generalisation and simplified rhetoric. This need to have regard to historical and policy context is nicely encapsulated in Geoffrey Fear's argument concerning the earlier phase of cartel activity:

> In general, cartels were voluntary, private contractual arrangements among independent enterprises to regulate the market. State-managed cartels or forced cartelization during wartime are important exceptions to this rule. Both Robert Liefmann and Harm Schröter stressed cartels' fundamental orientation toward security and stabilization, a sort of risk management strategy. Some definitions of cartels include the *intent* to monopolize markets, but the motivations to form cartels were so varied, so few cartels actually achieved monopolies, and many were established with the explicit aim to *preserve* competitors rather than competition, that this assumption is unnecessary. Early German cartel theorists

---

73 See for instance the following account from within the Marine Hose Cartel: 'I think that the majority of people causing cartels are usually doing it not for personal gain but for their business, for their firms. I don't think from what I've seen that many individuals are doing it for their own ends. They are doing it because it's expected of them, because they've always done it, or because it's the only way they are going to survive. I don't view it as dishonest. I can distinctly recall when the OFT interviewed me they said, 'Do you accept that your behaviour was dishonest?' I knew I had to say yes in order to get the deal, but it stuck in my throat having to say it because I have always considered myself an honest, truthful person. I was always the last person to expect to end up in jail, but I did'. (Interview transcript: Michael O'Kane, 'Does Prison Work for Cartelists? The View from behind Bars' (interview with Bryan Allison), 56 (2011) *The Antitrust Bulletin* 483).

viewed cartels as an anti-merger policy, contrasting dangerous American-style
trusts with responsible cartels. Empirical studies have confirmed that prohibiting
cartels sped concentration.[74]

'*Das Kartellproblem*' has not been resolved, but if anything has become more
complex and more challenging.

What may be said with greater certainty is that, as cartels have gone
underground and become more hidden and shadowy, so *Das Kartellproblem* has
become more prominent in policy and legal regulation – the subject has become
more obscure but discussion and public intervention in relation to the subject have
become more manifest and substantial. The last one hundred years have witnessed
a transition from a situation of largely private management of 'market anarchy'
to one of external regulation of market subterfuge and subversion. As part of this
transition, open and formal structures have given way to informal interactions
of less certain shape. And finally, as part of this process, changes in economic
policy have required increasing public intervention and legal control, resulting in a
significant expansion of law and a new regulatory industry. It is this last aspect, the
normative basis of cartel control and the emerging regulatory infrastructure and
process, which will be the subject for discussion in the next chapter.

---

74   Jeffrey Fear, 'Cartels and Competition: Neither Markets nor Hierarchies', Harvard
University Working Papers, October 2006.

Appendix One: One Phenomenon but Different Narratives

This provides a comparison between a lawyer's preference for a factual or neutral account and a researcher's preference for an interpretative and analytical account.

The 'Page One Thousand' story

Extract from the European Commission's formal decision on the Soda Ash Cartel (1990) as a legal process account of investigation and evidence:

> In a new ICI/Solvay agreement made in 1945, the terms of which were set out in a document discovered at ICI and headed 'Page 1000', Solvay and ICI placed on record their belief that 'the pre-war co-operation between them (which had gone on for nearly 70 years) in the technical and commercial development of the alkali business had been of benefit to both of them ... '. They stipulated that as in the past each would continue to pursue a commercial policy designed to encourage a steadily increasing overall consumption of alkalis: 'Each party intends to increase the volume of its sales by this means and not to increase them simply at the expense of the other party'. 'Page 1000' recorded that Solvay's manufacturing and selling organization was almost wholly within the continent of Europe while that of ICI was mainly the British Commonwealth and other countries of Asia, Africa and South America.
>
> ... The alleged desuetude of the 'Page 1000' arrangement did not however manifest itself in any significant change in the commercial policy of Solvay and ICI in the soda-ash sector, either in 1962 or at any later stage'.
>
> [European Commission, decision of 19 December 1990, 91/297/EEC. *Soda-Ash – Solvay-ICI*, OJ 1991 L152, at paragraphs 23 and 25]

'Page One Thousand' as a poem narrating an 'analytical history' of cartel behaviour and anti-cartel enforcement (Christopher Harding, 2001)

> Page One Thousand,
> Wrote some bold entrepreneurs
> Back in Nineteen Forty Five,
> To celebrate many days of good fellowship -
> Thriving days of yore,
> Many dollars in the corporate chest.
> And, hey lads,
> Good times are here again!
> The arguments are over,
> We can recover our smart project,
> Peace will revive our wealth.

Page One Thousand,
That's code for the bond we shall not sever,
Let's renew our trust for ever,
And ever.
Page One Thousand,
Discovered in a dusty document
In Nineteen Ninety One,
An indictment of too many days of bad fellowship -
Thriving days to be sure,
Many dollars in the corporate chest.
And hey lads,
Look what we have here!
The search is complete,
We can recover our good repute,
And their wealth will rest in peace.
Page One Thousand,
That's code for conspirators' play,
Now proof for their judgment day.

Chapter 3

The Normative Basis of Regulation and Sanctions: Pathology and Mythology Revisited

The need agreed to control this breed, but should criminal law take the lead,
Or is this Sherman Act creed, and a possible regulatory misdeed?[1]

Competition governance: The changing context

When anti-competitive business activities such as price-fixing and market sharing become an object of critical attention and concern, especially in their more organised and systematic form which has led them to be described and identified as cartels, the question of some measure of control or regulation of such activities in a wider social or public interest moves to the forefront. Naturally enough, the initial critical assessment is economic in nature, and what may be seen as unacceptable about cartel activity is a matter of analysing the economic, and then following on from that, the social and political impact of the activity. *It is important to remember in this way that the starting point of critical discussion and legal control is a question of economics and economic policy*, and that the conduct in question is deemed unacceptable and bad because in the first place it disturbs what is seen as the desirable operation of the economic and trading system. That disturbance may then have political consequences (for instance, the accumulation of political power through gaining an economic monopoly) or social consequences (for instance, poverty or deprivation for those who are unable to gain access to essential commodities). Such economic, political and social arguments are the drivers of normative reaction and explain the degree of intervention and choice of method in regulation and legal control. These considerations of competition governance explain the American reaction to 'trusts' at the end of the nineteenth century, the German reaction to 'Kartelle' in the early twentieth century, and the European Community reaction to 'concerted practices which affect trade between Member States' in the later twentieth century, and the different systems of regulation and legal control which emerged from such reactions. This observation is emphasised here in order to counter the facile assumption that business cartels

---

1 Research poem (Christopher Harding, 2013). See Christopher Harding, 'The Relationship between EU Criminal Law and Competition Law', contribution to Valsamis Mitsilegas, Maria Bergstrom and Theodore Konstadinides (eds), *Research Handbook on EU Criminal Law* (Edward Elgar, 2016, forthcoming).

have been universally viewed as inherently bad wherever and whenever they have occurred. Enough has been said already in Chapters 1 and 2 to demonstrate the falsity of such an assumption.

Having said that, it should also be recognised that, by the beginning of the present century, the critical assessment of cartel activity in economic, political and social terms had advanced to a high point of condemnation, accompanied then by a rapidly developing infrastructure of global legal control. As part of that process, the determined move towards criminalisation of cartel conduct in a number of legal systems had contributed a further dynamic of political and legal control. This later view of cartel activity as highly illegal or even criminal has had three major consequences:

- it has transformed the perception of the conduct and its moral evaluation (from business hero to entrepreneurial villain – the cartelist as the 'well-dressed thief');
- it has driven the activity into a delinquent underworld, in effect adding another layer of condemnation (the cartel as a conspiracy and site of subterfuge); and
- it has spawned a growing infrastructure of legal control – more incursive legal process, more significant sanctions, and additional resources to give effect to so much new law (a developing anti-cartel regulatory industry).

And in epistemological terms, as cartel conduct has become increasingly a matter of crime and criminal law, legal boundaries have been reconfigured and it has become meaningful to refer to a criminology of cartels and cartel conduct.

To see the matter in these terms will enable a clearer appreciation of this critical present moment in competition governance. Although the move towards a stronger regime of control and in particular the use of criminal law signals a forceful resolve in policy, the policy itself remains a contestable matter. It is this very fact of a significant but contested development which renders the present discussion both important and timely, since it allows for an enquiry into the use of criminal law in a particular context and for a particular purpose. A critical line of discussion and analysis may and should be employed here and is summarised and prefaced by Stephen Wilks in his recent argument, drawing upon Teubner's idea[2] of competition law as part of an 'economic constitution':

> The economic constitution idea becomes more challenging when we go deeper into an examination of 'the market principles' and ask what kind of market do the competition rules require? ... There are several alternative theoretical paradigms which yield differing conclusions about desirable competitive behaviour. In practice, however, policy makers have made a clear move away from the static defence of certain market structures which grew out of German

---

2   G. Teubner (ed.), *Juridification of Social Spheres* (de Gruyter, 1987), at p. 26.

ordo-liberalism towards a more dynamic and conduct-based approach which draws upon sophisticated economic analysis and game theory ... It can be argued that this shift privileges a conception of the market which is neo-liberal, or perhaps Anglo-American, in its basic assumptions about how firms and individuals behave.[3]

He then refers to challenges to this neo-liberal orthodoxy 'from outside the enforcement community of competition economists from both economic and ideological perspectives', and adds that:

These dissenting voices throw doubt on the assumption that the economic theory underlying current competition enforcement is sufficiently authoritative to provide the robust basis necessary to establish illegality to a criminal standard.[4]

In short, the contemporary normative basis for strong anti-cartel enforcement, and then criminalisation, is the (now 'orthodox') policy preference for a concept of competition which is located in the ideology of the open market, and as such is open to some critical assessment (see below, under 'Cartel delinquency').

Normative escalation: Illegality to a criminal standard

In the context of this prevailing orthodox scheme of competition governance there is a strong consensus that there should be some regulation of the activities of business cartels – 'a need agreed to control this breed'. But the question remains of how such control might be appropriately achieved. The official position adopted now by a significant number of governments and intergovernmental organisations, and therefore of many competition authorities, is to advocate strong and determined methods of legal control, culminating in the move towards what Wilks has referred to as 'illegality to a criminal standard'. There has emerged a rhetoric of tough and uncompromising regulation, with an emphasis on the need for strong dissuasion and deterrence, and the resulting infusion of the method of

---

3   Stephen Wilks, 'Cartel Criminalisation as Juridification: Political and Regulatory Dangers', chapter 15 in Caron Beaton-Wells and Ariel Ezrachi (eds), *Criminalising Cartels: Critical Studies of an International Regulatory Movement* (Hart Publishing, 2011), at pp. 350–51.

4   Ibid. The particular dissenting voices referred to by Wilks are O. Budzinski, 'Monoculture versus Diversity in Competition Economics', 32 (2008) *Cambridge Journal of Economics* 295; M.E. Stucke, 'Am I a Price Fixer? A Behavioural Economics Analysis of Cartels', chapter 12 in Beaton-Wells and Ezrachi (eds), *Criminalising Cartels*, note 3 above; and A. Wigger, 'Towards a Market-Based Approach: The Privatization and Micro-Economization of EU Antitrust Law Enforcement', in H. Overbeek et al. (eds), *The Transnational Politics of Corporate Governance Regulation* (Routledge, 2007).

criminal law into this sphere of economic regulation. As noted above, the outcome has been the transformation of corporate and individual cartelists into economic underworld delinquents, pursued within an increasingly complex and powerful culture of law enforcement.

It may be helpful at this point to give some brief account of how this process of normative escalation has come about, by presenting a short biography of enforcement.[5] As in any retrospective account, it may be possible to identify some key transformative moments as seminal events or tipping points in the history of the subject. Over the past half-century, the EU has been an important site for such a narrative of cartel control,[6] and two such transformative moments might be chosen for this purpose: the prosecution of the quinine and dyestuff suppliers at the end of the 1960s, and that of the wood pulp suppliers in the 1980s.

The quinine and dyestuff cases stand out historically as the first European prosecutions, in the sense of Commission investigations of cartels leading to the application of penal sanctions. During most of the 1960s, despite the original award of investigatory and sanctioning powers under Regulation 17 of 1962, the Commission had dealt with supplier cartels in a largely administrative fashion, often as part of the notification procedure laid down in Regulation 17, sometimes as a result of customers' reports and complaints, but not through investigation on its own initiative.[7] The Quinine and Aniline Dyes Cartels came to the Commission's attention after being dealt with by national authorities, in the US and Germany, and involved companies who were seasoned cartelists; and there was a sense of the Commission exploiting an opportunity to move against two substantial but obvious targets by way of an example to others.

Quinine: Cinchona bark, medicines and the Vietnam War

For an excellent summary biography of the Quinine Cartel, reference may be made to the account in Goyder's work on Competition Law,[8] which sketches the longer

---

5   This account will draw to some extent on the narrative already presented by Christopher Harding and Julian Joshua, *Regulating Cartels in Europe* (2nd edn, Oxford University Press, 2010), chapters 5 and 6. See also Lee McGowan, *The Antitrust Revolution in Europe: Exploring the European Commission's Cartel Policy* (Edward Elgar, 2010), especially chapter 6, 'European Cartel Policy: Deployment and Combat, 1963–1998' (this is a political science study of anti-cartel enforcement in Europe); and Alan Riley, 'The Consequences of the European Cartel-Busting Revolution', 12 (2005) *Irish Journal of European Law* 3.

6   Indeed, it might be said that the EU has been the single most important actor in the globalisation of cartel control, even though the US has been forceful for so long in promoting a particular agenda. See, for instance, the emphasis presented by Alan Riley, 'The Consequences of the European Cartel-Busting Revolution', note 5 above.

7   See Harding and Joshua, note 5 above, in chapter 5.

8   See D.G. Goyder et al., *Goyder's EC Competition Law* (5th edn, Oxford University Press, 2009), at p. 172.

history of a well-established industry arrangement, dating back to 1913, and setting the companies' strategies in the context of changing economic circumstances of the market for quinine and quinidine as components in the manufacture of a number of important medicines.[9] The latest of these cartel arrangements during the earlier 1960s occurred at a crucial time in both legal and economic terms. With the coming into force of Regulation 17/62 in the Common Market the European companies considered a number of options – termination of the 'agreement', or 'open' notification, or continuing in secret, and opted for the latter. However, for economic reasons, the companies decided to disband the cartel in 1965.[10] The Cartel was first investigated and dealt with by the US authorities, and arising from this the EEC Commission instituted its own proceedings in 1967, culminating in a decision and fines[11] and an appeal to the Court of Justice, which handed down its judgment in 1970.[12]

This episode provides a valuable case study. The case related to an economic sector which had a long experience of cartelisation and the parties were sophisticated and significant economic actors at the international level, operating a cartel with classic organisational features.[13] These were companies, therefore, with cartelisation in their corporate 'DNA',[14] and their deliberation between an open strategy of notification or to continue in secret – to go underground into

---

9   Quinine and quinidine are derived from cinchona bark and are important in the manufacture of medicine for the treatment of fever (such as malaria), pain and inflammations Quinine is listed by the WHO as an Essential Medicine. There is an intriguing historical connection with aniline dyes: William Perkin, in experimenting with the development of synthetic quinine, discovered the organic dye mauveine in 1856. Historically, chemistry and cartelisation appear to have a close relationship of some kind. See also Peter Hayes, 'Carl Bosch and Carl Krauch: Chemistry and the Political Economy of Germany, 1925–1945', 47 (1987) *Journal of Economic History* 353.

10   Notably an increase in demand, following the American involvement in the Vietnam War and the need for more supply of anti-malaria medicine.

11   *Re Quinine Cartel*, decision of 16 July 1969, OJ 1969, L 192/5.

12   Case 45/69, *Boehringer Mannheim v Commission* (1970) ECR 771. A closer study of the personnel involved in this proceeding is instructive. One of the counsel for the company was Arved Deringer, a German lawyer and politician and expert on competition law (author of, inter alia, *The Competition Law of the EEC: A Commentary* (Commerce Clearing House, 1968), regarded then as one of the leading English language publications on the subject), and whose name is celebrated in that of the large law firm Freshfields Bruckhaus Deringer. The appeal rehearses some powerful legal arguments which were to be played out in appeals to the European Courts in years to come.

13   Strategies such as price-fixing and market sharing were maintained through regular meetings and mechanisms to ensure cartel loyalty.

14   The parties were German, French, British and Dutch: the Dutch company, Nedchem (later ACF Chemiefarma) served as ringleader; there were two German companies, Buchler and Boehringer Mannheim; four French companies (the 'French group'); and two British companies, Carnegies, and Lake and Cruickshank (the latter, outside the EEC, were not fined).

a delinquent underworld – was a kind of defining moment in the legal history
of the subject. Their collective decision affected their own self-perception and
also then that of the Commission, which was able to attribute to the companies a
clear outlaw status that merited the application of penal sanctions. The proceeding
became an inaugural quasi-criminal case of 'prosecution', penalisation and appeal
on procedural and evidential issues,[15] which in effect set the tone and policy of
anti-cartel enforcement in Europe for the future. From the Commission's point of
view, this was a well-chosen test case: the facts were clear and it was to prove a
classic example of a new kind of furtive arrangement (the 'gentlemen's agreement'
and 'concerted practice') which was seriously anti-competitive in the context
of the new Common Market in Europe. If, for reasons of historical neatness, a
transformative moment of new outlaw status is sought, then this was that moment.

Dyestuffs: A heritage of cartelisation[16]

> Like many a physical or chemical invention
> pioneered by the British I could mention
> Perkin's valuable synthetic dyes
> which will always, for yours truly, symbolise
> the magic of chemistry, Germans monopolise.[17]

At the same time that the Commission acted against the Quinine Cartel, it also
took aim at the Aniline Dyes Cartel in Europe. This was a sector of the chemicals
industry with again a rich history of cartelisation, the latter triggered, as in other
economic sectors, by national trading rivalry in earlier twentieth century, pre-
trade liberalised Europe, especially as between Germany and Britain. In relation
to dyestuff, Carl Duisberg (mentioned already[18] as the cartel 'architect' from the
German firm Bayer) had remarked in 1914 that England really had

> no cause for complaint about her success and position in the world, and especially
> no cause for complaint that perhaps one or another country has superseded her
> in one or other industry,

---

15   Most importantly, issues relating to the companies' rights of defence, the
sufficiency of reasoning and evidence, and the possibility of double jeopardy (violation of
the principle *ne bis in idem*) arising from the fact that the German companies had already
been convicted and fined in relation to the cartel under US law. See Case 41/69, *ACF
Chemiefarma v Commission* (1970) ECR 661; Case 44/69, *Buchler v Commission* (1970)
ECR 733; Case 45/69, *Boehringer Mannheim v Commission* (1970) ECR 769.

16   For a lively and engaging account of the development of the dyestuff industry, see
Simon Garfield, *Mauve* (Faber and Faber, 2000).

17   From the play *Square Rounds* by Tony Harrison (1992), words given to Sir William
Crookes, historian, physicist and chemist.

18   See Chapter 2 above.

and referring to British advantage in coal and steel, spinning and weaving and colonial expansion, he opined that only in the coal-tar industry was Britain lower ranked, and

why should Germany in this one instance not take a leading position?[19]

In due course such rivalry was tamed in the form of the 'Aniline Dyes Cartel', which had its origins in the German Interessengemeinschaften of the interwar period, and progressive international collaboration with rivals such as the major Swiss producers, ICI in Britain, and later Du Pont in the US.[20] The Cartel had an established membership in the 1930s when IG Farben joined with Swiss companies Ciba, Geigy and Sandoz to form the 'Tripartite Cartel', later adding ICI in the 'Quadrapartite Cartel'.[21] When the Commission took legal action in the later 1960s against the group identified as the 'Aniline Dyes Cartel', following complaints from buyers' associations, it was moving against firms known to be seasoned cartelists in a sector almost renowned for this kind of business strategy, and indeed for pioneering the modern cartel method. The cartel dealt with by the Commission comprised four Italian firms, four German firms (all IG Farben successor companies – Bayer, Hoechst, BASF and Cassella), four Swiss companies, two from the UK (including ICI), one from France, one from the Netherlands, and one from the US (Du Pont). Again, this was a major international cartel, comprising sophisticated and long-established businesses accused of classic anti-competitive activity, in this case price alignment. Involving a number of non-EEC participants, the case had an important jurisdictional element which was fully explored, and resolved, in the appeal to the Court of Justice.[22] But there was an important point of difference with the Quinine Cartel, which concerned the evidence of cartel activity, and this turned the proceeding into a different kind of test case.

The proceeding (and this was not so much of an investigation as such) against the dyestuffs producers was triggered by complaints from associations of buyers of the dyes, who pointed out that there had been simultaneous and similar price changes in 1964, 1965 and 1967, suggesting that these price changes had been coordinated by the suppliers.[23] Whereas the business strategies of the quinine suppliers were blatant and well evidenced, this was not the case with the dyestuff producers. There was evidence that there had been meetings (for instance one in

---

19 As quoted in Garfield, note 16 above, at pp. 152–3.

20 For a fuller account, see George W. Stocking and Myron W. Watkins, *Cartels in Action* (Twentieth Century Fund, 1946), chapter 9, 'The Chemical Industries'.

21 For a discussion of why the cartel never extended its membership to Japan, see Harm G. Schröter, 'Competition and Cooperation or Why Japan Was Not Included into the International Dyestuffs Cartel 1929–1939: A New Explanation Based on Communication', 50th Congress of Business History Society of Japan (2014).

22 Case 48/69, *ICI v Commission* (1972) ECR 619.

23 See the Commission's decision: *Re Dyestuffs Cartel*, OJ 1969, L195.

Basle in August 1967) but not what had been actually decided or agreed then, so that the case against the companies was essentially circumstantial, linking market outcomes with insufficiently specific evidence of contact. As a test case, this proceeding quickly raised a host of legal and evidential issues,[24] and again served as a rehearsal for and prediction of what was to come in subsequent years – in practical terms, the resort to expert evidence on both sides and the length of time taken for the appeal to be decided (three years after the date of the Commission's decision) served as a pointer to the future regarding the complexity of such cases and the volume of legal business which would be generated. The most controversial issue was the reliance on circumstantial evidence, which provoked a quick critical response from a heavyweight lawyer and academic, F.A. Mann.[25] In parallel German proceedings, both the Berlin Court of Appeal and the Bundesgerichtshof were unwilling to accept such evidence as sufficient proof of illegal cartel activity.[26] But the Court of Justice eventually decided otherwise, thus setting the scene for an ongoing debate for some time on the economics of oligopoly (argued to be the situation in the dyestuffs market) and sufficiency of evidence for this kind of legal proceeding, awaiting resolution for a number of years in the seminal Wood Pulp case. At the stage of its Dyestuffs judgment in 1972, the Court appeared to have an underlying policy reason for supporting the Commission's view that the circumstantial evidence would be sufficient to establish behaviour 'designed to substitute for the risks of competition, and the hazards of … spontaneous reactions, a co-operation which amounts to a concerted practice'.[27] The Court referred to an imperative of competition in the context of the European Common Market:

> the function of competition in relation to prices is to maintain prices at the lowest possible level, and to encourage the movement of products between member-States so as to permit an optimum sharing out of activities on the basis of productivity and the adaptive capacity of undertakings. The variation of price rates encourages the pursuit of one of the essential aims of the Treaty, namely the inter-penetration of national markets, and hence the direct access of consumers to the sources of production of the whole Community.[28]

This analysis clearly privileges the 'open market' goals of the free flow of trade and consumer access and choice over supplier needs for market stability and then

---

24　Most importantly: what constituted evidence of collusion; jurisdiction over the non-EC firms; procedural and due process questions; and a limitation period for the application of fines. See case 48/69, note 22 above.

25　F.A. Mann, 'The Dyestuffs Case in the Court of Justice of the European Communities', 22 (1973) *International and Comparative Law* Quarterly 35.

26　Harding and Joshua, note 5 above, at p. 126.

27　Case 48/69, note 22 above: (1972) ECR at p. 661 (at para 119).

28　Ibid., at p. 60 (paras 115–116).

firmly locates the treatment of cartel activity in the agenda of trade liberalisation, which was gaining dominance in the second half of the twentieth century. In this way the Court's Dyestuff judgment clarifies, via its interpretation of the idea of the concerted practice affecting trade between Member States, the normative basis for the EC/EU regulation of business cartel strategies.

A history of enforcement in three main episodes

Thus, by the turn of the 1970s, there had been a significant normative leap forward which had identified certain types of cartel activity as especially detrimental to the interests of the Common Market. The Quinine Cartel proceedings in particular indicated a consciousness of this development on the part of both businesses (the companies' decision not to notify and so keep secret their 'gentlemen's agreement') and regulators (the Commission's decision to formally condemn and penalise the companies involved). In essence, this was the outlawing of business cartels in Europe, and was the first main episode in a major normative shift. This in turn led to the second main episode – having driven cartels underground, there was then likely to be an increasing problem of gaining evidence, especially in the context of a legal process which was escalating towards criminal law standards. The drama of the second episode revolved around the Commission's play for easy proof – just look at the market, there is no need to show any more. As will be seen shortly, when the Commission eventually lost that argument (as happened in the Wood Pulp proceeding), the scene was set for the third main episode, comprising the search for categorical evidence of collusion, and that takes the history of the subject into dawn raids and, most significantly, leniency programmes, as the key to effective legal control.

Wood Pulp: A tale of the Northlands or pulp fiction?

Returning to the biography of enforcement, the Court of Justice's *Dyestuff* judgment left matters hanging in the air somewhat, apparently confirming the Commission's ability to prove a case by pointing to market and circumstantial evidence; but this was clearly still very much a contested issue, as can be seen from the critical argument presented in F.A. Mann's paper, published quickly after the judgment.[29] Indeed, this issue was part of a wider ongoing debate concerning what was necessary to prove the existence of prohibited cartel activity and thereby in effect the very existence of a cartel. American regulators and courts had also struggled with this question and evolved a theory of evidence which combined, first, a concept of 'conduct plus' or 'plus factors'[30] – proof of something in addition

---

29   Mann, note 25 above. Mann opens his broadside attack by deploring a lack of persuasive analysis of facts and cogency of reasoning (at p. 35).

30   Mainly: hard evidence of meetings and other types of contact; parallel conduct that cannot reasonably be interpreted as individually spontaneous; elements of market structure

to what appears on the market – with, secondly, the overall impact of a range of plus factors, resulting in a panorama of evidence which would be cumulatively probative so as to point inevitably to real collusion.[31] A somewhat similar approach appears to have been adopted by the Court of Justice in Anilines Dyes, although its exposition in the judgment there was not wholly unambiguous:

> Although parallel behaviour may not by itself be identified with a concerted practice it may however amount to strong evidence of such a practice if it leads to conditions of competition which do not correspond to the normal conditions of the market.[32]

But the jurisprudence of the Court of Justice eschewed the much more explicit American listing and ranking of plus factors, contenting itself for instance with the argument that in Aniline Dyes a number of meetings occurred, and could be coupled with the timing and amounts of subsequent price changes and the similarity of messages sent out to subsidiary companies, to point inexorably to a finding of collusion.[33] So matters stood until the Commission was eventually tempted to bid for a powerful evidential card in the Wood Pulp proceedings in the 1980s.

Like quinine and dyestuffs, the market in wood pulp was characterised by a long history of cartelisation. Again, this was an example of a basic product, significant in its industrial and commercial application, but by its nature not lending itself to vibrant competition, so that once more economists' arguments about oligopoly could be brought into play.[34] Naturally enough most of the suppliers in this market were geographically based in northern countries – this is a sector sometimes described as 'forest industry' and the members of this alleged cartel were from Canada, the US, Finland, and Sweden, although also Spain and Portugal (and all of these countries were, at the time of the cartel's operation, outside the EC). Pulp and paper export cartels were a long-standing and established feature of this economic sector in the Nordic countries.[35] As Niklas Jensen-Eriksen has commented:

that are conducive to coordination.

31   Harding and Joshua, note 5 above, at p. 158.

32   (1972) ECR 619, at paras 65–68.

33   (1972) ECR, at p. 660.

34   For an overview account of the EC proceedings against the wood pulp suppliers, see Harding and Joshua, note 5 above, pp. 133–36, and pp. 160–66, The judgments of the Court of Justice are reported in Cases 114/85 etc., *Ahlström Oy and others v Commission* (1988) ECR5193; Cases C89/85 etc., *Ahlström Oy and others v Commission* (1993) ECR I-1307.

35   See Niklas Jensen-Eriksen, 'Disband or Go Underground? The Nordic Pulp and Paper Export Cartels and European Competition Policies, 1970–1995', unpublished paper, 11th Annual Conference of the European Business History Association, September 2007, Geneva; Birgit Karlson, 'Cartels in the Swedish Forest Industry in the Interwar Period', chapter 13 in Sven-Olof Olsson (ed.), *Managing Crises and Deglobalisation* (Routledge, 2010).

In 1932 the Nordic (Swedish, Norwegian and Finnish) producers of kraft paper set up a cartel called Scankraft. One observer called it in 1943 'the most perfect type of cartel that has ever existed in the paper trade'.[36]

To a large extent this evident pattern of cartelisation in the forest industries in the northern countries was left undisturbed, attracting critical regulatory attention quite late in the day. The Commission turned its attention to the alleged major international wood pulp cartel in the 1977, investigating its operation from 1973 onwards. This was a time-consuming matter and following a hearing in 1982 there were attempts to reach a negotiated settlement between 1982 and 1984. This last strategy was also protracted and appeared to suddenly break down in December 1984, at which point the Commission adopted a formal decision against the Cartel, and refused then to budge from the position taken in this decision.[37] The Commission's obstinacy in the legal argument that followed is one of the most notable features of the case.

The report of the legal proceedings,[38] both the Commission's role and the two appeals to the Court of Justice, is full and informative, not least for its depiction of a shift in the dialogue from one between the Commission and the companies to one between the Commission and the Court and its Advocate General.[39] Moreover, the Judge Rapporteur in the second appeal (which dealt with the contentious issue of evidence of collusion) was René Joliet,[40] an early critic (alongside Mann) of the Court's Dyestuffs judgment, and this would have contributed an important edge to the legal discussion. It is clear that both Commission and Court struggled to understand each other fully and there are parts of both the Commission's

---

36   Jensen-Eriksen, note 35 above, at p. 2.

37   There is a revealing account of this stage of the proceeding in the opinion of Advocate General Darmon in his opinion given in the second of the appeals to the Court of Justice: see (1993) ECR I-1503.

38   Again for a fuller account of the legal proceedings, see Harding and Joshua, note 34 above, pp. 133–6, and pp. 160–66. The first appeal related to the problem of jurisdiction, while the second appeal dealt, inter alia, with the question of evidence of cartel activity.

39   Advocate General Marco Darmon's opinion in the second appeal stands as a remarkably detailed study of the case and clear and insightful legal analysis of the issues, and his frank comments on the Commission's presentation of its argument and the quality of expert reports used by both sides in the case should be noted.

40   Like Arved Deringer and F.A. Mann, René Joliet was a leading academic commentator on the then new field of EC competition law in the 1960s and 1970s, well known then for his work, *The Rule of Reason in Antitrust Law: American, German and Common Market Law in Comparative Perspective* (Martinus Nijhoff, 1967). Joliet, like the British commentator Valentine Korah, was an early critic of what he saw as a too categorical and sweeping view of anti-competitive activity on the part of the Commission. Korah once remarked to one of the present authors: 'If I had to recommend just one work on the subject to students, it would be Joliet's book.' Equally, via informal comment, it would seem that Joliet was not a favourite among some officials in Commission DGIV.

presentation of the case and the Court's judgment which remain perplexing, although Advocate General Darmon's discussion is clear and insightful.[41] Suffice it to say that there was evidence of some collusion,[42] but the Commission was insistent that its case should stand, or fall, on the market evidence of price announcements. The Commission stated in its 14th Report on Competition Policy, that the proceedings in Wood Pulp were:

> the first time that concertation on prices is proved by an economic analysis showing that under the given circumstances the similarity of prices was inexplicable unless there was concertation beforehand.[43]

Suffice it to say for present purposes that eventually the Court, seemingly almost goaded by the Commission's resolve to use this approach, categorically disagreed, finding that parallel behaviour on the market cannot of itself be used to establish collusion if there are other plausible explanations from economic analysis for such parallelism, and then it would be necessary to show reciprocal co-operation through direct or indirect contact between the parties to establish collusion. Given that economic evidence in such cases will almost certainly be conflicting (as in the Wood Pulp proceeding),[44] this means that in practice evidence of contact will be crucial for a convincing case to be made of cartel activity. This was indeed a 'devastating' outcome for the Commission, in the words of Van Gerven and Navarro Varona,[45] although not a 'victory for economic theory' as those authors asserted. Far from it, this was a victory in favour of hard legal evidence of contact and communication between the alleged cartelists and in that sense a seminal moment in the history of anti-cartel enforcement. The judgment, whatever its varying qualities, settled the matter for the future and set a standard of proof for regulators. By raising the stakes in enforcement, the Commission had also raised the standard of proof: the allegation, to use the terminology of English criminal law, would have to be proven beyond reasonable doubt. And evidence of that kind would require the use of investigatory methods such as the dawn raid and the insider confession, gained through leniency programmes.

Summary: Three episodes of normative and penal escalation

Episode One: condemnation – the move to outlaw status and the subject goes
    underground (*Quinine*).

---

41   See Harding and Joshua, note 34 above, at pp. 162–65.

42   For instance, evidence from one of the Canadian companies concerning a meeting in Stockholm in September 1977: see Harding and Joshua, note 34 above, at p. 163.

43   *14th Report on Competition Policy* (1985), point 56 (pp. 57–8).

44   See Harding and Joshua, note 34 above, at p. 165.

45   Gerwin Van Gerven and Edurne Navarro Varona, 'The *Wood Pulp* Case and the Future of Concerted Practices', 31 (1994) *Common Market Law Review* 575.

Episode Two: problems of gaining evidence in a context of more exacting probative requirements – how much must be proven (*Dyestuffs*)?

Episode Three: stricter requirements of clear proof and a changing dynamic of evidence collection (*Wood Pulp*) (leading to the use of leniency programmes).

The outcome: juridification, penalisation and criminalisation in the domain of business regulation.

The enforcement imperative and deterrence argument as a driver of legal control

The analysis provided so far suggests an upward spiral of both legal enforcement and cartel delinquency: stronger condemnation begets a stronger enforcement effort and both lead to a stronger outlaw identity, which in turn justifies the call for stronger sanctions and more incursive powers of investigation to probe increasingly covert activity. By the 1990s the main issue of enforcement had become the problem of detection. As cartelists became more aware of the serious illegality of their conduct, in so far as they persisted in that conduct they naturally became more covert and more sophisticated in their efforts to cover the traces. And by the early 1990s in Europe it had become clear that regulators required convincing evidence of contact and communication as collusion in order to establish both the existence of a cartel and the extent of individual corporate participation in an alleged cartel. Success in enforcement therefore became very much a matter of success in first uncovering the cartel activity and then in dissuading the companies from further cartel participation. Within that regulatory mind-set, deterrence theory, or at least talk about deterrence, came very much to the fore. Claims were made that business persons and companies, as rational actors and profit seekers *par excellence*, would desist from cartelisation only if deterred, and then that cartels could only be detected only if they feared the prospect of discovery and punishment, and the latter would happen more easily through insider reporting encouraged by leniency programmes. In short, the natural nervousness and apprehension of cartelists could be exploited by offering the first party to self-report complete immunity from prosecution and punishment. But that temptation to blow the whistle depended on a real prospect of a severe penalty – the 'big stick', typically in the form of huge fines or prison terms for individuals. In this way, the theory and policy of deterrence came to the front of the stage for two main purposes: as a justification for incursive and hard-hitting legal control, and in effectively uncovering the existence and evidence of cartel activity. As Harding commented, writing in 2010:

> Thus at the present time, regulatory language is replete with the need to achieve deterrence. For instance, in a speech in October 2009, EU Competition Commissioner Neelie Kroes proclaimed: 'I don't want to merely destabilise cartels. I want to tear the ground from under them. This requires effective

deterrence across a range of competition systems'.[46] And, at an OECD roundtable discussion on anti-cartel enforcement in 2005, a national representative had opined that: 'No single sanction is a sufficient deterrent, but it was important that a panopoly *[sic]* of sanctions is available to combat cartels'.[47] The regulatory message is clear: combating cartels has become a priority and legal action to do so must comprise effective deterrence.[48]

Arguments drawing upon deterrence theory in this context include in particular those aimed at the calculation of 'optimal' penalties and sanctions,[49] particularly as used by economists to demonstrate the amount of financial penalty which will dissuade a rational business actor carrying out a cost-benefit analysis, and those used to justify criminalisation and prison terms for individual cartelists as effective 'non-indemnifiable' sanctions which will dissuade individuals from entering into cartel activity or induce them to report such activity to gain immunity.[50] Many of the deterrence-based arguments have a regulatory and official (governmental and intergovernmental) provenance, and are bolstered to some extent in academic literature and critical commentary, emanating from both economists and also some legal scholarship.[51] Yet much of the argument rests upon assumption and there is a dearth of reliable empirical research which tests such assumption.[52] Indeed, the theoretical basis of deterrent claims in this context remains to some extent contestable – for instance, the assumption that the business person, either corporate or individual, is a quintessential rational actor. As Peter Whelan has observed in relation to deterrence-based claims justifying the criminalisation of cartel conduct:

> These types of statement expressly approve of the application of the justificatory criminal punishment theory of deterrence to the concept of cartel activity. It is submitted that, given the significant resources required for the creation of a criminal antitrust regime, not to mention the potentially very serious

---

46   Neelie Kroes, address at Brasilia, 8 October 2009, press release, speech/09/454.

47   OECD, *Sanctions against Individuals*, roundtable discussion (OECD, 2005), per the Canadian representative, at p. 105.

48   Christopher Harding, 'Cartel Deterrence: The Search for Evidence and Argument', 56 (2011), *The Antitrust Bulletin* 345, at p. 347.

49   Sometimes referred to as the 'unlawful gain' model – for a penalty to have an efficient deterrent impact it must be set at a level which at least matches the unlawful gain of the offender, otherwise the offender would not be deterred.

50   A non-indemnifiable sanction is one which will not be undermined by a compensatory counter-measure, such as a financial payment by a company or employer to off-set the disadvantage to an individual having to pay a fine. But theorising imprisonment as non-indemnifiable may be misjudged, since a company may look after the interests of imprisoned employees in a number of ways: see the discussion in Chapter 7, regarding Japanese corporate practice.

51   For an overview, see Harding, 'Cartel Deterrence', note 48 above, at pp. 357–60.

52   Ibid.

consequences which face an individual cartelist subjected to a criminal process (i.e. imprisonment), one should not take these statements simply at face value. A robust analysis should be undertaken concerning the application of deterrence theory to cartel activity before deciding whether to introduce criminal sanctions (including imprisonment) as punishment for such activity.[53]

This is an important argument, calling up practical and ethical concerns which require convincing grounds for any resort to deterrent argument as a basis for legal action in this context. Whelan seeks to establish a surer and clearer theoretical framework for the use of deterrence as a justification and his efforts may be usefully drawn upon in later discussion in this work. Suffice it to say for the present that Whelan identifies four main objections or doubts regarding the likely deterrent effect of criminal sanctions in dealing with cartels: that cartel conduct may be regarded as morally neutral, that businesses are risk averse, that firms and individuals are not rational actors, and that the personal cost of criminal sanctions may be disproportionate, so that deterrence argument 'is not as robust as some commentators would have one believe'.[54]

Nor has the deterrent impact of anti-cartel sanctions been convincingly demonstrated as yet in a social scientific way, and indeed it may be argued that this is a research exercise which needs to be followed further. A few researchers have attempted to assess the impact of anti-cartel sanctions.[55] Some economists, rooted in rational actor assumptions, have constructed models of optimal fines to be imposed on companies,[56] but these are econometric projections which resolutely disregard evidence of recidivism.[57] Other investigations have used models of cartel stability and formation,[58] 'before and after' case studies of particular markets,[59] calculation of cartel abandonment rates based on selective interviews,[60] and the study of post-enforcement 'diversion' of cartel activity to other jurisdictions).[61] All

---

53 Peter Whelan, *The Criminalization of European Cartel Enforcement: Theoretical, Legal and Practical Challenges* (Oxford University Press, 2014), at pp. 44–45.

54 Ibid., at p. 78; see generally his discussion in chapter 3 of the book.

55 For an overview, see Harding, 'Cartel Deterrence', note 48 above, at pp. 352–68.

56 For a useful discussion and summary, see E. Combe and C. Monnier, 'Fines against Hard Core Cartels in Europe: The Myth of Over Enforcement', 56 (2011) *The Antitrust Bulletin* 235.

57 See the critique by Maurice E. Stucke, 'Behavioural Economists at the Gate: Antitrust in the 21st Century', 38 (2007) *Loyola University Chicago Law Journal* 513.

58 Paul A. Grout and Silvia Sonderegger, 'Predicting Cartels: Discussion Paper' (Office of Fair Trading, OFT 773, March 2005).

59 For instance, Deborah L. Spar, *The Competitive Edge: The Internal Politics of International Cartels* (Cornell University Press, 1994).

60 Deloitte and Touche, for the OFT, 'The Deterrent Effect of Competition Enforcement by the OFT', Office of Fair Trading, OFT 962, 2007.

61 For example, Julian L. Clarke and Simon J. Evenett, 'The Deterrent Effects of National Anticartel Laws: Evidence from the International Vitamins Cartel', 48 (2003)

of these approaches suffer from (sometimes admitted) methodological limitations[62] often characteristic of such social scientific investigation.

A number of basic problems bedevil this subject. In particular, and arising partly from a lack of an agreed definition of cartels, it is probably impossible to estimate the total amount of cartel activity at any one time.[63] It is then difficult to establish a yardstick for any measurement of deterrent effect. But there is also a significant problem of agency. Cartel activity involves the conduct of both corporate and individual human actors and policies and measures of deterrence need to address the question of *whose* action is being dealt with as productive of delinquent behaviour. Much of the research to date blithely skates over this complication of agency. But anti-cartel policy needs to address little known or understood internal relationships between corporate entities and individual employees or executives, moving beyond a few anecdotal accounts of such relationships. Overall, then, there is a need for a surer approach to the evaluation of this significant body of legal development. As explained in Chapter 1, the biographical method proposed in the present work has the advantage of drawing upon a now substantial body of reliable recent historical (rather than predictive) data, derived from rigorous legal process. This material can then be used, along with other historical data relating to the periods preceding and subsequent to the course of the legal proceeding, to analyse the impact to date of different kinds of legal process and sanctioning, with reference to a set of relevant variable factors which may be grouped in four main clusters: market, corporate identity, jurisdiction, and normative character of the subjects of legal control. This methodology will be explained in more detail in the following chapter.

Sanction accumulation: The multiplication of victims and jurisdictions

One particular outcome of the increasing resort to deterrence-based argument in favour of strong legal control of cartel activity, and especially what may be referred to as the 'panoply' argument mentioned above ('no single sanction is a sufficient deterrent, and it is important that a panoply of sanctions is available to combat cartels')[64] is what may be described as the phenomenon of sanction accumulation. An important feature of international business cartels arises from their international scope, in terms of markets affected and jurisdictions which are covered by their operation. Self-evidently, in economic terms such cartel activities may affect markets in a number of countries and then the position and interests of other traders and consumers located in a number of jurisdictions. In this way the operation of an international cartel may be subject to legal proceedings severally and either sequentially or simultaneously in different systems in so far as the

---

Antitrust Bulletin 689.

62   Harding, 'Cartel deterrence', note 48 above, at p. 352 *et seq.*

63   Ibid., at p. 352.

64   Note 47 above.

conduct is illegal in each of those systems (which is more and more likely to be the case). In turn, this gives rise to the possibility that a number of different sanctions may be applied in a number of different systems to a range of individual and corporate actors involved in basically the same activity.[65] This shotgun or cluster-bomb method, justified by reference to the needs of effective enforcement, gives rise to a number of practical, ethical and legal issues, especially in relation to the regulation of large-scale international cartels.

Such accumulation of sanctions is for the most part a little regulated legal phenomenon, subject at present to a limited amount of control, mainly through the normal limits of jurisdictional reach and the generally accepted prohibition on double jeopardy (*ne bis in idem*) – but the latter would not apply if the effects of the cartel's operation are disaggregated for each jurisdiction, as separate offences. Little attention has been paid to how sanctions may add up, across jurisdictions, in relation to the operation of a single cartel. This is a matter which is complicated by issues of agency – the fact that a number of both human and corporate actors may be involved in the overall operation of a single cartel. There are outstanding and unresolved questions concerning the quantification of sanctions and their overall impact in such a context and how this might relate to the damage caused by a cartel, or what might be termed its victimhood. If it is felt as a question of basic justice that there should be some proportionality between the nature and extent of wrongful conduct and the harm that it brings about, then there is a need to address these matters and how the offending conduct and its damage may be measured and assessed.

The matter may be simply illustrated through a standard example. Suppose that a cartel involves the participation of x companies and y individuals working for those companies, and covers the markets in z countries or national jurisdictions during the period of its operations. (The device of the *cartel as a box* may be used to further illustrate this example by reference to the three essential components of cartel operation used in that graphic – participation, geographical space or markets, and duration, and multiplying the quantities relevant to those three axes of involvement – see the discussion in Chapter 2) Additionally, given that different kinds of legal sanction (for example: financial penalty, prison term, disqualification, compensatory damages) may be applied to a number of those actors in a number of jurisdictions either sequentially or at the same time, the total number of different sanctions applied per actor per jurisdiction (t) may be added to the calculation of sanction accumulation over time.

A formula for the calculation of total application of the sanctions might be:

$$[x \text{ (companies)} + y \text{ (individuals)} = x + y \text{ actors}] \times z \text{ jurisdictions} \times t \text{ applied sanctions}$$
$$= a. \text{ (total number of sanctions)}$$

---

65   Although bearing in mind that it may be open to argument what counts as the 'same' cartel activity, a problem of definition and identification discussed already in Chapter 2, and what may be referred to in shorthand as the problem of the *idem*.

The above is just one model of calculation, and is simply a quantitative count of the sanctions applied.[66] That leaves aside the qualitative experience of suffering the sanction – for example, some idea of the adverse impact of a financial penalty compared to a prison term. It is not clear how that might be estimated and whether for instance notional weightings might be agreed for a relative valuation of such impacts (especially taking into account different likely impacts for corporate and individual actors as the recipients of sanctions).

More concretely, a historical instance of one international cartel and the sanctions applied to date, might be cited as a way of illustrating this attempt at calculation. The *Marine Hose Cartel* might be taken as an example, describing below the sanctions applied, by jurisdiction (see Appendix One at the end of this chapter).

The discussion in Appendix One of the *Marine Hose Cartel* begins to probe the total quantitative impact of the transnational sanctioning process, although still in a limited way, since it does not move on to the qualitative effect of sanctions (such as the personal impact of a prison term or financial penalty, or damage to corporate or individual reputation and effect on later career), or indirect quantitative consequences (such as damage to competitive position or corporate financial stability). Indeed, the approach to and methods of measuring such impacts remain far from agreed as a matter of social science. How far should the enquiry be taken? Economists who talk about optimal sanctions refer in relatively simple terms to the amount of the sanction in itself (for instance, the amount of a fine) and a notional amount of harm arising from the offending behaviour (for instance, an estimated supra-competitive gain from the selling price). Yet criminologists may well argue – should argue – that the quantum of the sanction is much more than that, and that quality of sanction should also come into the reckoning.

Moreover, there are both practical and theoretical grounds in policy and law for arguing that there should be an agreed limit to the quantum of sanction. Contrary to the rhetoric of some regulators that the 'full panoply' of sanctions should be used and that the sky is the limit, an endless accumulation of sanctions in relation to one case is neither practically sensible[67] nor normatively acceptable. Justice and policy concerns might be mediated through the application of some basic legal principles, in particular *ne bis in idem*, subsidiarity, and proportionality.[68] In

---

66 See generally on the question of quantitative assessment in this context: Peter Davies and Eliana Garcés, *Quantitative Techniques for Competition and Antitrust Analysis* (Princeton University Press, 2009).

67 As demonstrated for example by the arguments presented by some corporate cartelists that the imposition of very large fines will serve to put them out of business – see Andreas Stephan, the 'Bankruptcy Wild Card in Cartel Cases', (2010) *Journal of Business Law* 510.

68 European Commission Communication, 'Towards an EU Criminal Policy: Ensuring the Effective Implementation of EU Policies through Criminal Law', COM (2011) 573 final.

relation to the latter, there is a strong normative (retributive) argument in favour of a proportionate relation between the quantum and nature of the harm arising from offending behaviour and the quantum and nature of the sanction used in response. Yet estimation of the former is also problematical in relation to cartel activity. What is the nature of such harm (economic and otherwise), to whom is it caused (who are the victims), and how long does it endure as harm? Such questions are not yet fully resolved in either policy or theory. There is an incomplete theory of cartel victimhood, and such victimhood is also a matter of historical contingency, as a policy and legal shift from other traders as main perceived victims to consumers as main perceived victims easily demonstrates.

In short, assessment of the impact of anti-cartel sanctions is problematic in relation to the measurement of both sanctions and victimhood, and there is a significant agenda here for theoretical clarification, policy formation and legal development.

Cartel delinquency: Probing the outlaw status of the cartelist

Having discussed deterrence as a basis for the legal control of cartel activity, in normative terms the other principal justification is *retributive* in character, relating to the moral content of cartel behaviour, what may be summarised as its inherent badness. Such a justificatory basis is particularly important when efforts of legal control move to the stage of criminalisation, since it is widely accepted that the important expressive function and severely incursive character of the criminal law sanction demand a clear and strong retributive justification.[69] In broad terms such justification is often seen as residing in three main criteria: a strong and convincing moral condemnation of the conduct, seriously harmful actual or likely consequences of that conduct, and the proper attribution of this harmful morally objectionable behaviour to the accused actor. The justification, in summary, then rests on the bad behaviour of a responsible person.[70]

Indeed, for some, retributive justification of this kind should be considered first, ahead of any justification based on deterrence or other 'consequentialist' argument. But in the context of cartel regulation, as noted already, deterrence talk has always been high on the agenda. As Whelan notes,[71] in the European cartel criminalisation debate so far, the deterrent effect of sanctions has occupied

---

69   See, for instance, the European Commission Communication on EU Criminal Policy (2011), note 68 above.

70   On the established rationale of retributive justification in the context of criminal law, a key reference point for discussion remains H.L.A. Hart's *Punishment and Responsibility* (Oxford University Press, 1968). For more recent discussion of this theoretical basis, in the context of cartel activity, see Peter Whelan, *The Criminalization of European Cartel Enforcement*, note 53 above, at chapter 4.

71   Whelan, note 53 above, at p. 80.

most attention, reflecting Wils' assertion that deterrence is the generally accepted rationale for public antitrust sanctions.[72] There are a number of possible explanations for this ordering of discussion: the arguably morally neutral character of much economic offending; the significant contribution of economists to the debate, stressing efficiency rather than the normative imperative; and more recently the emphasis placed by regulators on the apparently self-evident effect of criminal sanctions ('if there is one thing business persons will certainly fear it is the prospect of a jail term in the US' type of argument). In that sense, so far in the literature there has been a relative deficit of retributive debate, and much of the resort to retributive justification has been based on assertion in a way similar to that of many deterrent claims. Indeed, some of the arguments pointing to the moral badness of cartel conduct have advanced quickly to striking comparisons and extreme metaphor, drawing analogies with racketeering[73] and serious property offences,[74] and employing colourful and highly pathological descriptions, such as the action of 'well-dressed thieves',[75] 'cancer on the open market',[76] and the 'supreme evil of antitrust'.[77] And the term 'egregious violation' has come into vogue. But, as Whelan correctly notes:

> a comprehensive retribution-based argument in favour of (or indeed against) antitrust criminalization has not been established in the literature and … consequently, the theoretical challenge of retribution in this context has yet to be examined in any great detail.[78]

This is an important point to take on board. Enough has been said already in the present discussion to show that the perception of cartel activity has changed over time, and continues to differ from place to place, as is shown by the ongoing discourse on criminalisation (again, a collection of varying voices on the subject may be consulted in Appendix Two to this chapter). But it is not just a matter of

---

72   Wouter P.J. Wils, 'Is Criminalization of EU Competition Law the Answer?', chapter 4 in Katalin J. Cseres, Maarten Pieter Schinkel and Floris O.W. Vogelaar (eds), *Criminalization of Competition Law Enforcement* (Edward Elgar, 2006).

73   Robert Kennedy as Attorney General – see the quotation in Appendix Two to this chapter.

74   For a summary of the numerous comparisons with theft and deception, see Whelan, note 53 above, at p. 81.

75   Joel I. Klein – see the quotation in Appendix Two to this chapter.

76   Mario Monti, EU Commissioner for Competition, Address, Stockholm, 11 September 2000, 'Fighting Cartels – Why and How?' See also Graeme Samuel, Chairman of the Australian Consumer and Competition Commission (ACCC), arguing that cartels are 'a cancer on the Australian economy and an insidious attack on consumers by well-dressed thieves' (Radio broadcast, 2 November 2007).

77   US Supreme Court in *Verizon Communications v Law Offices of Curtis V Trinko* (2004) 540 US 398, at 408.

78   Whelan, note 53 above, at p. 111.

how bad, or objectionable, or damaging, such conduct may be judged, but – prior to that question – what is *the way* in which it may be judged to be so – its inherent, cardinal as much as ordinal badness. It is interesting in this regard that most of the legal prohibitions are superficially descriptive and do not convey very precisely the essential substantive objection to the conduct, referring to the most part to form and method. Thus, for example, the language of the Sherman Act and of Article 101 of the Treaty on the Functioning of the European Union (TFEU) speak in broad terms about collusion ('conspiracy', 'combination', 'concerted practice') and anti-competitive business methods ('in restraint of trade or commerce', 'prevention, restriction or distortion of competition'), leaving aside the evocative word 'cartel' (whatever that may mean!) Section 188 of the UK Enterprise Act uses the heading 'cartel offence', without repeating the term in the text of the section or attempting to define the word. There is here almost an assumption that what is being referred to is so 'egregious' that its offensive nature speaks for itself. Yet the real point of the objection has not been fully articulated across a range of jurisdictions – whether for instance it resides in the kind and extent of damage to competition (but, then, to which and whose interests more precisely), or in the resort to conspiracy and collusion, or in a display of contempt for the values of trade liberalisation, or in the elements of subterfuge and cover-up of known illegality, to mention some main possibilities. If the basic principles of legal certainty and specificity of legal prohibition[79] are taken seriously, a significant criticism may be levelled at a host of legal definitions of infringement and offence. Part of this problem of insufficient discussion doubtless resides in the fact that the starting point for discussion (as noted at the beginning of this chapter) is an assertion of economic harm, which has led to some feeling that cartel infringements are morally neutral in character (*mala prohibita* rather than *mala in se*), and in that way may be distinguished from 'classic' or 'core' offending', such as violent behaviour or the direct damage to or disregard of property interests. Moreover, the nature and consequences of such economic harm – anti-competitive damage – remain open to argument.

Despite the force of the expressed objection to cartels, particularly in American sources, there are a number of arguments which may be drawn upon to challenge the assumptions underlying this categorical condemnation. For ease of exposition, these arguments[80] may be grouped together as relating to the following main issues:

79　Specificity is well described by Antonio Cassese as 'an articulation of the principle of legality' in the following terms: 'criminal rules must be as specific and detailed as possible, so as to clearly indicate to their addressees the conduct prohibited ... the principle is aimed at ensuring that all those who fall under the prohibitions of the law know in advance which specific behaviour is allowed and which conduct is instead proscribed'. Antonio Cassese, *International Criminal Law* (1st edn, Oxford University Press, 2003), at p. 145. The concept is closely related also to the principles of legal certainty and non-retroactivity.

80　For a detailed and critical overview and analysis of these arguments, see Whelan, note 53 above, at p. 86 *et seq.*

- the model of competition governance: acceptance of the political and economic values which inform the open market of economic regulation;
- the nature of anti-competitive damage: the fact that consumer victimhood is highly dispersed and not easily amenable to remedy through conventional juridical process;
- competing economic and social claims and values, for instance the interest of suppliers (protecting *competitors* as distinct from competition), the maintenance of employment, and the viability of local economies;
- the anti-competitive motive and intention: the reasons for engagement in cartels, which may be more complex than pure economic self-interest on the part of individual and corporate actors.

When considered further such objections tend to undermine easy analogies between cartel conduct on the one hand and core criminal offending in the categories of theft, deception and cheating on the other hand. As Whelan points out, preferring a consumer welfare standard over a total welfare standard facilitates the argument that cartel activity may be conceptualised as stealing, but on the other hand a total welfare standard may be presented as more efficient in producing longer term social and political justice and competition policy may be less efficient than taxation systems in dealing with unwanted distributive consequences.[81] There are also complex yet insufficiently explored issues concerning the relation between cartel formation and company merger as alternative competition reducing strategies – cartels may reduce competition but preserve a number of formally independent competitors, whereas after merger both disappear, yet a merger is rarely regarded as illegal per se.[82] Then as well, the identification, quantification and rectification of victim injury is a legal minefield which in the case of the US legal system has generated work and remuneration for lawyers but with a less certain benefit to those identified as victims of cartelisation.

Whelan's conclusion regarding this agenda of doubts and critical argument is compelling: there is much here, as in the domain of deterrence-based argument, which is a matter of assumption and assertion and needs to be further tested. He concludes that the scarcity of empirical evidence should be addressed:

> a thorough examination of the motivations of cartelists is vital for a comprehensive understanding of some of the complexities of the theoretical challenges of antitrust criminalization. Until definitive empirical data is forthcoming, assertions that cartel activity inevitably entails 'morally wrongful' conduct remain vulnerable to challenge … Likewise the complexities of the challenge of deterrence theory for antitrust criminalization will also persist.[83]

---

81   Whelan, note 53 above, at p. 98.

82   See Jeffrey Fear, 'Cartels and Competition: Neither Markets nor Hierarchies', Harvard University Working Papers, October 2006.

83   Whelan, note 53 above, at p. 113. Note that the European Commission's Communication of 2011 on EU criminal policy, note 68 above, emphasises the need for

Searching for theoretical order: Offences of conduct and offences of outcome

A possible solution to the issue of justification, at least for the present, may be to argue that a combination of (a) economic damage and (b) legally evasive and obstructive mind-set, in the sense of engagement in secretive collusion, determined recalcitrance and defiance of legal order, and actions designed to frustrate or sabotage efforts of legal enforcement, serve to transform the cartelist into a significant outlaw. But such a justification for strong legal control has yet to be clearly or fully articulated in legal definitions, and would have to be read into the legal texts, by extrapolating that reasoning from commentary and from subsequent 'sentencing' practice in deciding on sanctions. Certainly, the matter has not been fully and systematically considered at the beginning of the legislative process of offence definition.

In line with this argument and to take discussion forward, two profiling exercises may be carried out: first, a typology of anti-competitive strategies and conduct which may be subject to different forms of legal control; and secondly, a categorisation of individual cartelist intentions and mind sets.

A typology of competition infringements and spectrum of delinquency

Harding has recently argued:

> The whole field of competition regulation is very broad and diverse, and it may be argued that there is a world of difference between resource-effective joint ventures or trade promoting licensing or distribution agreements on the one hand, and aggressively predatory or exclusionary market tactics or highly profitable self-serving collusion on prices and markets at the other extreme of the spectrum. This is now clear in the vocabulary of '*per se* violations', and 'naked' or 'egregious' 'hard core' anticompetitive behaviour, used to describe the latter as categories of action which attract stronger and less equivocal condemnation and in relation to which there may be elements of bad conduct as well as bad outcome. Some effort at typology might indicate then more clearly this strongly outlaw fringe where categorisations of anti-competitive and criminal more comfortably overlap.[84]

The following typology may be then suggested:[85]

---

criminalisation impact studies in advance of the introduction of new measures of criminal law.

84 Christopher Harding, 'The Relationship between EU Criminal Law and Competition Law', chapter 12 in Valsamis Mitsilegas, Maria Berström and Theodore Konstadinides (eds), *Research Handbook on EU Criminal Law* (Edward Elgar, 2016, forthcoming)..

85 For a more detailed discussion, see Harding (2015), note 84 above.

- abusive but not collusive strategies: abuse of market power, for instance in the form of a very exploitative, exclusionary or predatory use of market strength and dominance (conduct covered by Article 102 TFEU);
- bilateral but not hard core anti-competitive conduct: regulated in principle but may well be allowed and is not subject to punitive sanctions (mergers, for example, would fall within this category);
- classic hard core competition delinquency: collusive cartel activity (the main subject of discussion here);
- conduct at the fringe of fraud and corruption: for instance, bid-rigging in some contexts and circumstances (most importantly, at the interface of collusion and corruption in relation to public procurement);[86]
- subterfuge which is criminally underhand and subversive: cartel facilitation, design and the obstruction of justice.

Such a typology provides a framework for and perspective on the range of legal control which arises within contemporary competition governance and can be used in the ordering and navigation of strategies of legal control (for instance, as between administrative scrutiny and regulation, administrative offences and sanctions, criminal procedure and sanctions, or civil procedure compensation). It may also bring to light what may seem anomalous in some ways, for instance the non-use (for the most part) of criminal law in relation to highly anti-competitive and abusive exploitation of market power (as in the domain of Article 102 TFEU). Most importantly, however, this kind of exercise works out a *spectrum of delinquency*, by relying on main categories such as collusion, corruption and criminal facilitation in relation to a range of coexisting and inter-relating anti-competitive conduct. In a move towards using more criminal law, it may then be sensible to distinguish, for instance, collusion in itself, bid-rigging as anti-competitive fraud and corruption, and facilitation and obstruction of justice offending, as indeed happens already in varying ways in a number of jurisdictions.[87] For present purposes, an important function of this kind of analysis would be to distinguish what may be termed infringements and offences of *outcome* and of *conduct*, further discussed below.

Profiling the individual cartelist

Just as there is a range of anti-competitive business strategies and practices, so too within the category of cartel activity there is a range of individual participation, in

---

86   See, for instance, OECD, Policy Roundtable, *Collusion and Corruption in Public Procurement* DAF/COMP/GF (2010)6, 15 October 2010.

87   For example, the separation of bid-rigging as a criminal offence from other cartel infringements as administrative offences under German and Austrian law. As another example, due to double criminality problems, the cartel defendant Ian Norris was extradited from Britain to the US in relation to obstruction of justice offences rather than the substantive Sherman Act offence.

terms of role, motivation and more precise intention, and this may be relevant and important to take into account in working out effective legal control, and in the resort to criminal law and sanctions in particular. Again a typology of offending conduct at the individual level may be attempted, on the basis of the evidence and perception of how cartels actually operate. The subject here comprises differing individual and personal features of motivation, interest, preference, role and ultimately (for purposes of criminal liability) intention, which may relevantly inform decision-making in the process of legal control, regarding issues of investigation, prosecution and the application of sanctions. Such a typology may also be mapped on to a scale of delinquency, as a form of moral assessment, which in turn may be translated into a more legal scale of offence seriousness, and then a form of 'sentencing tariff'. Such a typology is sketched out in Table 3.1.

This kind of analysis may be used possibly to construct different kinds of cartel offence, or alternatively in some instances provide a mitigating defence or ground for immunity. Certainly it is the kind of analysis which may be and is employed in the determination of individual role and responsibility for purposes of selecting sanctions or deciding on the quantum of penalty.

Outcome and conduct

The line of argument which emerges from this kind of analysis leads to a distinction which may be drawn between two main forms of involvement in cartel activity: first, the employment of anti-competitive business strategy in itself evaluated in terms of its market outcome (as a simple example, price-fixing with a certain economic outcome for consumers); secondly, the manner in which that strategy is used (for instance, knowing that it is illegal, in a determined and recalcitrant way, taking action to cover the traces and destroy evidence). The first kind of involvement may be described as an offence of outcome and as matter of economic damage. The second kind of involvement may be described as an offence of conduct, and is more a matter of individual or corporate mind-set, attitude and motivation.

The value of this distinction between outcome and conduct lies in the differing evaluation of two key features of prohibited anti-competitive activity. 'Outcome' in this context refers to the essential *economic* harm arising from an anti-competitive activity. In one sense, this is the primary reason for intervention; nonetheless, it is harm of a particular kind and established as such by a process of applying economic policy and market analysis. This gives rise to the argument that the activity and conduct in question has a morally neutral character and to consequent doubts regarding the appropriate application of criminal law sanctions and also the idea that the relevant agent is an economic actor and typically corporate rather than a human individual. In turn, this may lead to a policy preference for the use of a non-criminal law or administrative process and sanctions, as is favoured in some European legal systems and most significantly used in the EU system of legal control. 'Conduct' refers to the motivation for and manner of resorting to the anti-competitive strategy and comprises a number of behavioural characteristics

Table 3.1   Individual cartelist profile

Profile	Short Description	Examples
Cartel leader, organiser, facilitator, enforcer	Cartel general or secretary-general	Whittle (Marine Hose) Norris (Carbon Products)
Knowing and calculating profit seeker	Cartel foot soldier	Greg and Fiona in *The Marker* (ACCC film)
Passive operative, following instructions or compliant with established culture	Cartel recruit	Martin in *The Marker*
Moralistic and reflective inside objector, eventual whistle blower or complainant	Cartel rebel	Internal legal office in Christie's (Art House Auctions) or Virgin Atlantic Air Fuel Surcharges) Power Pipe (outsider and complainant in Pre Insulated Pipes)
Defender of other interests (competitor survival, saving employment, preserving local industry)	Crisis champion	Respondent in Melbourne project survey Allison (Marine Hose)

of the actor, whether the latter be corporate or, perhaps more relevantly, individual. It is this element of conduct which may then be identified and treated separately as a matter fit for control by means of criminal law. As Harding has argued, this is:

> a matter of undertaking anti-competitive conduct *in a certain way and in certain circumstances*. After all, not all price fixing, market sharing and the like is viewed as illegal, let alone criminal (consider the example of the Organization of Petroleum Exporting Countries (OPEC), or production quotas under the old European Coal and Steel Community). What appears to be very objectionable about anti-competitive action that is now prosecuted as a cartel is the consciously and defiantly illegal manner of its performance. ('a great initiative, but don't put it in writing, it's highly illegal')[88]

---

88   Harding, in Beaton-Wells and Ezrachi (eds) (2011), at p. 377. The quoted line is taken from the evidence in *Hasbro Toys and Games*, Office of Fair Trading, OFT CA98/2/2003, 21 November 2003 (73).

In very broad terms, this is then a question of attitude and intention and something which may be more easily cast as *mens rea* for the purposes of criminalisation, and in the context of a business cartel described alliteratively as a mind-set which is conscious, contumacious, collusive and conspiratorial.

Such a disaggregation of the whole cartel 'package' into an economic offence of outcome which may be more easily and sensibly attributed to corporate actors and a more behavioural offence of conduct, which may be attributed to corporate or (perhaps more appropriately) individual actors[89] may be seen in practice, although perhaps not so much by intention, in some contemporary legal ordering. One example would be the distinction drawn in the UK between the Competition Act infringement of the competition rules which may be dealt with by civil penalties[90] and the cartel offence under Section 188 of the Enterprise Act 2002, a criminal offence applicable to individuals, although this distribution of legal control was not explicitly designed on the basis of such a theory. In the same way the division of jurisdiction as between the EU, dealing with infringements of Article 101 TFEU committed by 'undertakings' by using non-criminal law penalties and some EU Member States applying criminal law to cartel activity as perpetrated by companies and/or individuals illustrates the different approaches to legal control on this basis. On the other hand, the Sherman Act in the US happily eschews any such differentiation, simply applying the single criminal offence to companies and individuals seen as conspiring together in a single activity. The overall legislative picture across jurisdictions is haphazard – a hotchpotch which lacks any agreed theoretical basis and design.

The above distinction between the delinquency of bad outcome and that of bad conduct, which draws upon an established sense of the morally neutral and the morally offensive, the conceptual terminology of *mala prohibita* and *mala in se*, and distinct processes of criminal and administrative regulation and penalty in some jurisdictions,[91] is offered as a critical template for further debate, but should also be borne in mind in the following discussion of the impact of sanctions applied to cartels and cartelists. For much of the upcoming discussion here will need to address the fact that rules and sanctions have been applied to both corporate and individual actors and that these rules and sanctions are found, sometimes operating

---

89   For some background to this argument, see the discussion in Harding and Joshua, note 5 above, at pp. 56–62.

90   Under Section 36 of the Competition Act 1998, undertakings may be required to pay a penalty in respect of infringements of 'Chapter I or Chapter II prohibitions'. In some respects, this runs parallel to fines which may be imposed by the EU Commission in respect of violations of Article 101 or 102 TFEU.

91   For further discussion, see Christopher Harding, 'The Interplay of Criminal and Administrative Law in the Context of Market Regulation: The Case of Serious Competition Infringements', chapter 9 in Valsamis Mitsilegas, Peter Alldridge and Leonidas Cheliotis (eds), *Globalisation, Criminal Law and Criminal Justice: Theoretical, Comparative and Transnational Perspectives* (Hart Publishing, 2015).

in parallel, in different legal domains, criminal law and non-criminal law. The normative framework and the underlying basis of legal control remains mixed and uncertain, and that fact will inform any critical assessment of anti-cartel regulation and the application of sanctions in that context.

Appendix One: Accumulation of Sanctions Relating to the Marine Hose Cartel

(For a full narrative of the Cartel, see Chapter 5)

The UK

Following an agreed transfer from the US, criminal convictions were handed down in relation to three UK nationals under Section 188 of the Enterprise Act 2002 on 10 June 2008. Defendants Whittle and Allison received three years imprisonment and were each subject to director disqualification orders that would last for seven years, while defendant Brammar, less involved than his co-conspirators, was to spend two and a half years in prison and was disqualified for five years. Each term of imprisonment was subsequently reduced on appeal – to two and a half years, two years and twenty months respectively. Two of the defendants were subject to confiscation orders and the other required to pay substantial legal costs.

The EU

The Commission levied total 'administrative' fines of €131,510 on Bridgestone, Dunlop Oil and Marine, Trelleborg, Parker ITR and Manuli, that was divided between the five companies and their subsidiaries in the way detailed in Table 3.2:

Table 3.2   Marine Hose Cartel: EU fines

Company	Dates of cartel participation	Amount of fine in Euros
Bridgestone Corporation (parent)	1 April 1986–2 May 2007	58 million
Bridgestone Industrial Ltd	19 December 1989–2 May 2007	48.1 million
Dunlop Oil and Marine Ltd	12 December 1997–2 May 2007	18 million
Contitech AG (parent)	28 July 2000–2 May 2007	16 million
Continental AG (parent)	9 March 2005–2 May 2007	7.1 million
Trelleborg Industrie SAS	1 April 1986–2 May 2007	24.5 million
Trelleborg AB (parent)	28 March 1996–2 May 2007	12.2 million
Parker ITR Srl	1 April 1986–2 May 2007	25.61 million
Parker Hannifin Corporation (parent)	31 January 2002–2 May 2007	8.32 million
MANULI Rubber Industries SpA	1 April 1986–1 August 1992 3 September 1996–2 May 2007	4.9 million

Yokohama, as the successful immunity applicant, had the fine which would otherwise have been imposed (€14,400,000) reduced by 100 per cent. Manuli, because of its transitory and occasionally passive role within the cartel, was granted a 30 per cent reduction, and Bridgestone and Parker ITR, in recognition of their leadership roles within the cartel, had their base fines increased by 30 per cent to the total shown in the above table.

Three appeals were made against these fines: one by Parker Hannifin, the parent of Parker ITR; one by Manuli; and the third by Trelleborg Industrie SAS, the French subsidiary of Trelleborg AB. According to Parker Hannifin, when the cartel was in operation, the entity that would become Parker ITR was owned and operated by a separate group of companies. It changed hands several times while the cartel operated, and was only acquired by Parker Hannifin and renamed Parker ITR in 2002. The appeal centred on the fact that despite this, the Commission held ITR liable for the entire period of the infringement, and the General Court, in agreement with Parker Hannifin, held that if an entity involved in a cartel transfers part of its business to an independent third party – as did the previous owners of what would become Parker ITR – the third party cannot be held liable for cartel conduct it had not participated it. Thus, that part of the Commission's decision that Parker ITR had participated in the cartel prior to 2002 was annulled, reducing ITR's fine by nearly 75 per cent.

Manuli, however, did not succeed. The General Court, exploring Manuli's appeal, noted that the Commission had been mistaken in the amount of credit it gave the company for cooperating with its investigation, but the gravity of its infringement was such that no changes were made to the amount of the fine.

The final appeal, Trelleborg's, like that made by Parker ITR, concerned the manner of its participation in the cartel. Here, the General Court concluded that the period of greatly reduced involvement that began around 1990 had interrupted its participation in the cartel for around 18 months (see the Ontology web page, Harding and Edwards, 2012). This interruption turned what was a single continuous infringement into a single repeated infringement, something that the Commission had discounted when calculating Trelleborg's fine. Despite this mistake, however, no change was made in the penalty apportioned.

Japan

The Japanese Fair Trade Commission (JFTC), like the British authorities, were treading new ground in terms of applying the relevant legislation (Article 2(6) of the Anti-Monopoly Act). Its decision was issued on 20 February 2008, and enjoined Bridgestone to both cease and desist its participation and to pay a ¥2,380,000 'surcharge'. The other members were likewise instructed, the first time non-Japanese firms had been so – but were not subject to financial penalties. Yokohama, as the successful immunity applicant, avoided sanctions.

Australia

The Australian Competition and Consumer Commission (ACCC) took proceedings against participants in the cartel in 2009 ACCC Chairman Graeme Samuel stated:

> Since the customers were mostly large oil and gas producers, the cost of the cartel ultimately fell on oil and gas end-users, namely the general public … Such losses are not ascertainable, but nevertheless real, and it is clear that the price of marine hose rose significantly in the period after the making of the marine hose club arrangement.

It was estimated that the cartel effected Australia between 2001 and 2006, affecting corporate customers such as BHP Billiton Petroleum, Woodside Energy and ConocoPhillips. Fines were imposed upon four of the cartel members, Trelleborg receiving the highest (AUS$3.2 million), Dunlop the second highest (AUS$2.68 million), Bridgestone the third (AUS$1.68 million) and finally Parker ITR (AUS$675.000).

South Korea

This was the first time that the Korean Fair Trade Commission (KFTC) imposed penalties upon foreign companies involved in an international bid-rigging cartel. Like the Australian authorities, it sanctioned four of the six participants – Bridgestone, Dunlop, Trelleborg and Parker ITR – imposing a total fine of 557 million Korean Won (approximately US$447,900). Of this, US$256,000 was imposed upon Bridgestone; US$117,400 upon Dunlop; US$40,200 upon Trelleborg; and US$33,700 upon Parker. Manuli was also implicated, but the KFTC decided not to impose a fine upon it. Yokohama again benefited from leniency.

US

The Sherman Act in the US allows for both corporate and individual criminal law fines and also prison terms to be imposed on individuals. The sanctioning process was set rolling in the US system following the cartel busts in Houston and San Francisco in 2007, with some of the individual executives deftly arrested following the infiltrated meetings (although some implicated individuals evaded US justice – the German Bangert (Dunlop) is still fugitive, while the Italian Pisciotti (Manuli) was arrested at Frankfurt Airport in 2013 before being extradited from Germany to the US in 2014 and only then convicted and sentenced). Five of the companies (leaving aside the whistle blowing Yokohama) agreed to plead guilty and pay fines totalling over $40 million and eventually a number of executives from a number of countries also entered guilty pleas, agreeing to fines and prison terms. But not all was plain sailing for the Department of Justice. Two of the Manuli executives – Francesco Scaglia, a product manager, and Val M. Northcutt, a technician and installer of marine hose – were testified against by their former bosses, Robert L. Furness and Charles J. Gillespie, as part of an agreement on the part of the latter for reduction of sentence. Peter Whittle, one subject of the UK's first use of the cartel offence under the Enterprise Act, also testified against them under the same understanding. The legal defence for Scaglia and Northcutt successfully cast doubt on these testimonies and secured acquittals (see the account by Marissel Descalzo, Michael S. Pasano, Paul A. Calli in *US v Val M Northcutt* et al.*: An Antitrust Case Study*, www.cfjblaw.com).

Table 3.3 shows in summary how each of the corporate and individual participants were subject to sanctions across six jurisdictions.

Another way of reading the cumulative impact of sanctions is to aggregate the more human impact of the process and sanctions imposed on a group of individual executives as a sample: the three British individuals (Whittle, Brammar and Allison) dealt with under US and UK law. The fate of the British defendants in the *Marine Hose Cartel* proceedings

> provides an instructive example of the totality of sanctions which may be applied in a single case … All three defendants were arrested at the time of a cartel meeting in Houston in Texas in May 2007, and then *held in custody* and subsequently *subject to curfew and tagging* while their plea bargains were being worked out, for a period of seven months. They agreed to pay *fines for the offences committed under US law*. On their return to the UK, they were *convicted of the British cartel offence*, and each sentenced to *imprisonment (two and a half, or three years, each sentence reduced later on appeal)*. All three were subject to *disqualification orders (either five or seven years)*. Two of the defendants were made subject to *confiscation orders (totalling £ 1 million)*, while the third was ordered to pay *prosecution costs*.
>
> (Harding and Joshua, 2010, at p. 357, emphasis added)

Any calculation of sanction accumulation should also take into account the possibility of 'follow-on' claims for damages, in a number of legal systems but especially in the US. Civil claims for compensation under the Sherman Act are for treble damages and so have a quasi-penal character, and may be facilitated as class actions. For instance, in relation to the *Marine Hose Cartel*, all the companies except Manuli collectively settled class action liability for a total of just over $21 million (which could be then added to the $40.3 million collected in criminal fines, a total corporate pay-out of over $60 million in the US).

Table 3.3 Marine Hose Cartel: Total sanctions

Jurisdiction	Manuli	Dunlop	Bridgestone	Yokohama	Parker ITR	Trelleborg
Japan	Cease and desist order	Cease and desist order	Cease and desist order plus a surcharge payment of ¥2.380.000	–	Cease and desist order	Cease and desist order
Australia	–	AUS$2.68 million fine	AUS$1.68 million fine	–	AUS$675.000 million fine	AUS$3.2 million fine
South Korea	–	US$117.400 (equivalent) fine	US$256.000 (equivalent) fine	–	US$33.700 (equivalent) fine	US$40.200 (equivalent) fine
US	US$2 million corporate fine Furness $75K fine 14 months Gillespie $20K fine 12 months 1 day Pisciotti extradited 2014 $50K fine 24 months	US$4.5 million corporate fine Bangert – still fugitive Allison £100K fine Brammar $75K fine Whittle $100Kfine A, B and W – prison terms transferred	US$28 million corporate fine Hioki $80K fine 24 months	–	US$2.3 million corporate fine	US$3.5 million corporate fine Calleca $75K fine 14 months Cognard $100K fine 14 months
UK	–	Whittle 30 months; Dq, 7 years Allison 30 months; Dq, 7years; £25.000 costs Brammar 20 months; Dq, 5 years B, W – confiscation (£1 million in total)	–	–	–	–
EU	€4.9 million fine	€18 million fine	€58.5 million fine	–	€25.6 million fine	€24.5 million fine

Appendix Two: Cartel Quotations – Look Out Towers on the Subject (A Narrative of Comment)

Over a hundred years or more of discourse and writing on the subject of business cartels, many people, expert or otherwise, have expressed views on the matter, and some of these opinions and arguments, especially when they are forceful statements of position, are nicely quotable in ongoing discussion. The collection of quotations can provide the opportunity for useful and interesting exercises in reflection and analysis. Below are a small number of such quotations about cartels, which are offered for critical reflection and deconstruction. Some of these statements are now so well cited as to have a kind of classic or iconic standing, but they each provide the chance to consider the theoretical and policy underpinning of the enterprise of cartel control. Collected together in this way they also stand as a number of 'look out towers' on the subject in the way described by Henning Mankell below, with the aim of shifting perspective in order to gain a meaningful overview and to see the matter simply, in the best sense of that word. After all, working out what to do about business cartels is rather like dealing with the problem presented in a Swedish crime story.

Henning Mankell (novelist, writer, humanitarian activist)

> Many years ago Rydberg had taught him a way of approaching an investigation
> in a new light. We have to keep moving from one look out tower to another,
> Rydberg had said. If we don't, our overviews become meaningless … No matter
> how complicated an investigation is, it has to be possible to describe it to a child.
> We have to see things simply, but without simplifying.
>
> *(The Man Who Smiled* (Harvill Press, 2005), at p. 261)

'You can quote me on this' Adam Smith (Scottish moral philosopher and writer on political economy)

> People in the same trade seldom meet together … but the conversation ends in a
> conspiracy against the public, or in some contrivance to raise prices.
>
> *(The Wealth of Nations* (1776), Book I, chapter X)

Oliver Wendell Holmes Jnr (American jurist and judge in the Supreme Court)

The Sherman Act is 'a humbug based on economic ignorance and incompetence' and 'an imbecile statute' aimed at 'making everyone fight and forbidding anyone to be victorious' (Holmes' *Letters*).

Presenting the view from 'inside' German industry: 'these industrial combinations are the consequence of necessity. Doubtless, the underlying idea of their establishment is thoroughly economic, the need to economize.'

28 September 1929, quoted in Ervin Hexner, *International Cartels* (1946).

Harry (1st Baron) McGowan (Chairman of Imperial Chemical Industries (ICI))

Described cartels as a way of assuring orderly marketing, planned expansion of international trade, elimination of cut-throat prices, and 'all that is admirable and reasonable'.

1926, quoted in George W. Stocking and Myron W. Watkins,
Cartels in Action (1946).

Francis D'Arcy Cooper (Head of Lever Brothers)

I do not think that any business, whether it be great or whether it be small, can exist, if such things go on. All business is based on confidence between the employers and the employees, and if you have corruption at the top, it spreads right through a business, and they are bound to fall.

Comment (1932) on insider speculation based on price-fixing by
the chairman and vice chairman of the Niger Company, quoted in
Catharine MacMillan, 'The Trial: How Procedure Shapes Substance',
19 (2008) *King's Law Journal* 465.

Franklin D. Roosevelt (President of the United States)

Unfortunately, a number of foreign countries, particularly in continental Europe, do not possess such a tradition against cartels. On the contrary, cartels have received encouragement from some of these governments ... I hope that you will keep your eyes on this whole subject of international cartels, because we are approaching the time when discussions will almost certainly arise between us and other nations.

Letter from the President of the United States to the Secretary of State,
6 September 1944.

Robert F. Kennedy (American Attorney General and Senator)

We are talking about clear-cut questions of right and wrong. I view the business-man who engages in such conspiracies in the same light as I regard the racketeer who siphons off money from the public in crooked gambling ... A conspiracy to fix prices or rig bids is simply economic racketeering and the persons involved should be subject to as severe punishment as the courts deem appropriate.

Quoted in Gordon B. Spivack, *Comparative Aspects of Anti-Trust Law*
(BIICL, 1963) at p. 45.

Richard Hofstadter (American Historian)

The antitrust movement and its legislation are characteristically American ... In America competition was more than a theory: it was a way of life and a creed. From its colonial beginnings through most of the nineteenth century, ours was overwhelmingly a nation of farmers and small-town entrepreneurs – ambitious, mobile, optimistic, speculative, anti-authoritarian, egalitarian, and competitive. As time went on, Americans came to take it for granted that property would be widely diffused, that economic and political power would be decentralized.

'What Happened to the Antitrust Movement?', in E. Thomas Sullivan, *The Political Economy of the Sherman Act* (OUP, 1991) at p. 20.

Joel I. Klein (Attorney General, US Department of Justice)

'The War against International Cartels: Lessons from the Battlefront –
Let me start with the obvious: cartel behavior (price-fixing, market allocation and bid-rigging) is bad for consumers, bad for business and bad for efficient markets generally. And let me be very clear: these cartels are the equivalent of theft by well-dressed thieves and they deserve unequivocal public condemnation.'

14 October 1999, Fordham Corporate Law Institute Annual Conference.

Mario Monti (Italian economist and prime minister, EU Commissioner for Competition)

Cartels differ from most other forms of restrictive agreements and practices by being 'naked'. They serve to restrict competition without producing any objective countervailing benefits ... Cartels, therefore, by their very nature eliminate or restrict competition. Companies participating in a cartel produce less and earn higher profits. Society and consumers pay the bill. Resources are misallocated and consumer welfare is reduced. It is therefore for good reasons that cartels are almost universally condemned.

Address, Stockholm, 11 September 2000, 'Fighting Cartels – Why and How?'

Julian Joshua (EC Commission official, DGIV)

Business delinquency on a truly massive scale has been revealed ... The very success of the Commission in uncovering these violations in three of Europe's biggest 'blue chip' industries is itself disquieting. It is a strong indication that the message that cartels are harmful, damaging and illegal may not have got through.

'Attitudes to Antitrust Enforcement', 1995
Fordham Corporate Law Institute at p. 110.

Graeme Samuel, Chairman of the Australian Consumer and Competition Commission (ACCC)

Cartels are 'a cancer on the Australian economy and an insidious attack on consumers by well-dressed thieves'.

Radio broadcast, 2 November 2007.

Australian business person (research survey respondent)

The key reason for us to enter into these arrangements was not to make profits, but for survival and to retain jobs within Australia ... I am very emotionally committed to Australian manufacturing and keeping jobs here ... At the time I knew I was breaking the law. I knew all the basics of the TPA [Trade Protection Act] ... I had been involved in retrenching people and that had involved a lot of pain ... In that time fines were relatively small – A$100,000. Fines that small were unquestionably palatable in the context.

Quoted by Christine Parker, 2006, 'The Compliance Trap', 40 *Law and Society Review*, at p. 607.

PART II
Narratives and Analysis: Tales of Anti-Cartel Enforcement as Criminological Testing

At this point the discussion moves on to a more specific aspect of the subject – an investigation of the impact of anti-cartel sanctions, using what is being termed here a 'biographical' method. Chapter 4 discusses the kind of data and material which may be used for a criminological study of business cartels, and then proceeds to explain the 'biographical' method employed in this part of the book, in order to investigate more specifically the impact of legal sanctions which are used in the contemporary regulation of cartel activity. Six major international business cartels which have been subject to legal proceedings across a number of jurisdictions since the early 1980s have been selected as the subject of a detailed narrative, providing an account of their background and 'pre-history', their actual operation, and events following their termination and legal sanctioning (their 'after-life'). After presentation of the biographies in Chapter 5, the remaining three chapters then provide some analysis, argument and conclusions regarding the application of anti-cartel sanctions in these cases. First, Chapter 6 explores some of the conceptual and methodological difficulties which occur in the exercise of measuring the impact of sanctions in this context. Chapter 7 then analyses the material contained in the biographies in terms of assessing the impact of the sanctions, leading to some conclusions in Chapter 8 regarding what may be learnt from this research and method of studying the subject.

Chapter 4
Data and Method:
Historical Narrative and Analysis

It becomes possible to develop a politics of reading that draws its legitimacy from explicit political positions, not from any fictitious 'real' knowledge – let alone 'neutrality'. And once we acknowledge both the necessity and the strategic nature of limits to interpretation, we move from the question of the author back to the question of interpretation.[1]

Information, sources and interpretation

In social science the subjects of investigation, research and discussion are often rich in data and information. This is especially so when the matter under examination comprises events and activities that are recent or contemporary so that 'evidence' relating to these matters is relatively well available and accessible. So the social scientific researcher may quickly amass a body of material and information to use as a basis for knowledge and understanding of the subject and there may be full accounts and narratives to tell to the world. In some respects this is obviously true of the subject of business cartels. It is known that such practices are widespread and there is now a virtually global activity of regulation and legal enforcement, so that much is happening and there is much that can be investigated and analysed. But, then, business cartels have become like crime more generally, in that, as they have been subject to more stringent legal control, they have naturally become more hidden and the 'evidence' has then become less accessible. In that sense, any research into this subject has taken on some of the character of criminological research, so that it has become meaningful to talk about 'a dark figure' relating to the actual extent of the phenomenon, it has become less easy to penetrate and be confident in explaining the reasons and motivations for involvement, and equally in the later stages of the account there is less certainty about the effects of legal intervention since ongoing and future actions are likely also to be obscure. Moreover, as the subject becomes increasingly one of confrontational and adversarial legal process, what comes to light is naturally contested through conflicting 'prosecution' and 'defence' accounts of what has happened, and problems of selection of information and its interpretation serve to complicate the reading and understanding of the data and evidence.

---

1   Mieke Bal, *Narratology: Introduction to the Theory of Narrative* (3rd edn, University of Toronto Press, 2009), at p. 10.

Two main points should therefore be made about the search for, the retrieval and the discussion and interpretation of sources and data relating to the subject of business cartels. First (and in contrast to the position some hundred years ago when the 'scientific' study of cartels was more open and straightforward), the subject is, like crime, one of some obscurity. Now, cartelists themselves are not likely to be forthcoming about their activity and the researcher will then take on something of the role of a legal investigator. Secondly, this search for information may have to draw upon a number of narrative accounts which are not wholly consistent with each other and are also based upon political positions in the sense used by Mieke Bal in the quotation above. For obvious reasons the cartelist's account from the 'inside' may differ from the regulator's, or lawyer's or researcher's account from the outside, and indeed different cartelist's inside accounts and different lawyer's outside accounts may oppose each other for again obvious strategic reasons. As Bal argues, it is then difficult to sustain a belief in either a 'real' or a 'neutral' version of the matter and what is claimed to be reality or truth is as much a fiction as any other version. For those reasons, the line of investigation, interpretation and analysis undertaken in the present work has been determinedly agnostic in its approach, fully accepting that the researcher will be confronted by a number of narratives or stories of the same subject and that the researcher's task is then to select and in some way read such accounts in reaching any understanding of an conclusions on the matter. As Bal argues, 'we move from the question of the author back to the question of interpretation'. The 'authors' of this study are more properly interpreters, as are in turn the readers of what is presented in this account.

Sources

Having made that statement of research position, what then are the main sources of information on the subject? As stated already, in earlier times and in a context of less invasive and hostile legal control, businesses themselves were more forthcoming about the nature and extent of their own activity, and so the research investigation carried out by the like of Piotrowski,[2] Hexner,[3] and Stocking and Watkins[4] did not face the kind of obstacle in the way of present researchers. For the greater part, none of the above writers were looking at the matter as crime, they were in no proper sense criminologists, and in so far as they were examining something as a an economic or political pathology, it was not described or discussed as such a serious disorder as it is now. The record for examination would thus have been fuller, clearer and perhaps then more honest, and less riddled with conflicting versions. By the later twentieth century, the research picture is much more obscure

---

2   Roman Piotrowski, *Cartels and Trusts* (George Allen & Unwin, 1933).

3   Ervin Hexner, *International Cartels* (Pitman, 1946).

4   George W. Stocking and Myron W. Watkins, *Cartels in Action: Case Studies in International Business Diplomacy* (Twentieth Century Fund, 1946).

and research enquiry and analysis has often involved a resort to the *prediction* of cartel formation, dissolution or desistance and over-confident claims based on common sense and anecdote ('every business person fears an American jail'). In short, the clear written record of events, participation, reasons and outcomes has become more elusive.

The approach taken here has departed from econometric, legal or criminological predictions of how sanctions may operate (the staple method of deterrence theory and policy) and turned to the examination of historical record. Bearing in mind that there is now a good 30 years or more experience of legal proceedings against cartels in a some jurisdictions, particularly in the US and Europe (EC and EU), reference may now be made to a full and reliable documentary source of information about cartels which have been investigated and formally established as such, and then sanctioned in particular ways. Leaving aside for the moment the fact that such cases are in an important sense a sample, selected in a particular way according to the demands of enforcement policy and legal process, there is nonetheless from the 1970s a sufficient critical mass of significant international cartels being dealt with in this way to provide factual information regarding business behaviour and the operation of markets to enable some informed conclusions to be drawn. This is especially true of the record emanating from the EC/EU. Once the stage has been reached for a formal Commission decision against a cartel, that decision will be published as a report on the market and companies' conduct and any following appeal will contain detailed evidence and argument contained in the parties' pleadings, sometimes an advocate general's opinion, and then the judgment of the Court of Justice or General Court (formerly Court of First Instance).[5] All completed proceedings before the EU Courts are published in the *European Court Reports*. Since the 1980s, appeals against Commission decisions, launched individually by companies as cartel participants, have become frequent, even verging on the automatic,[6] and the official reports of such proceedings in the *European Court Reports* (ECR) run altogether into thousands of pages. For instance, the report of the main judgment of the Court of Justice in relation to the Wood Pulp Cartel (discussed in Chapter 3) runs to 325 pages, with a great deal of factual information contained in the first section (facts and arguments of the parties – some 130 pages), a detailed report and opinion drafted by Advocate

---

5   For information on the lay-out and role of reports of such cases as published in the *European Court Reports*, see Institute of Advanced Legal Studies, *European Union: A Guide to Researching the Law of the EU* (Hester Swift, 2014) (libguide.ials.sas.uk) The Court of First Instance was established in 1989, and took over the jurisdiction of the Court of Justice in relation to appeals against the Commission's formal decisions in competition cases, although a number of judgments of the Court of First Instance then would be appealed to the Court of Justice. The Court of First instance was renamed the General Court in 2009.

6   For a study of the appellate process in this context, see Christopher Harding and Alun Gibbs, 'Why Go to Court in Europe? An Analysis of Cartel Appeals, 1995–2004', 30 (2005) *European Law Review* 349.

General Darmon (125 pages), and finally almost 50 pages of the actual judgment of the Court.[7] The comparable American sources may be less full, on account particularly of the greater rate of out of court or negotiated settlement in the American criminal justice system. Nonetheless, taken together these legal reports provide a large amount of information about the operation of cartels, and the reliability of this information has naturally been tested within the legal process itself. It was therefore decided to establish for this research a summary database of all 'cartel' cases dealt with in the US and EU jurisdictions between 1980 and 2010 as a starting point for data collection.

The database provides information on salient features of international anti-cartel proceedings in the European Union and the US during the period 1980–2010. This period extends from the beginning of confrontational legal action against significant anti-competitive collusion of a secretive and unreported nature (in violation of Article 101(1) of the TFEU or the US Sherman Act) until a relatively recent point in time. A 30-year period represents a significant body of legal proceedings to enable both comparative (EU and US) and temporal analysis to be undertaken from such data. All the summary information in the database was collected from the publicly available official record of such proceedings and is of an essentially factual nature – for instance in relation to 'recidivist status', the information does not comprise a qualitative assessment of repeat offending,[8] but whether factually an earlier or other offending cartel action has been mentioned or taken into account in the decision taken against the instant cartel. The information for each cartel proceeding was organised into 10 categories:

- name of cartel/market description;
- type of anti-competitive strategy employed by the cartel, e.g. price-fixing, market sharing;
- corporate participants;
- location of companies (nationality/place of registered office);
- jurisdiction of the legal proceeding;
- sanctions imposed on the members of the cartel;
- any recidivist status;
- aggravating and mitigating factors taken into account in the decision taken against the cartel;
- any recorded role of individuals in the cartel's operation or modalities;
- dates of the first and last activities of the cartel (duration).

While the database provides a starting point for an examination of cartel activity and for comparative analysis, it may be supplemented by further material, both more detail derived from the legal sources, including other jurisdictions where cartels have been subject to legal proceeding, but also contextual data, in particular

---

7   Cases 89/85 etc., *Ahlström and others v Commission* (1993) ECR 1-1307.
8   For a further discussion of the issue of recidivism in this context, see Chapter 6.

the 'pre-history' of the legal proceeding against the cartel comprising the earlier corporate and market history as drawn from a range of other source material, and also the 'afterlife' of the cartel participants following the completion of the legal process, again drawn from other sources. In this way a longer-term biography of a cartel may be provided, locating its actual operation and legal fate in a salient context, in order to appreciate better its origins and also then the outcomes of legal process.

The legal sources referred to just above therefore comprise factual information, economic and market data and analysis, and legal argument. Although in some respects this may be seen as rigorously generated and well attested, as part of a formal legal procedure, it nonetheless should be handled with some care. In the first place, such data has a selective quality – it has been chosen and put forward for particular legal purposes. Secondly, some of the information recorded in the legal record may still be contestable in itself, a good example again from the Wood Pulp proceeding being the specially commissioned 'expert' reports of economists supplied on both sides of the case (see the critical comments of Advocate General Darmon).[9] Put another way, all this data may be interpreted as a number of different narratives of the same events and situation which somehow need to be interweaved into a single informative and credible narrative – the role of the present authors and readers.

Moving beyond such formal reportage and record of legal process, there is then a potentially rich and more diverse field of information and discourse to draw upon for the more contextual aspects of cartel biography. There is, first, a large existing 'literature' on the subject, both older and more recent, comprising both factual accounts and analytical and critical discussion of the subject. Reference has been made already to the flourishing of scientific study of cartels, especially in Germany, in the earlier part of the twentieth century, while in the last 20 years there has been a developing momentum in critical scholarship and practical commentary to cover the global boom in regulatory action, so that a work such as this present study will merit a substantial bibliography.[10] Secondly, governmental and intergovernmental policy papers, reports and public presentations provide a large body of information and argument, subject of course to a health warning that there is often an underlying or accompanying message.[11] Thirdly, and similarly, there has at different times appeared an interesting body of 'campaigning' literature and material, ranging from the 'muckraking' written accounts and press cartoons directed over 100 years ago at the American trusts[12] to more recent documentary and fictional presentations

---

9   (1993) ECR 1-1307, at p. 1546.

10   See the contents of the bibliography the end of the book.

11   Reports from government departments and issued by intergovernmental organisations may be objective in tone but motivated by policy positions, more especially the public presentations of antitrust officials from the US Department of Justice or the EU Commission.

12   For instance, Ida Minerva Tarbell, *The History of the Standard Oil Company* (McClure, Phillips & Co, 1904).

of the subject in literature and cinema.[13] Finally, press and media accounts may be informative, although in a usually selective and haphazard way, in relation to both the history of the subject (for instance, intensive reporting in the *Daily Mail* and *Daily Mirror* in Britain regarding William Lever's 'Soap Trust' of 1906)[14] and also more contemporary perceptions (for instance American media reports on the fate of high-profile cartelist Diana 'Dede' Brooks[15]in relation to the Art House Auctions Cartel). The subject-matter has not been consistently high-profile in either public perception or on political agendas, and even at present, despite the impressive explosion of regulatory action, may still struggle to capture wider attention (compared for example to subjects such as the traditional domains of organised crime, or financial misconduct in the banking sector). Thus, some of the above sources may not be obvious, although there is much to be found upon closer searching. All these sources, however, should be considered subject to the usual social scientific caveats regarding reliability, selectivity and representativeness.

One further source deserves some separate mention: the autobiographical account from within the cartels and the voice of the cartelist himself (or more rarely, herself). Reference has already been made in Chapter 1 to the problem of gaining access to a reliable inside outlaw cartelist account of the subject and naturally enough what may emerge after the event (beyond the legal record) is haphazard. Some former cartelists disappear from view (for instance, Diana Brooks of Sotheby's)[16] while others reappear in different guises. The small spectrum of cartelist autobiography covers the fully repentant and born-again (Mark Whitacre, Lysine),[17] the exploitative educator (Keith Packer, Fuel Surcharges),[18] the regretful but hardly repentant (Bryan Allison, Marine Hose),[19] and the brashly unrepentant (Alfred Taubman, Sotheby's).[20] Such accounts are informative and thought-provoking, but naturally raise questions regarding reliability. After the event autobiographical narratives may also feed into biographical work in the

---

13   For instance see Appendix Two to this chapter on the emergence of 'cartel cinema'.

14   See Charles Wilson, *The History of Unilever*, Volume 1 (Cassell, 1954), at pp. 72–88 ('The Crisis of 1906').

15   See Chapter 5, at p. 175–6.

16   Tellingly, actor Sigourney Weaver was keen to make an HBO film based on the Brooks story, but the latter was not willing to engage with the project, which then faltered.

17   'Mark Whitacre – Lysine Cartel Whistleblower on Price Fixing and Rebuilding his Life after Prison', Feedinfo News Service, 13 January 2009.

18   Erik Larsen, 'Ex-BA Executive Shares Prison Tales to Sway Violators', *Bloomberg*, 22 October 2010; Keith Packer, 'A Cautionary Tale: How a Competition Law Breach Led to a Jail Term for One BA Exec', *Legal Week*, 22 September 2011.

19   Michael O'Kane, an interview of Bryan Allison: 'Does Prison Work for Cartelists? The View from behind Bars', 56 (2011) *The Antitrust Bulletin*, issue 2.

20   Alfred Taubman, *Threshold Resistance: The Extraordinary Career of a Luxury Retailing Pioneer* (Harper Business, 2007).

conventional sense (such as Kurt Eichenwald's *The Informer*[21]and Christopher Mason's *The Art of the Steal*)[22] and even the occasional biopic film (such as *The Informant*, mentioned in Appendix Three below). But for the most part, rigorous social scientific interrogation of either corporate or individual cartelists to elicit their own accounts remains in its infancy.

The selection and presentation of information: A biographical dilemma

In presenting explanatory or analytical accounts of actual life situations researchers commonly construct narratives which interpret the actuality from different kinds of source. In this process, the methodology of research (such as the identification, collection and ordering of data) is combined with the interpretation and presentation of information as a 'reading' or 'story', but the latter may depend crucially on the kind of information and how it has been found and selected. This may seem a self-evident point, but the outcome and character of much research and writing is the product of method as much as substance and it is important not to lose sight of this truism. Criminologists' and lawyers' accounts of the same situation may then appear very different, each selecting from the raw material of the subject different kinds of information, to be used for different purposes, so presenting the same matter in very different perspectives and leading to qualitatively different conclusions. Such is the challenge and perhaps also potential confusion, or at least complication, of interdisciplinary approaches. What is true of disciplines may also be true of methods. Researchers may not easily agree on a choice of method, and readers of research accounts should be sensitive to this common pitfall of academic understanding.

The construction and writing of cartel biographies is fraught with such methodological choice and anxiety. This project has sought to collect information about and thereby understanding of the working of business cartels. As explained already, given the problem of source (a largely hidden and disguised type of activity as the main subject), the collection of full and accurate data is problematic. Some researchers have addressed this problem by presenting accounts and drawing conclusions from hypothesised and predictive econometric models by assuming a rational course of behaviour, then a reliable typical scenario, and drawing therefrom conclusions which are quantitative in nature. An alternative approach, adopted in the present study, is more empirical, and draws upon the close observation of an actual instance ('case') or number of such instances of the activity in question, using the rigorously tested collection of evidence via legal process, and presents such observed data as a reliable basis for discussing

---

21 Kurt Eichenwald, *The Informer* (Broadway Books, 2000); Kurt Eichenwald, *The Informant: A True Story of Greed, Conspiracy and Whistleblowing* (Portobello Books, 2009).

22 Christopher Mason, *The Art of the Steal: Inside the Sotheby's-Christie's Auction House Scandal* (Putnam Publishing, 2004).

and understanding the subject. An objection to this approach is that it is likely to be quantitatively limited, a 'sample', which may not be representative of an (unknowable) whole, and so potentially misleading. This objection will draw its greatest force in relation to one or a small number of intense accounts, which may provide considerable detail, but as an 'anecdote', 'vignette' or 'biography' risk a picture and understanding which is dangerously different from the rest of the field. The dilemma is this: can more be learned and understood better from quantification, either through the calculations based upon a rational abstracted model or the safety of larger (hence more representative) numbers, or through the sharp actuality of a limited empirical experience?

To some extent this project has attempted to draw advantage from both approaches. On the one hand, a large database of cartel 'cases' dealt with through legal process over a significant period of time has been constructed, to gain some assurance in number, and this provides a landscape or geography within which a number of biographical accounts may be located. On the other hand, a small number of such cases have been selected for closer analysis and report, so as to draw upon greater detail and acquire a surer sense of historical experience at an individual and subjective level. For those seeking an objective, *external* view, drawn from numbers, to tell a story of how many companies in how many cartels, in how many and which markets and countries, over what period of time, a graphic tale of maps, charts and graphs can be used to weave a narrative of pattern, scale and dimension, and indeed this may possess some explanatory force. But there will still be limitations. The raw material of such accounts is necessarily selective, and dependent on the forces which drive and determine legal process, leaving aside a suspected large dark figure, and so representative only up to some point. Moreover, this is an account externally observed, which may provide little insight into motive and incentive, beyond intelligent guesswork based upon the patterns of time and place. An understanding of the 'why' of cartel behaviour, and its dynamic and strategy, requires more qualitative information drawn from a more individualised account of particular corporate and human actors, at the risk of becoming anecdotal but the gain of being more insightful.

This discussion is located in the familiar methodological territory of quantitative versus qualitative approaches, of what might be gained or lost by opting for one rather the other. But it does prompt some further reflection, in the context of cartel research at least, on the use of the more qualitative 'anecdotal' approach, and the role of such individualised story-telling, both for purposes of research and also in the process of anti-cartel enforcement activity in itself.

The problem with anecdotal evidence

Scientists and lawyers tend to be dismissive of anecdotal evidence, distrusting its seductive but possibly unreliable character. After all, an anecdote is necessarily a short account or story, drawn from an individual or personal experience, a snapshot and not the full story (whatever that might be – and that is another issue for biographers!) but presented in such a way as to impress, and perhaps even allow a theme or lesson to be drawn from the telling. The term 'vignette' is now also used in a similar way in the context of research, to convey the idea of something presented in a short and focused way in order to provide a strong impression of a character, idea or object.[23] The impressive power of an anecdote is evident, for instance in Joseph Stalin's famous example: 'the death of one man is a tragedy, the death of millions is a statistic'. This reveals another important aspect of anecdote, the possibility that the person hearing that account can relate more easily and immediately to the situation being described, so that it then becomes more credible.

The reservations about anecdote in the research context concern anecdote *as evidence*, and as such the main objections relate to its nature as observation rather than fact, its 'unscientific' and casual presentation, and that it often takes a 'word-of-mouth' rather than full documentary form. Another way of viewing anecdotes as evidence for argument is to see them as 'telling cases' and the analogy with cases in the (common law) legal sense is also important. In the practice of law a case is one instance – a lived, and perhaps in some respects dramatised, example – of a wider phenomenon. Legal process will usually then analyse such cases comparatively in order to generalise from such examples in order to find solutions or construct norms, so that the case law approach may be seen as a method of testing and exploiting the anecdotal rendering of one or a number of cases to reach generally applicable conclusions. The point to note, then, is not the invalidity of anecdote, but the care which should be taken in using anecdotal evidence in any kind of argument.

Despite the 'scientific' reservations regarding anecdotal evidence, there is nonetheless some recognition of its value and practical significance. Thus in medical practice, a 'case report', while not accepted as conclusive, may still be seen as a valuable trigger for further research, as something suggestive which could then at a later stage be confirmed by other evidence and so ultimately validated. This is just one example of the use of anecdote for working out hypotheses which merit further examination and testing in a research context, or as part of a process of analytical or detective argument. Another way in which anecdote may prove of value is through its social or political utility in promoting an awareness or understanding of phenomena. Thus, when Department of Justice official Scott Hammond lauded the impact of the publication of the famous Lysine Cartel tapes (a kind of official criminal investigation anecdote), he noted that people contacted

---

23   For an example of the use of research vignettes, in relation to qualitative data gathering, see the University of Melbourne Law School Cartel Project, when 'factorial vignettes' were used to test business people's perceptions of cartel activity. University of Melbourne Law School, *The Cartels Project.*

him to say: 'Now I finally get what you do for a living – go and nail the crooks'.[24] This is referring to an educating force and outcome. It is also a nice example of 'double-anecdoting' – using anecdotal evidence to educate public opinion, and then reporting on this as another anecdote, to convince professional and official opinion elsewhere.

Daniel Kahneman has also demonstrated the power of anecdotal evidence in everyday decision-making.[25] As a matter of choice theory, it may be shown how models of choice used in various contexts may be contingent on accounts or anecdotes that frame or influence an individual's choice to do x or y. Focusing on the impact of rare events on future decision-making, Kahneman has commented: 'My current view of decision weights has been strongly influenced by recent research on the role of emotions and vividness in decision-making ... Emotions and vividness influence fluency, availability, and judgments of probability – and thus account for our excessive response for the few rare events that we do not ignore.'[26] Kahneman discusses the matter in terms of vivid outcomes and vivid probabilities in order to examine the hypothesis that people (a) overestimate the probabilities of unlikely events and (b) overweight unlikely events in their decisions. This line of enquiry is relevant to deterrence theorising and cartel control if the example of Scott Hammond's account of the Lysine Cartel bust is taken again. Is it the case that Hammond's vivid and celebratory (therefore emotive) account of the Lysine Cartel bust might incline would-be cartelists to overestimate the probability of being detected in that way and weight highly the possibility of a prison term as the outcome of any future involvement in cartels? Certainly the way in which Hammond presents his anecdote suggests that such may well be his purpose. Note the title of his paper and presentation: 'From Hollywood to Hong Kong: Criminal Antitrust Enforcement is Coming to a City near You'. Equally, it may be asked of that example – how should researchers and other readers take into account the Hammond anecdote, in understanding the reality of anti-cartel enforcement and the behaviour of cartelists? At one and the same time the anecdote has a political force and also a research value, although care has to be taken in gauging and acting upon such force and value.

The use of biography and vignette in the present context

In seeking to understand the dynamics of cartel collusion and cartel control, the decision has been taken here to employ in particular a method of data selection

24 Scott D. Hammond, 'From Hollywood to Hong Kong: Criminal Anti-Trust Enforcement is Coming to a City near You' (US Department of Justice), Address, 9 November 2001, Chicago.
25 Daniel Kahneman, *Thinking Fast and Slow* (Penguin Books, 2011), chapter 30, 'Rare Events'.
26 Ibid., at p. 323.

and of presentation of argument which narrates the subject-matter as a series of 'biographies' or stories about the actual operation of business cartels and the effects of legally regulating such activities. The narration of such biographical accounts of itself gives rise to a number of questions and problems, regarding the selection and amount of information and its narrative presentation. One of these problems relates to the anecdotal nature of some of this data, not only in terms of its evidential quality and subjective origin, but also its place in the overall story of a cartel – its significance in, for instance, strategic or economic terms, as distinct from its personal vividness. The following three examples may be taken for present purposes of illustration, without trying to answer for the moment that question of what weight should be given to such elements in the narrative of cartel biography. But this will be, at a later stage of discussion, a decision as to how to use such material, if at all.

Airfield rendez-vous

The airport meeting between CEOs Diana Brooks and Christopher Davidge as part of the high-level collusion in the case of the Christies' and Sotheby's Cartel. Davidge arrives in New York, flying by Concorde, at 9.25 p.m., meets with Brooks in her car in a parking lot, and Davidge takes the 12.30 return flight to London.[27]

Cartel bust in Houston

The personal account of one of the Marine Hose Cartelists of the discovery of the meeting in Houston and his subsequent arrest and detention by the US authorities.[28]

Antipodean whistle-blowing

The film made by the Australian Competition and Consumer Commission (ACCC)[29] presenting a fictional but intended realistic account of involvement in a cartel and its legal aftermath (*The Marker* see Appendix Three to this chapter).

Each of these examples presents an account of cartel activity and legal enforcement, the first two as real life historical episodes and the third as a dramatised story of involvement and legal action, although seriously intended as an accurate though fictional version of that subject. Each has an anecdotal quality, in providing an illuminating snapshot of the broader subject, and saying something

---

27 See the accounts by Orley Ashenfelter and Kathryn Graddy, 'Anatomy of the Rise and Fall of a Price-Fixing Conspiracy: Auctions at Sotheby's and Christie's' 1 (2005) *Journal of Competition Law and Economics* 3; Christopher Mason, *The Art of the Steal*, note 22 above.

28 See note 20 above.

29 Australian Competition and Consumer Commission (ACCC): film, *The Marker* (2012). ACCC News Release, 19 August 2012.

(significant?) about the individual human role of business persons in cartel activity. What use can or may the interested cartel observer (such as a researcher) make of such material? For instance, a comparison may be drawn between how the conduct is presented in the ACCC film with the argument made by Warin, Burns and Chesley(2006)[30] regarding the way in which members of the American public and jury members in contested US federal trials of Sherman Act offences may view cartelist defendants.

More widely, and beyond the question of the (problematic) power of anecdote, some consideration should be given to the relation between forms of narration in this context – for instance, biography, case study, anecdote, vignette – and the way in which the use of each will employ a particular selection and interpretation of data. For some quick insights, it is interesting to compare for example John Connor's 'case study' of the 1990s Citric Acid Cartel[31] with Ashenfelter and Graddy's study[32] of the Sotheby's-Christie's auction cartel, both of which present very interesting and thought-provoking conclusions. Connor, at the start of his discussion, refers to the tradition of 'industry case studies from court records' by industrial organisation economists ('IO work'). His own narration and analysis of the Citric Acid Cartel selects and uses primarily economic and legal process data (as a 'legal-economic' study) and so may be taken as a 'law and economics' story in terms of narration. Interestingly, Connor's appendix – headed 'Citric Acid Chronology' – presents a linear chronological account of events in the citric acid market, as an easily usable and readable historical narration.

How to read the biographies: The agenda for narration

Using the kind of source material referred to above, and bearing in mind the argument presented there about selection, presentation and interpretation – in short, the *reading* of that material, the following chapter will contain a series of narratives relating to six selected international cartels. The events and situations described in these narrative accounts occur in the context of business activity and regulation of economic and legal significance but there is also some diversity in these selected examples. The intention is to present these instances of cartel activity as a descriptive narrative, leaving analysis and critical comment to the following chapters, and that is also then the way in which these' biographies' should be read. It has to be accepted, however, that no narrative can be purely descriptive or neutral in its presentation – at the very least the selection of material

---

30   F. Joseph Warin, David P. Burns and John W.F. Chesley, 'To Plead or Not to Plead? Reviewing a Decade of Criminal Antitrust Trials', *The Antitrust Source*, July 2006.

31   John M. Connor, 'What Can We Learn From the ADM Global Price Conspiracies?', Staff Paper #98–14, August 1998, Department of Agricultural Economics, Purdue University.

32   See note 27 above.

for narration will be based on a certain agenda of interest and relevance.[33] In this case, there is a social scientific agenda underlying the presentation (rather than for instance an ambition to excite dramatic interest or effect). Remembering that this work is conceived as a 'criminology' of cartels, constructed around the themes of pathology and mythology, the narratives need to serve that purpose. That having been said, the reader should proceed to the next section with the idea of reading largely factual biography, in a text unencumbered with critical reflection and analysis.

---

33 Following the method used in chapter 5 of Christopher Harding and Julian Joshua, *Regulating Cartels in Europe* (2nd edn, Oxford University Press, 2010): 'A Narrative of Cartel Regulation in Europe'. As those authors comment, at p. 119 – 'Although the discussion in this chapter is therefore mainly of a descriptive character it can also serve to bring out a sense of historical development, and provide some insight into the role of the main players in this ongoing drama of investigation and litigation', thereby indicating some agenda and parameters for the narrative.

Appendix One: Contesting Accounts of the Same Subject

1. Business, Lies and Videotape

- A US Department of Justice official's account of the regulator/investigator's role based upon the publication of the Lysine Cartel videotape:

This was a monumental case for the Division's criminal enforcement efforts because it grabbed the attention of so many groups that we were urgently trying to reach – including the media, US consumers, the business community and foreign governments ...
... I know that I had friends ... call me about the case and say 'Oh, now I finally get what you do for a living – go and nail the crooks!' When the public viewed the tapes, they saw with their own eyes an unmitigated, undeniable crime of fraud and deceit. One could not have asked for a better introductory lesson for the US public as to why price fixing is a crime and why those who commit it are criminals ...

> Scott D. Hammond, 'From Hollywood to Hong Kong – Criminal Antitrust
> Enforcement is Coming to a City near You', Department of Justice paper,
> presented in Chicago 2001.

- A cartelist's reflection on business delinquency in an interview after conviction and sentence for his participation in the Marine Hoses Cartel:

I think that the majority of people causing cartels are usually doing it not for personal gain but for their business, for their firms. I don't think from what I've seen that many individuals are doing it for their own ends. They are doing it because it's expected of them, because they've always done it, or because it's the only way they are going to survive. I don't view it as dishonest. I can distinctly recall when the OFT interviewed me they said, 'Do you accept that your behaviour was dishonest?' I knew I had to say yes in order to get the deal, but it stuck in my throat having to say it because I have always considered myself an honest, truthful person. I was always the last person to expect to end up in jail, but I did.

> Interview transcript: Michael O'Kane, 'Does Prison Work for Cartelists?
> The View from behind Bars' (interview with Bryan Allison),
> 56 (2011) *The Antitrust Bulletin* 483.

2. Evidence and Dramatic Presentation

- The transcript of recorded conversation from the Lysine Cartel meetings, read as evidence to be used in legal proceedings.

- The same used a research 'vignette', used as a trigger for reflective and critical discussion within a selected group of discussants, to whom it is presented as a text or as a dramatic re-enactment.

3. Tales from Business History

- An American economic historian on early German cartelisation:

In general, cartels were voluntary, private contractual arrangements among independent enterprises to regulate the market. State-managed cartels or forced cartelization during wartime are important exceptions to this rule. Both Robert Liefmann and Harm Schröter stressed cartels' fundamental orientation toward security and stabilization, a sort of risk management strategy. Some definitions of cartels include the *intent* to monopolize markets, but the motivations to form cartels were so varied, so few cartels actually achieved monopolies, and many were established with the explicit aim to *preserve* competitors rather than competition, that this assumption is unnecessary. Early German cartel theorists viewed cartels as an anti-merger policy, contrasting dangerous American-style trusts with responsible cartels. Empirical studies have confirmed that prohibiting cartels sped concentration. Antitrust policy is a misnomer; it is more accurately an anti-cartel policy.

Jeffrey Fear, 'Cartels and Competition: Neither Markets nor Hierarchies', Harvard University Working Papers, October 2006.

- President Roosevelt's 1944 letter to the Secretary of State:

During the past half century the United States has developed a tradition in opposition to private monopolies. The Sherman and Clayton Acts have become as much a part of the American way of life as the due-process clause of the Constitution. By protecting the consumer against monopoly these statutes guarantee him the benefits of competition ... Unfortunately, a number of foreign countries, particularly in continental Europe, do not possess such a tradition against cartels. On the contrary, cartels have received encouragement from some of these governments ... Cartel practices which restrict the free flow of goods in foreign commerce will have to be curbed ...

Letter from the President of the United States to the Secretary of State concerning cartel policies, 6 September 1944.

Appendix Two: The Cartel Cinema

There is a growing body of filmed and dramatised depiction of business cartel activity which may be viewed for both basic information on and discussion of cartel behaviour and also, and perhaps more significantly, as an interpretation and perception of the nature of such conduct.

Several of these films have been made and released for public viewing by competition authorities. As the International Competition Network (ICN) has commented:

> Several competition agencies have used broadcast media in their cartel awareness efforts, by producing videos, radio and television advertisements, short films and animations. Many additional agencies are currently exploring the use of social media, such as posting short films on YouTube and using Twitter to communicate its anti-cartel message.

ICN, *Anti-Cartel Enforcement Manual*, Cartel Working Group, Subgroup 2: Enforcement Techniques, Chapter on Cartel Awareness, Outreach and Compliance, March 2012, at p. 6.

As such, this particular sub-genre may be analysed for its particular presentation and interpreta of the subject and as a means of conveying officially a kind of 'antitrust message'.

Listed here are some of the 'cartel films' which are at present easily accessible for such viewing (a number via YouTube).

* *The Lysine Cartel.* US Department of Justice 'Lysine' videotapes from its investigation of the Cartel in the 1990s: covert footage of actual cartel meetings. This is both legal evidence and live documentary, but is low in terms of dramatic quality.
* *The Raid.* Probably a collector's item and potential art-house classic. Made as part of an in-house training and compliance programme for the Finnish Neste Corporation. A dramatisation, at times engagingly tongue-in-cheek, but not far-fetched. 29 minutes. May be viewed via Chillingcompetition. com, *Antitrust Oscars* web page.
* *The Dutch Construction Cartel.* A documentary made for the Dutch current affairs programme, *Zembla*, director Jos van Dongen, 65 minutes (edited in co-production with the Amsterdam Centre for Law and Economics (ACLE) from four 45-minute episodes as televised in 2001). Highly recommended by Daniel Sokol.
* *Clementie in Kartelzaken* (Leniency in Cartel Cases). By the Dutch Competition Authority, NMaMovie, 2008, 9 minutes.
* *The Informant.* US feature film, 2009, directed by Steven Soderbergh, and based on the book, *The Informant*, by Kurt Eichenwald (Broadway Books, 2000), a journalistic account of the Lysine Cartel. Actor Matt

Damon in the role of whistle blower Mark Whitacre. The film achieves an odd, uncertain tone – sometimes described as a 'biography-comedy-film'.

- *Kom Forst (Be the First to Tell: A Film About Leniency)*. By the Swedish Competition Authority (the Konkurrensverket), February 2010, 5 minutes. Intended to promote awareness of the Swedish leniency programme. Has been shown daily on the train between Stockholm City and Arlanda Airport.
- *Understanding Competition Law*. From the UK Office of Fair Trading (OFT), a competition compliance film, June 2011, 20 minutes. A rather stilted, semi-dramatised aware-raising film. Features Professor Richard Whish.
- European Commission documentary, *Fighting against Cartels*, July 2012, 9 minutes. Features Professor Richard Whish again, talking about cartel basics.
- *The Marker*. By the Australian Competition and Consumer Commission (ACCC), August 2012. 16 minutes. A lively dramatisation. 'A short film that shows the devastating effects involvement in a cartel can have on individuals and businesses'. Bonus features: presentations by ACCC chairman Rod Sims, Qantas CEO Alan Joyce, and University of Melbourne researcher Caron Beaton-Wells.
- *Cartel Limode* (Lemonade Cartel). By the Brazilian Competition Authority (CADE). Animated film.

It is interesting to reflect comparatively on this body of work, regarding any cultural variation in presentation (for instance, the rather feisty and youthful Australian cartel in *The Marker*, operating in a world of urban wine bars; the more sedate and middle-aged Swedish cartel in *Kom Forst*, drinking coffee in home meetings; and the rather prim British investigation in the OFT film). The recent educational, awareness-raising films are useful presentations of how cartels operate in a basic way and have a common purpose – to send out warning and encourage reporting in the context of leniency programmes. The Swedish and Australian films both tell the story of an 'innocent' (respectively Stefan and Martin) caught up in cartels against their better instincts and eventually drawing relief and reward from going for leniency. Note the differential sanctions applied to the hard core cartelists, Gordon and Fiona, in *The Marker* – reflecting their gender perhaps? The earlier in-house film, *The Raid*, does not preach the virtues of whistle-blowing, probably reflecting its origins in pre-leniency days in Europe, and interestingly its hero Markku decides for himself, cannily but rightly, to resist the temptation to join the cartel, to the chagrin of the regulators who carry out the raid. Some of these films have highly quotable lines. For instance, in *The Marker*, Fiona tells Martin that it is 'the nature of the industry – you get to know everyone and everything', while Gordon quips in relation to their bid-rigging arrangement 'What goes round, comes round, mate'. In *The Raid*, Markku is tempted by the argument 'there is nothing to lose, plenty to gain' and the sexy Spanish intermediary, Christine, who whispers 'your secret is safe with me', but eventually resists both ploys to ensnare him in the cartel. In *Kom Forst*, the voice-over opines that 'the reasons may vary, but the cartel is a fact'. And that last view may fairly well sum up some of the research argument here.

This body of cinema is at the least interesting and entertaining and presents a fascinating subject for academic deconstruction.

Chapter 5

Cartel Biographies: Six Narratives of Cartel Prehistory, Lifetime and After-Life

This chapter contains narrative accounts of six major cartels subjected to legal process over the past 30 years. These six instances of cartel activity have been chosen on the basis of their international scope, economic significance and distinctive and illustrative legal features. In terms of their actual cartel life-span, taken together they cover the period 1945 to 2007. They overlap each other in their time of operation, although for the most part the predominant period of cartel action covered here is during the 1990s and into the early years of this century. The cartels span a range of products and services, some or perhaps even most of which will not be evident or familiar to non-expert readers. Although each example will embody the resort to 'classic' anti-competitive strategies, such as price-fixing and the sharing of markets, these accounts will also exhibit some diversity of circumstance and motivation, a point which will be taken up in the following analysis and argument in later chapters.

The first issue of narration to be decided upon is the order of telling the stories. Since an important objective of this chapter is to remain as factual as possible and enable the reader to make up his or her own mind, as it were, from the facts presented, any temptation to introduce a thematic ordering has been resisted to maximise the opportunity for 'neutral' interpretation. For that reason, the order of telling is based simply on the historical start point for proven cartel activity in each case. That results in the following order of appearance:

1. Soda Ash (1945–1989).
2. Marine Hose (1986–2007).
3. Pre-Insulated Pipes (1990–1995).
4. Lysine (1991–1993).
5. Art House Auctions (1993–2000).
6. LCD Panels (2000–2009).

Henceforward, as lawyers like to say, '*res ipsa loquitur*' – let the facts speak for themselves.

The Soda Ash Cartel: Cartel heritage and long-term litigation

Some prehistory

Sodium carbonate – also known as washing soda, soda ash and soda crystals – is a sodium salt of carbonic acid. Pure sodium carbonate is a white, odourless powder that absorbs moisture from the air, has an alkaline taste, and forms a strongly alkaline water solution. It is domestically well known for its everyday use as a water softener, and can be extracted from the ashes of many plants growing in sodium-rich soils. Vegetation from salt-bearing soils (found in the Middle East), kelp (from Scotland), and seaweed (most predominantly sourced from Spain) produces so noticeably different an ash than timber (that is used to create 'potash' potassium carbonate) that it became known as 'soda ash'.

The cultivation of plants known to be rich producers of soda ash reached a historical high in the eighteenth century. There was increasing demand from Europe's burgeoning soap, glass and textile industries for alkali, and to meet this need the French scientist Nicolas Leblanc developed what would become known as the Leblanc process – a method to manufacture soda ash synthetically using salt, limestone, sulphuric acid, and coal.[1] Popular because of the increases in output it made possible, this process dominated alkali production during the early nineteenth century, although its expense and pollution-ridden byproducts (hydrochloric acid gas to name but one) made it far from a sustainable solution to the problem of increasing demand.

An alternative process for producing synthetic soda ash was developed in 1861 by the Belgian chemist Ernest Solvay,[2] whose company was destined to become a major player in the history of soda ash. Solvay's invention – a 24-metre tall gas absorption tower in which carbon dioxide bubbled up through a descending flow of brine, together with efficient recovery and recycling of the ammonia – proved to be much more economical and less polluting than the Leblanc method. In the ensuing three years Solvay and his brother Alfred accrued sufficient financial backing to construct a plant in Charleroi in Belgium, in 1863, and the process was patented In 1872, from which date the huge Solvay enterprise (Solvay et Cie) and network of cartel activity may be dated.

The beginning of this international soda ash industry and its collusive activities is neatly summarised by Stocking and Watkins from their mid-twentieth perspective in the following terms:

---

1   This process is believed to have been first developed in 1791. Nicolas Leblanc committed suicide after his prize money for developing the process was withheld by both the Revolutionary Government and Napoleon Bonaparte.

2   Ernest Solvay was, again, a man typical of his time, combining entrepreneurial and intellectual achievement – he also organised scientific conferences, and became a scientific and research philanthropist.

One of the oldest chemical cartels centers around the network of companies set up by the Solvay brothers and their foreign partners in the leading industrial countries to exploit their newly developed ammonia soda process for making alkalies. In 1872 Ernest Solvay and Ludwig Mond organized Brunner Mond in Great Britain and the Solvay brothers granted it an exclusive license for the British Empire. In 1881 Brunner Mond and Solvay et Cie jointly organized the Solvay Process Company of New York, with exclusive rights to the United States market. Solvay Process and Brunner Mond then formed a joint subsidiary, Brunner Mond of Canada. From time to time thereafter the original Solvay company (Solvay et Cie), whose exclusive territory was the European continent, established subsidiaries in Germany, Holland, France, Italy, Russia, and, in partnership with Aussiger Verein, Czechoslovakia, Poland, Yugoslavia, Hungary, and Roumania.[3]

This was an industrial sector permeated from the start by a culture of collaboration, achieved through strategies of financial connection, licensing, marketing arrangements and the sharing of information. Solvay maintained close relations with IG Farben in Germany and the successor companies in Britain, ICI,[4] and the US, Allied Chemical and Dye. When the dominance of the Solvay process was threatened by the development of brine electrolysis, Solvay, IG Farben and ICI and American companies acting through the US Alkali Export Association, Alkasso, worked together to manage their interests in that new market. ICI and Alkasso were leading representatives, for instance concluding an international agreement in 1929, when ICI stated that 'it is understood that there will be complete co-operation between us in order to avoid competition in any part of the world'.[5] This was, broadly speaking, the historical backdrop for Solvay and ICI's memorandum of agreement in 1945, in the 'Page 1000' document,[6] which was a blueprint for the

---

3   George W. Stocking and Myron W. Watkins, *Cartels in Action: Case Studies in International Business Diplomacy* (The Twentieth Century World Fund, 1946), at p. 430. Of the corporate founders, Ludwig Mond was another chemist, originally German, and Sir John Brunner was another typical example of the time – industrial chemist, business manager, politician and benefactor. The Czech enterprise Aussiger Verein was absorbed into IG Farben in 1938.

4   ICI was formed by the merger in 1926 of four major chemical companies that were based in Great Britain: Nobel Industries; Brunner, Mond and Company; the United Alkali Company; and the British Dyestuffs Corporation. Its main areas of production were chemicals, explosives, fertilisers, insecticides, dyestuffs, non-ferrous metals, and paints, and it quickly established a reputation as an innovator.

5   Stocking and Watkins, note 3 above, at p. 434.

6   See Appendix One to Chapter 2, 'The Page One Thousand Story'. The nature and terms of the agreement are described in more detail in the Commission's 1990 decision relating to the Soda Ash Cartel (OJ 1991, L152, at paras 23 and 25). The incriminating document was discovered during a dawn raid carried out by the Commission at an ICI office in Northwich, Cheshire in 1989 (see further below).

European wide co-operation, allocating the British and Commonwealth markets along with other countries in Asia, Africa and South America to ICI and the continental European market to Solvay.

The Cartel in the 1980s: The 'evergreen' co-operation

The Solvay/ICI soda ash arrangement,[7] while it should be seen in this broader temporal and spatial context of extensive industry-wide collaboration and cartelisation, had some distinctive features. It was certainly a long-standing and durable co-operation, determinedly anti-competitive to the clear advantage of the partners, and also secretive from an early date – the parties claimed to the Commission that their earlier practices were no longer in operation.[8] But the 'Page 1000' agreement remained operative after the United Kingdom entered the European Economic Community, regardless of the fact that it was formally ended in 1973, and the companies continued to consult regularly so as to ensure that a mutually beneficial status quo – 'evergreen' in the sense that it remained unchanged despite time passing – was maintained. For instance, following the closure of one of ICI's plants in the early 1980s, Solvay continued to provide long-term support for ICI's position by supplying it with large tonnages for resale in ICI's traditional markets. ICI and Solvay thus saw themselves not so much as competitors but as partners and conducted themselves accordingly. The whole purpose of the arrangements was to maintain the territorial status quo so that they did not compete and each was dominant and able to control the market in its own allotted territory. For the most part, and in so far as the ICI/Solvay co-operation is described and defined as a particular cartel in itself, it was also a duopoly[9] as much as or even rather than a multipartite collusion or concerted practice. There was one other German firm connected with Solvay in market sharing, which was brought within the scope of the Commission's investigation and formal decision against the soda ash producers – Solvay had a concurrent agreement with Chemische Fabrik Kalk (CFK) to divide up the market in Germany[10] – but this could be seen almost as an incidental feature of the main operation.

---

7   Should it be described as a cartel, or more than one cartel? This again is a question of definition and identification of a cartel. In her Opinion for the 2011 European Court of Justice judgment (see below), Advocate General Kokott refers to 'cartels' in this case, separating the arrangement between Solvay and ICI on the one hand, and that between Solvay and CFK on the other hand: Case C-109/10P, *Solvay v Commission* (2011) ECR 1–1044.

8   See the Commission's decision, note 6 above, and the judgment of the European Court of Justice in 2011, note 7 above.

9   The term used to describe a two-party oligopoly arising from the dominant position on a particular market of those two parties.

10   See the Commission's decision, note 6 above, and the CFK box in the text.

As a two-party cartel or duopoly the main parties were to be dealt with by the Commission on three legal bases: ICI and Solvay in respect of a market sharing cartel in violation of Article 81 of the EC Treaty (Decision 297/90), Solvay and CFK in respect of their market sharing cartel also in violation of Article 81 (decision 298/90), and Solvay and ICI for abuse of their positions of market dominance in violation of Article 82 of the Treaty (decisions 299 and 300/90). With a very large share of the market respectively in Western Europe and in Britain, it was alleged that the two companies had used their dominance to protect their territories from serious competition, in particular through a system of 'top-slice rebates' to customers.[11] On the one hand, therefore, the Commission was dealing here with a classic anti-competitive cartel arrangement, what amounted in effect to a market sharing arrangement between Solvay and ICI, continuing a long-standing practice, hard core and well proven in legal terms, and there was little serious attempt to deny the substantive infringements. On the other hand, this was also a legally distinctive case in some respects, based on an enforcement strategy which appeared to carve out a particular arrangement of just two significant industry actors from a wider history and culture of industry cartelisation. In theory, this may have appeared as a strong case for the Commission, once it had the incriminating evidence against the two companies. However, the case was to evolve into a 20-year long legal saga, culminating in a final annulment of the Commission's decision and sanctions in 2011.

CHEMISCHE FABRIK KALK: THE GERMAN QUESTION

In the middle of the 1980s, Solvay came to realise that CFK had adopted a policy of price cutting that it was using to retain or regain its market share. In response to this, representatives from Solvay and its German subsidiary DSW discussed the possibility of an 'armistice' with CFK. An agreement was made between Solvay and CFK: Solvay would ensure that CFK achieved an annual minimum sales tonnage on the German market in return for a cessation of its aggressive price cutting practices. If CFK's sales in Germany fell below the guaranteed minimum – a figure of around 179,000 tons was set based on CFK's sales figures in Germany during 1986 – Solvay would buy up the shortfall. Under this system, CFK's sales rose above the guaranteed minimum in both 1987 and 1988 – reaching 183,000 tons and 180,000 tons respectively – and this, added to an unexpected increase in demand for Soda Ash in Germany, allowed the company to end 1988 with an 8.3 per cent increase in total sales over the previous year.

---

11   See the CFK box. Another aspect of Solvay's dominance was its large market share as a supplier of salt, used in the process of manufacturing synthetic soda ash.

SOLVAY AND ICI TOP SLICE REBATES

Added to their history of mutual support and non-competition, during the 1980s Solvay and ICI established a system of rebates designed to avoid any danger of real competition in their respective territories. Most large users of soda ash have one main supplier for their 'core' requirements (80 per cent of their needs, say) but like to have a secondary supplier for the remaining 20 per cent as a counterbalance for the core supplier. In order to minimise the competitive effect that this method engendered, ICI and Solvay developed a two-tier pricing system where the 'core' tonnage was sold at normal prices but the additional quantities (the remaining 20 per cent or 'top slice') which the customer would otherwise buy from a second supplier were offered at a substantial (and secret) discount. In some cases these discounts meant that the additional tonnage was being offered by Solvay or ICI at virtually half-price, and it was made clear to customers that their being availed of these exclusive rates depended on their agreeing to take most, if not all, of their requirements from the dominant producer. While inducements of this kind cost this producer very little, suppliers quoting for the remaining tonnage would need to offer a price that fell below the cost of their outgoings if they wished to get any business.

The legal saga

The main chronology of the legal proceedings is summarised in the box just below.

Legal timeline	Legal action
April 1989	Dawn raids
December 1990	Four Commission decisions and fines, OJ 1991 L152/21
May 1991	Appeals by Solvay and ICI to CFI Case T-32/91 (Solvay), Case T-36/91 (ICI)
June 1995	All decisions annulled by CFI, 1995 ECR-II 1825
August 1995	Appeal by Commission to ECJ, Case C-288/95P
April 2000	Appeal dismissed by ECJ, 2000 ECR I-2391
December 2000	Commission re-adopts decisions and fines, OJ 2003 L10/10
March 2001	Appeal by Solvay to CFI, Case T-57/01
December 2009	General Court judgment, 2009 ECR II-4621
March 2010	Appeal by Solvay to ECJ, Case C-109/10 P
February 2010	Solvay's application under the ECHR
April 2011	Opinion of Advocate General Kokott in Case C-109/10 P
October 2011	Judgment of ECJ and annulment of decision and fines 2011 ECR ...

The Commission had been aware of ICI and Solvay's collaborative relations for some time. Earlier in the 1980s there had been some examination of the two companies' 'tonnage' contracts, and an agreement by the companies to modify their practice, so that the Commission closed its file on that particular arrangement. But during the 1980s, Solvay's 'total requirements' contracts with three Belgian glassmakers triggered legal proceedings in the Belgian courts on the part of an American soda ash producer, so that there would have been a general awareness of the continuation of cartel activity. The Commission's case against what was then identified as the Soda Ash Cartel (see the Legal Timeline box above) commenced with dawn raids mounted by the Commission in April 1989, leading to the discovery in particular of the 'Page 1000' document in one of ICI's offices. A number of companies in the soda ash market were investigated in this way: Solvay and ICI, but also the 'small producers' – AKZO in the Netherlands, CFK and Matthes and Weber in Germany, and Rhône-Poulenc in France.[12] In the event, legal proceedings were taken only against Solvay, ICI, and CFK in respect of the violations of Article 81 and 82 of the EC treaty, as described above. In December 1990 the Commission adopted four decisions finding infringements of Article 81 and 82 of the Treaty and imposing substantial fines on Solvay and ICI, and a smaller fine on CFK.[13] There then followed a series of appeals, by the companies to the Court of First Instance, and then by the Commission to the Court of Justice, lasting until April 2000.[14] The companies succeeded in their claim for annulment of the Commission's three decisions on the ground that they

---

12 AKZO and Rhône-Poulenc both appear in a number of other European cartel cases, qualifying therefore as 'usual suspects' – see further in the discussion of the Bleaching Agents Cartel, just below. On the after-life of CFK, it may be noted that for this company (a subsidiary of BASF since 1971) the financial situation deteriorated in 1992 when the price for sodium carbonate fell sharply, a change that was partly caused by the European Commission lifting anti-dumping regulations on sodium carbonate imports from the American Natural Soda Ash Corporation (ANSAC). Following this change, CFK's revenue decreased to 225 million DM and losses increased to 9.6 million DM. In December 1993, all remaining production was shut down at its Kalk facility, and all of the remaining 700 workers were laid off. Since then *Chemische Fabrik Kalk GmbH* has been a wholesale distributor of chemicals and subsidiary of Kali und Salz AG (K&S AG since 1999).

13 Commission decision and fines, note 6 above, OJ 1991 L152/21. Soda ash accounts for up to 60 per cent of the raw material costs of glass making, so the adverse effect of restrictive arrangements and abusive behaviour is ultimately felt by millions of consumers as well as by the many industries which use glass, such as cars and construction. In view of the seriousness of the case, the Commission imposed fines of ECU 10 million on ICI, and a further ECU 3 million on Solvay for its dealings with CFK. CFK itself was fined ECU 1 million.

14 CFI: Case T-32/91 (Solvay), Case T-36/91 (ICI), (1995) ECR-II 1825; ECJ: Case C-288/95P, *Commission v Solvay* (2000) ECR I-2391.

had not been properly authenticated when issued to the parties, an essential procedural defect, and also, in relation to the decision addressed to Solvay and CFK, in respect of a failure to give proper access to the file.[15] In December 2000 the Commission re-adopted the decisions, in proper form and imposed the fines once more on Solvay and ICI[16] (CFK had not appealed against the original decision in so far as it was addressed to itself, and had paid the fine of €1 million). Solvay proceeded to challenge this second decision on some different procedural grounds: first, again, that the Commission had infringed the company's defence rights by refusing to grant access to its file,[17] and secondly, that the case had not been decided in reasonable time,[18] and again violated the company's basic rights. These appeals were considered by the General Court in 2009 and then again by the Court of Justice in 2011.[19] In 2010 Solvay also made an application to the European Court of Human Rights, claiming that the excessive time of the proceedings violated the Human Rights Convention.[20] The final judgment of the Court of Justice found in favour of the company, just on the basis of denying access to the file, and annulled the decision (and the fines) completely.[21]

The Court of Justice found it unnecessary to deal with the claim of excessive delay. This had developed into a further contentious aspect of the whole proceedings, involving criticism of the General Court as well as the Commission, and bringing to light the loss of relevant documents and inadequate filing arrangements on the part of the Commission. Advocate General Juliane Kokott, in her thorough review and analysis of the case in her Opinion for the Court of Justice,[22] was willing to confront these issues and concluded that there had indeed been excessive delay.[23] But she also argued that, taking into account the seriousness of the original violation of the competition rules, the decision should only be partly annulled and the fine thus

---

15   (2000) ECR I-2391.The arguments relating to access to the file enabled the Court of First Instance to elaborate fuller rules on this question, so that this judgment provided a significant precedent on the matter (see the discussion in Christopher Harding and Julian Joshua, *Regulating Cartels in Europe* (2nd edn, Oxford University Press, 2010) at pp. 212–16).

16   OJ 2003, L10/10.

17   Case T-57/01, *Solvay v Commission* (2009) ECR II-4621.

18   Ibid.

19   Case T-57/01, note 17 above; Case C-109/10P, note 7 above.

20   See Advocate General Kokott's opinion, Case C-109/10P, note 7 above.

21   Case C-109/10 P, note 7 above.

22   Opinion of Advocate General Kokott in Case C-109/10 P, note 7 above.

23   It is interesting to speculate that the Court of Justice was being politically diplomatic in side-stepping this aspect of the case, especially since the General Court had become embroiled in the allegations of delay – it had taken eight years for it to hand down its judgment in 2009. The Advocate General no doubt felt less constrained in criticising both the Commission and the Court.

ACCESS TO THE FILE

Advocate General Juliane Kokott stated in her Opinion in Case 110/10 P (April 2011): 'A corollary of the principle of the protection of the rights of defence, the right of access to the file means that the Commission must give the undertaking concerned the opportunity to examine all the documents which may be relevant for its defence. These documents include both incriminating and exculpatory evidence, save when the business secrets of other undertakings, the internal documents of the Commission, or other confidential information are involved. It is common ground that, in the administrative procedure, Solvay was made aware only of the documents in the file that the Commission used against that undertaking in the contested decision. Numerous other documents from the file which Solvay would have been entitled to inspect by virtue of its rights of defence were withheld from it. The Commission thus infringed a fundamental rule of procedure, which is a corollary of the right to good administration. Such a procedural infringement cannot be remedied after the decision has been adopted, in particular not by submitting individual documents during subsequent judicial proceedings' (paragraphs 23–14 of the Opinion). This was the procedural breach which was used by the Court of Justice later that year as the ground for annulment of the Commission's re-adopted decision in December 2000 imposing fines on Solvay and CFK in respect of their cartel arrangement in violation of Article 81 of the EC Treaty.

reduced by 50 per cent. Although eventually removing all the fines, the whole legal saga, spanning 20 years, covered considerable legal ground and some diverse decisions within the system of the European Union courts. Advocate General Kokott opened her opinion, handed down in April 2011, with the following comment:

> Whether time really does heal all wounds, as the old saying goes, may seriously be called into question in the light of present dispute. This case has been occupying the European administrative and judicial authorities for over twenty years now. Generations of lawyers have worked on it. Documents have disappeared and the court proceedings have dragged on for years.[24]

---

24 Note 7 above, at point 1 of the Opinion.

Cartel after-life

In the meantime, and in the wake of the Soda Ash Cartel investigation, Solvay had been involved in further legal proceedings in relation to another cartel in another market. In 2002 the German company Degussa had reported the existence of a cartel in the bleaching agents market (hydrogen peroxide and sodium perborate), seeking immunity under the leniency programmes in the US and in the EU. This prompted investigations into the alleged cartel, involving alongside Degussa companies from Italy, Spain and France, and also Solvay in Belgium, in relation to a period of operation from 1994 until 2000. The Commission handed down a decision against the cartel members in 2006,[25] including a fine imposed on Solvay of €167 million– this fine was calculated with a 50 per cent increase since the company was regarded as a repeat offender (Degussa was also classified as a repeat offender but escaped a fine, being granted immunity for reporting the cartel). Commenting on these fines, EU Commissioner for Competition Neelie Kroes stated:

> These high fines take into account that certain companies are repeat offenders.
> Directors and shareholders alike should ask why these practices were allowed
> to continue.[26]

On appeal to the General Court, Solvay's fine was reduced to €139.50 million, on the ground that its involvement in the cartel for a particular period was not fully proven.[27] In the meantime, Solvay and Akzo Nobel paid a total of $72 million in fines in the US, having pleaded guilty to price-fixing as between 1998 and 2001 in relation to the cartel's operation in the US market.[28] Civil claims were also started in Germany in relation to the cartel's operation in the German market, totalling €475 million.[29]

In 2009–10 Solvay sold off its pharmaceutical division to Abbott Labs for €4.5 billion. Further wide-scale change followed this divestment in April of 2011, when the French chemicals company Rhodia merged with Solvay. This deal came to fruition in September 2011, and following it Solvay's Committee of Executive Members reorganised its numerous business units into five segments – Consumer Chemicals, Advanced Materials, Performance Chemicals, Functional Polymers and Corporate and Business Services, effective from 2013.

Turning to the subsequent history of ICI, there are some parallel aspects to be noted. In particular, ICI was apprehended in the Methacrylates or Acrylic Glass

---

25   *Hydrogen Peroxide and Perborate*, OJ 2006, L353/54.
26   Commission Press release IP/06/560, 3 May 2006.
27   Case T-186/06. Akzo Nobel had been fined over €25 million, but its appeal to the General Court was later removed from the Court's register.
28   Department of Justice Press Release, 06-137, 14 March 2006.
29   European Court of Justice Press Release, 170/14, 11 December 2014.

Cartel, proven to be operating from 1997 until 2002, the other participants being Arkema, Lucite, Quinn Barlo and Degussa. As in the case of the Bleaching Agents Cartel, Degussa reported the cartel's activities and benefited from complete immunity under the EU leniency programme. For its role in the Cartel, ICI was fined 91.4 million Euros, and failed to gain any reduction of the fine since, unlike the other parties, it was unable to provide any further useful evidence to the Commission. Again, there was castigation from Competition Commissioner Neelie Kroes, who proclaimed: 'Cartels are a scourge. I will ensure that cartels continue to be tracked down, and punished. I am shocked that companies like ICI and Arkema have been fined once again. If their management needs a wake-up call, then with these fines, I am happy to provide it'.[30] ICI appealed, but unsuccessfully, against the decision and the fine[31] (whereas co-cartelist Arkema succeeded in securing a reduction in its fine, on the basis of the Commission's miscalculation). By the time of the General Court's judgment in June 2012, ICI had become part of Akzo Nobel, and the latter was bracing itself to pay the fine, on the basis of the rebuttable presumption of parent and successor company liability, as laid down by the Court of Justice in an earlier case involving itself.[32] The demise of ICI had come about with its takeover by Akzo Nobel at the beginning of 2008, following a steady period of divestment during the 1990s and into the new century. The company had long before sold its soda ash production arm to Brunner Mond in 1991, so quickly exiting from that market. The proceedings taken against it for its involvement in the Acrylic Glass Cartel were to prove a legal swan song in the long narrative of its cartel activity.

Before and after: The longer-term historical view

Both Solvay and ICI had been the subject on several occasions of substantial fines imposed by the Commission for collusion in various areas of the chemicals industry. Those which pre-dated the decisions and sanctions in the Soda Ash case arose from the Dyestuffs Cartel in 1969 (ICI),[33] the Peroxides Cartel (Solvay) in 1985,[34] the Polypropylene Cartel in 1986 (Solvay, ICI),[35] the PVC Cartel in 1989 (Solvay, ICI),[36] and the LdPE Cartel in 1989 (ICI).[37] Cartel involvement continued after the Soda Ash Cartel, although Solvay and ICI were not proven to have worked together directly again in the way they did in the Polypropylene and

---

30   Commission Press Release IP/06/698, 31 May 2006.
31   Case T-214/06, *ICI v Commission* (General Court), (2012) ECR II-000, June 2012.
32   Case C-97/08, *Akzo Nobel v Commission* (2009) ECR 536.
33   *Dyestuffs*, OJ 1969, L185.
34   *Peroxygen*, OJ 1985, L 35/1.
35   *Soda Ash*, note 6 above.
36   *PVC*, OJ 1989, L74/1.
37   *LdPE*, OJ 1989, L74/21.

PVC cases: the Vitamins Cartel in 2001 (Solvay),[38] the Hydrogen Peroxide Cartel in 2006 (Solvay),[39] and the Methacrylates (Acrylic Glass) Cartel in 2006 (ICI).[40] But all along, they had other partners in common, and both then fell foul of the German company Degussa's deft exploitation of the leniency programme in more recent years.

The two companies' participation (indicated in italics) in the 1980s chemicals cartels dealt with by the Commission can be seen in Table 5.1.

Table 5.1   Better together: Regular co-operation in related markets

Peroxides	Polypropylene	PVC	LdPE
	ANIC		
Atochem (Produits Chimiques Ugine Kuhlmann at the time of the cartel)		Atochem	Atochem
	ATO Chimie		
	BASF	BASF	BASF
			Bayer
			BP
			CdF (Orkem)
Degussa AG			
			DOW
	DSM	DSM	DSM
		Enichem	Enichem
	Chemische Werke Huls		
	Chemische Werke Linz		
	Hercules Chemicals		
	Hoechst AG	Hoechst AG	Hoechst AG
		Huels	Huels
	ICI	*ICI*	*ICI*
L'Air Liquide			
Laporte Industries (Holdings)			
			Linz
		LVM	LVM
			Monsanto
		Montedison	Montedison
	Montepolimeri		
			Neste

---

38   *Vitamins*, OJ 2003, L56/1.
39   *Hydrogen Peroxide*, note 25 above.
40   *Acrylic Glass*, OJ 2006, L322/20.

Peroxides	Polypropylene	PVC	LdPE
		Norsk Hydro	Norsk Hydro
	Petrofina		
			Repsol
	Rhône-Poulenc		
		SAV	SAV
	Shell International Chemicals	Shell	Shell
Solvay	*Solvay*	*Solvay*	*Solvay*
			Statoil
		Wacker	Wacker

The Marine Hose Cartel: Global business and global legal action

The Marine Hose Cartel, identified as operating between 1986 and 2007, presents many of the features of a classic international cartel, in terms of its market, anti-competitive strategy and broadly based international participation (comprising companies from Europe, North America and East Asia). As an example, the story of the Cartel and its legal busting and sanctioning also embodies a certain degree of drama, while illustrating a wide range of legal responses across a number of jurisdictions.

The Marine Hose market

> Demand for marine hoses largely depends on the development of the oil sector, and in particular on oil exploitation in areas remote from the place of consumption. Demand has expanded over time. It is cyclical and to a certain extent linked with the development of oil prices. It started to become significant in the late 1960s and rose in the early 1970s, in particular from oil-producing regions in the Persian Gulf, the North Sea and North Africa. During the 1980s demand from national oil companies in South America increased. In the late 1990s demand moved towards West Africa.[41]

Oil is such a vital element in the global economy that it is easy to assume that it has been present on the world economic stage since the start of the industrial revolution, but the industry in its present form has mainly nineteenth-century origins, and evolved into a worldwide phenomenon only in the 1950s. Following

---

41 From the judgment of the General Court in Joined Cases T-147 and 148/09, *Trelleborg Industries SAS and Trelleborg AB v Commission* (2013) ECR 259, 17 May 2013, at point 7 of the Court's judgment. This is a major source of factual information. There is a concise description of the marine hose market in the first part of the Court's judgment.

naturally from the need to transport the newly commoditised oil, the marine hose business emerged in 1959 with the invention of floating and submerged hose systems by Uniroyal Scotland. They were and are used to both load sweet or processed crude oil and other petroleum products from offshore facilities onto vessels – from a derrick to a waiting tanker for example – and to offload them back to offshore or onshore facilities.

In the late 1960s the price per barrel of crude oil began to rise, and in 1980 it hit a historical high of \$36.83 (\$95.89 in today's figures). Demand for marine hoses increased more or less along with these prices,[42] more being needed when the prices were high because of an increased demand from oil companies for revenue, and likewise dipped deeply in the six years following the 1980 high. At the start of the 1986 fiscal year, the price per barrel was down to \$14.43 (\$28.25 at today's rate), and it was in this year, perhaps as an attempt by its participants to stabilise the market, that the Marine Hose Cartel appears to have started its activity.

The Cartel, like the industry it was based in, was worldwide in scope. It had 11 members in total, but because a number of them were subsidiaries or associated companies the European Commission arranged them as a cartel, in its decision on the case, into six main groups – Bridgestone, Yokohama, Dunlop Oil and Marine or DOM, Parker ITR, Trelleborg and Manuli, as detailed in the box below (with the parent companies in the left hand column and principal cartel members in bold).

Marine Hose Cartel: Participants

Bridgestone Corporation (Japan)	**Bridgestone Industrial Ltd (UK)**
Yokohama Rubber Company (Japan)	
Continental AG	Conti Tech AG; **Dunlop Oil and Marine (UK)**
Parker Hannifin Corporation (US)	**Parker ITR (Italy)**
Trelleborg AB (Sweden)	**Trelleborg Industrie (France)**
Manuli Rubber Industries (Italy)	**Uniroyal Manuli (US)**

First, then, in this narrative, something may be said about the cartel participants.

Bridgestone

Until 1984, the Japanese entity now known as the Bridgestone Corporation was called Bridgestone Tire Co. Bridgestone is a company that heads a group active in the worldwide manufacture and sale of a wide variety of rubber products, as

---

42　Ibid.

well as bicycles and other industrial and sporting goods. It has manufactured and marketed marine hoses on a worldwide scale since 1972.

Bridgestone's marine hose business is run by Bridgestone Corporation and several wholly owned subsidiaries. The subsidiaries involved are Bridgestone Industrial Limited (incorporated in 1989 and headquartered in the UK), Bridgestone Industrial Products America, Inc. (a Delaware incorporated company headquartered in Nashville in the US), Bridgestone Engineered Products of Asia Holdings, SDN, BHD (headquartered in Kuala Lumpur, Malaysia) and six Japanese subsidiaries. Marine hose sales outside Japan are carried out by one of the subsidiaries covering the relevant regions of the world.

Yokohama

The Yokohama Rubber Company Limited, originating in 1917 as a joint venture between Yokohama Cable Manufacturing and the American aeronautical company B F Goodrich, is now the head of a group active in the manufacture and sale of tyres and other rubber products like hoses, sealants and adhesives, aircraft products, and golf products worldwide. It is headquartered in Japan, and manufactures and markets marine hoses throughout the world. Yokohama's marine hose business is organised as part of its Industrial Products Division its Japan offices. Sales outside Japan are managed from the Industrial Products Overseas Sales Department. None of Yokohama's subsidiaries in the EEA, which focus on the sale of tyres, are involved in the marine hose business.

Dunlop Oil and Marine

Dunlop Oil and Marine, founded in 1955, had been active in the design, manufacture and supply of hoses for the oil, gas, petrochemical and dredging industries since then for both offshore and onshore based operations. After the cartel episode discussed here, the company merged with ContiTech Beatty in 2012 and is now part of the Continental group of companies, headed by the German Continental company. The latter is noted (like ABB based in Zurich and discussed as a 'dancing giant' later in this chapter in connection with the Pre-Insulated Pipes Cartel) for its decentralised corporate organisation, intended to promote innovation through the autonomy of its constituent companies and the synergies of group membership.

Parker ITR

The Italian company Parker ITR has a long and complex history. It began with Pirelli Treg SpA, which was part of the Pirelli group, and started a marine oil and gas hose business in 1966. Pirelli Treg SpA later merged with Itala, another member of the Pirelli group, and was renamed ITR SpA. ITR SpA was then purchased by Saiag SpA in 1993, and later, as ITR Rubber Srl, was purchased by the American company Parker Hannfin in January 2002, when it became Parker ITR Srl.

Parker Hannifin itself is based in Cleveland, Ohio, and is a diversified manufacturer of motion and control technologies and systems that provide precision engineered solutions for a wide variety of commercial, mobile, industrial and aerospace markets, and is divided into eight broad groups, the Fluid Connectors group covering the marine hose market. This group covers four geographic regions – North America, South America, EU and Asia.

At present, Parker Hannifin Corporation is the parent company of Parker Hannifin International Corporation, which is in turn the parent company of Parker Italy Holding LLC, itself then the parent company of Parker ITR Srl. The latter is active in the manufacturing and supply of industrial and hydraulic hoses, marine oil and gas hoses, and technical compounds. Parker ITRIt is headquartered in Veniano, Italy.

Trelleborg

Trelleborg AB is a Swedish undertaking that has been operating since 1905, and is involved in the production and supply of marine hoses through its French subsidiary Trelleborg Industrie SAS. The Trelleborg Group comprises four business areas – Trelleborg Engineered Systems (which includes marine hoses), Trelleborg Automotive, Trelleborg Sealing Solutions and Trelleborg Wheel Systems – and established Trelleborg Industrie in 1996 after purchasing Caoutchouc Manufacturé et Plastiques de Palport SA from the Michelin Group. Since then the French subsidiary has had a number of successive legal identities: Trelleborg Industrie SA in 1997, Trelleborg Industrie and/or Bergougnan in 1998, Trelleborg Industrie and/or Bergougnan SAS in 2004, and Trelleborg Industrie SAS from 2005.

Manuli

Manuli is a company that designs, manufactures and distributes machines and fluid conveying rubber and/or metal components and systems for industrial hydraulics and oil and marine applications worldwide. Manuli Rubber Industries SpA ('MRI'), the ultimate parent company heading the undertaking, is based in Milan, Italy, and manufactures and markets marine hoses throughout the world.

Manuli entered the oil and marine business in 1973, through a joint venture named Uniroyal Manuli SpA, owned in equal 50 per cent proportions by Uniroyal, and by Dardanio Manuli SpA and three individuals of the Manuli family. In May 1986, Dardanio Manuli SpA purchased Uniroyal's stake in the company and its name was changed into Uniroyal – Manuli Rubber SpA. This name was later changed on three occasions, finally to Manuli Rubber Industries SpA in January 1997.

Manuli's worldwide marine hoses business activities were initially conducted by MRI. In 1984 Manuli had established Uniroyal Manuli (USA) Inc. ('MOM') – a corporation that was based in Delaware and was wholly owned by MRI. Like its Italian forebear the MOM's name was changed on three occasions, finally to Manuli Oil and Marine (USA) Inc. in 1997.

MOM's board of directors was appointed by MRI. After the creation of MOM, Manuli's entire worldwide marine hoses marketing and sales were run by MOM. The company was eventually liquidated on 31 December 2006.

What emerges from this brief survey of corporate history is a varied picture of manufacturing and a complex narrative of corporate restructuring. The geographical background to the Cartel and main location of its members is evident from the map below. What is also evident, as a characteristic of this economic sector, is a certain fluidity and lack of definition in participation, or more exactly how that participation may be identified and described over time. This can give rise to some tricky legal questions regarding the definition of the cartel and the formal identification of who precisely was involved, in what role and at which time, as became clear as the legal process involving the cartel unfolded.

The cartel

(See also the circles of collusion and orbiting referred to in Chapter 2 as another way of reading the cartel narrative given here.) Between 1987 and 1992 cartel members usually held general meetings (which they came to refer to as 'Club meetings') twice a year, but the first meeting was a year prior on 1 April 1986. This meeting was that at which the cartel formed, and it was attended by representatives of five of the eventual six member groups – Dunlop Oil and Marine only coming into the cartel in 1997. In 1986, most likely because the cartel was being created, four meetings were held from April onwards. Representatives from Bridgestone, Yokohama, Parker ITR, Trelleborg, Manuli and three other firms or groups of firms the names of which are redacted in the Commission's report on the case, met and agreed on a one page 'Memorandum of Understanding' that was later referred to in at least three other cartel documents found during the Commission's investigation.

The second meeting, at the Oriental Hotel in Bangkok on 8–10 June 1986, involved the same parties as the first. Their original agreement evolved subtly in this meeting, and would continue to do so as the cartel progressed. Market shares were changed; geographic markets, Japan, the United Kingdom and Italy, were allocated to specific members as home markets; and a trial period for the prices to be quoted for goods was provisionally set until an envisaged next meeting on 6 October that year. This arrangement in fact lasted until December 1987; the October meeting in Copenhagen and the 'Autumn meeting' in Como, Italy affirming its efficacy and approving its continuation.

The April 1987 meeting is the next in which the cartel's nature evolved. Here the 'Rules' – a document incorporating the minutes of said meeting – provided for target market shares for all undertakings involved in the cartel at the time to be applied 'for the period 1/4/87 to 1/1/88'.

In 1990, Trelleborg did not attend meetings. It was quick to assure the other members of the cartel though that, 'whilst their corporate policy prohibits them from attending meetings of the Committee, they intend to pursue 'intelligent' pricing policy via co-operation with other members, as long as it coincides with their target ...'. Despite this seeming play for distance from the arrangement, Trelleborg was included in the market statistics and market share allocation during the meetings its representatives did not attend, and was in possession of comprehensive statistics for the same period. By the October 1991 meeting held in Florence, Trelleborg was again being represented.

1992 saw the next upheaval within the cartel. Manuli, which had participated in most of the cartel-wide meetings until April that year, did not participate in any of those that were held after August, and returned in only a partial role at some point in either 1996 or 1997. This absence could have been a symptom of caution, or perhaps reflective of the problems beginning to arise within the Cartel itself between 1997 and 1999. Internal friction and conflict appeared in this period, though the coordination of tenders did not cease, nor were there any withdrawals from the Cartel during the period.

It was June 1999 before the formal 'Club' structures that had existed until the early 1990s to increase prices were once again put to proper use, and along with them came the addition to the cartel of a new 'member' – Peter Whittle, working through his company PW Consulting. A former marine hose executive, Whittle owned and ran this consultancy firm specialising in the field. His role within the Cartel was that of coordinator. The suppliers would provide him with any information they received about upcoming marine hose contracts they were interested in, and he would designate amongst them, based on the rules established long before his entry into the Cartel, who would be contracted to perform it. The company thus designated was known colloquially as 'the champion', and Whittle, after making the nomination, would calculate how much the other cartel champion', and Whittle, after making the nomination, would calculate how much the other cartel members would need to bid on the job in question – rigging them, effectively – in order for the champion to earn it.

Whittle's membership was, if not the main cause, certainly a factor in the reinvigoration of the Cartel. Confidence in the arrangement amongst the members soared; so much so that in the December 1999 meeting in London it was confirmed by the undertakings involved that they 'will do everything (they) can to continue to cooperate as fully as they have always done in the past' and 'consider this to be the last chance to make the Club work'. In furtherance of this spirit of co-operation it was stated that 'any member who (violates) an instruction will be isolated by the other members'.

As well as cartel-wide meetings, between 1999 and 2002 a number of bilateral meetings took place, particularly between representatives of Parker ITR and Yokohama, and between the Cartel's coordinator and Trelleborg. These meetings supported the multilateral contracts in place between members, and became the cartel's standard method of coordination from 2003 onwards as various members had become wary of taking part in larger gatherings.

CARTEL FACILITATION: THE ROLE OF PW CONSULTING

(As reported by convicted cartelist Bryan Allison in a subsequent interview): 'But remember all communications were filtered to me. I never had any direct access to any of these people really. I never spoke to them on the phone or met them. Everything I got was filtered through Peter Whittle who was the coordinator of the cartel. He would receive the tenders from companies and would then administer the cartel by ensuring that particular companies won the tender through a rigged bidding process. In addition he coordinated the creation of global price lists. [He] would tell people largely what they wanted to hear and ... was basically running the cartel for his own ends rather than the benefit of the members'.[43]

In 2003 Manuli, as it had done in the early 1990s, again left the Cartel. It did so first by letter on 12 March, and then confirmed its decision in a meeting held with the Cartel's coordinator on 25 March. Manuli's subsidiary MOM remained in the Cartel however, and when it was dissolved on 31 December 2006, some of the employees who facilitated that involvement were transferred to Manuli and continued to maintain contact with other Cartel members. Yokohama was the next company to exit. In June 2006 it substantially undercut the cartel prices for a tender issued by Shell Asia, and formally withdrew from its collaboration at the start of that month. Bridgestone, Dunlop, Trelleborg, Parker ITR, and Manuli continued to coordinate through meetings, emails and phone calls until, after Yokohama's bid for immunity, a number of competition authorities (the US Department of Justice, the European Commission and the UK Office of Fair Trading) launched surprise inspections on the premises of Dunlop, Trelleborg, Parker ITR, PW Consulting, and at the home of Peter Whittle on 2 May 2007. This was the first instance of such broad-ranging, multi-agency co-operation in a case of this kind, and it led not only to the arrest of eight foreign executives in the US (three of whom were from the UK, two from France, two from Italy and one from Japan), but also to the first search of a home address in the UK under powers contained in the Enterprise Act 2002.

---

43 Michael O'Kane, 'Does Prison Work for Cartelists? – The View from behind Bars', 56 (2011) *The Antitrust Bulletin* 483, at p. 490. This is another valuable source of information.

THE JAPANESE DESERTION

(From Bryan Allison's interview): 'I had a reasonable degree of confidence in the Europeans. I was always a little wary of the Japanese ... The cartel was actually detected because they caught one of the participants [Yokohama] in another cartel and, in order to get out of that one, one of the people that was due to be prosecuted gave up the marine hose cartel.[44] If we hadn't been caught, would it have carried on? Yes, I think it probably would for a while. Now that I understand what has gone on, the cartel was starting to fall apart, that's quite clear. The Japanese were getting very cold feet and wanted to find a way out of it. It's quite clear that at some stage there would have been a move to China and low cost production by one of the participants and that, I think, would have sounded the death knell of the cartel'.[45]

The US busting operation was dramatic: on 2 May, after a meeting in Houston in Texas, those who had attended were arrested by the FBI and charged under the Sherman Act with being involved in a conspiracy to suppress and eliminate competition by rigging bids, fixing prices and allocating market shares for marine hose sold in the United States.[46]

A BAD DAY IN MAY: ARRESTS IN HOUSTON

(From Bryan Allison's interview): 'It was five in the morning, on May 2, 2007, and I was up doing some work when the phone went. It was reception, and they said the police were here to see me ... Six men came in, five with guns and Craig Lee, the DOJ trial attorney. [Lee is a staff attorney within the National Criminal Enforcement Section of the Antitrust Division of the US Department of Justice. The police were special agents of the Inspector General's Office of the US Department of Defence.] I was instantly handcuffed and made to sit down in a chair. I was bewildered, thinking what the hell is going on here. Craig Lee started talking. He said I was in a meeting yesterday and then showed photographs of me at the meeting. As soon as I saw these photographs I thought that the game was up. There was not much point in pretending that I haven't done anything. He then asked me a few questions which I tried to answer as best I could and he told me that other people were being arrested at the same time.'[47]

Following the arrests and dawn raids, the legal process against the cartel and the corporate and individual cartelists started in a number of jurisdictions (for an overview of the application of sanctions, as a discussion of sanction accumulation, see the discussion in Chapter 3, and in particular, Appendix One to Chapter 3).

---

44   A reference to the 'amnesty plus' procedure in the US, which enables a person or company to obtain a reduction of the penalty in relation to its present cartel conduct, in return for reporting another cartel, in respect of which it would then gain full immunity from sanctions.

45   'Does prison work for cartelists?', note 42 above, at pp. 490, 492.

46   Ibid., at p. 483 *et seq.*

47   Ibid., at p. 485.

The United States

In so far as the Cartel's activity had affected the US market and jurisdiction, the American interest in dealing with the Cartel and the action taken against it was decisive. The US was a crucial partner in the coordinated dawn raids at the start of May 2007 and was in a position to infiltrate the Houston cartel meeting and then swoop on a number of individuals who were rapidly taken into custody. This placed the US authorities in a particularly strong position to take action against foreign individual cartelists, eight altogether from four other countries including the British mastermind-facilitator Peter Whittle, apprehended red-handed, and the only practical question for whom was the kind of deal they could then cut with the US enforcers to minimise the penalties inevitably coming their way. From the point of view of the Department of Justice, this was an enforcement *coup de grace*, sending out a powerful message, since it demonstrated what could be achieved in gaining incriminating evidence and possible corporate fines and prison terms for executives, most of whom were non-US nationals and companies. The manner of arresting and taking into custody the apprehended cartelists was intended, at the very least, to overawe the conspiring businesses and others in the business community. The subsequent legal process brought in over $40 million in corporate fines, a number of prison terms and individual fines,[48] and set in train possible civil claims against the companies involved – for instance Parker ITR reached a settlement in March 2009, when it agreed to set up a fund for purposes of compensating injured parties, providing 16 per cent of its revenues from non-US sales of marine hose between 2002 and 2007 for this purpose.[49] There were also consequent legal developments of significance in the field of international collaboration: first, the agreement to send the three British cartelists back to the UK to be tried and convicted there in lieu of serving prison terms in the US (see further below), and secondly, the later extradition of the former Manuli executive Romano Pisciotti from Germany to the US in 2014 to face conviction and sentence some years after the event. It was not quite plain sailing all the way. Two other Manuli executives, Francesco Scaglia and Val M. Northcutt, pleaded not guilty and were acquitted, their defence lawyers claiming that evidence against them provided by their former co-conspirators (including the cartel facilitator Peter Whittle) had been discredited[50] – an example perhaps of the possible moral hazard inherent in leniency programmes when juries become involved. But overall, the legal outcome in the US demonstrated the significant potential of the legal process available in in that country – especially, the legal powers of surveillance, the nature of the system of plea negotiation, the readiness to use prison terms, and the established system of civil claims in this context.

---

48   See the table in Appendix One to Chapter 3 above.
49   Marine Hose Claims: www.marinehoseclaims.com.
50   See the discussion in Appendix One to Chapter 3, and further below.

The UK

The three British cartelists detained in the US following the raid in Houston, namely
Peter Whittle of PW Consulting, and Bryan Allison and David Brammar of Dunlop
Oil and Marine, agreed to plead guilty in exchange for being allowed to serve the
prison terms they were faced with in the UK. To do this they would need to be found
guilty of the 'cartel offence' under Section 188 of the Enterprise Act in the UK which
requires that the accused, 'dishonestly agree(s) with one or more other persons to
make or implement, or to cause to be made or implemented, arrangements' such as
price-fixing, bid-rigging or market sharing relating to at least two undertakings'.[51]

After their return to the UK, the three defendants were convicted and sentenced
at Southwark Crown Court in June 2008. Whittle and Allison each received three
year terms of imprisonment and were each subject to a director disqualification order
for a period of seven years while Brammar, participating at a less senior level than
the others, was to spend two and a half years in prison and was disqualified from a
director's role for five years. Each term of imprisonment was subsequently reduced
on appeal – to two and a half years, two years and twenty months respectively. The
Court of Appeal commented that the sentencing judge had worked form too high
a point on the sentencing tariff and the appeal judges were mindful of important
'mitigating factors' relating to the degree of co-operation offered to the prosecution
by the defendants (including the willingness of the cartel coordinator to return to the
US to testify against other accused cartelists).[52]

JUDGMENT ON A CARTEL CO-ORDINATOR
(From the sentencing decision of Judge Geoffrey Rivlin at Southwark Crown Court,
June 2008)
'Peter Whittle ... You worked for Dunlop for some considerable years but then when
you left you formed two companies, PW Consulting International and, later, PW
Consulting Oil and Marine Limited, which, from the latter part of the year 2000, and
throughout the period covered by the charges, you used in order to carry out your
work as what has been described as the cartel co-ordinator. This was a full-time job.
The cartel was run as it had to be with meticulous attention to detail. Code names
were used, clandestine meetings were organised and held, agreements were reached,
both in relation to the market share and for the bogus contract bids ... You were
very deeply involved in all this dishonesty; indeed, it formed the basis of your whole
working life ... You were the co-ordinator, and you did that job very efficiently ... this
was a serious crime and you played a leading role in it. The sentence of the court upon
you is one of three years' imprisonment. In addition, I am satisfied that, in your case,
the completely dishonest running of your companies requires that, in accordance with
the Companies Directors Disqualification Act 1986, you should be disqualified from
being a director of a company ... for a period of seven years'.[53]

---

51 For the details, see Sections 188(1) and 188(2) of the Enterprise Act 2002.
52 Court of Appeal Criminal Division, October 2008.
53 *R v Whittle, Brammar and Allison*, Southwark Crown Court, 10 June 2008.

The European Union

In comparison with the range of sanctions which could be drawn upon, and were in fact used, following the proceedings in the US and the UK – criminal fines, prison terms, disqualification, confiscation, and civil damages (see the sanctions accumulation table in Appendix One to Chapter 3), the EU sanctions would be limited to administrative fines to be applied to the companies, something which sets the EU apart from the national jurisdictions. Nonetheless, such fines may be considerable, and in a case of this kind involving complex corporate structure, spread across a number of main and connected parties. In total, the Commission imposed fines on 10 companies and amounting altogether to more than €220 million. The sanctioning process in the case of the EU, applying in practice to corporate actors, also then exploits the complexity of corporate structures to extend the scope of the sanction. This aspect was also evident in the appeals made against the fines, for instance in relation to the ownership of Parker ITR before 2002 and the consequent liability of Parker Hannifin for the actions of its subsidiary, bringing about the decision of the General Court to reduce the level of that fine by a large margin. As became increasingly the case in the EU system, many of the arguments raised before the General Court related to the way in which fines had been calculated and their proper legal basis, and sufficiency of evidence to justify the level of fine.[54]

The Pacific Rim

There were also proceedings relating to the Cartel in three Pacific Rim jurisdictions, involving decisions by Japan's Fair Trade Commission in February 2008, the Korean Fair Trade Commission in … and the Australian Competition and Consumer Commission (ACCC) in June 2009. Yokohama, as elsewhere, had successfully gained immunity in each of these jurisdictions. The Japanese FTC imposed a fine (or 'surcharge payment')[55] only on Bridgestone, and in Australia and Korea fines were imposed on Bridgestone, Parker, Dunlop and Trelleborg, but not Manuli (see the sanctions accumulation table in Appendix One to Chapter 3 for details). The Japanese FTC appeared to be dealing leniently with non-Japanese since this was the first potential application of penalties to foreign firms.

---

54 See the judgment of the General Court in Joined Cases T-147 and 148/09, note 41 above.

55 In relation to a breach of Article 2(6) of the Anti-Monopoly Act of Japan which defines an unreasonable restraint of trade as: '… such business activities, by which any entrepreneur, by contract, agreement or any other means irrespective of its name, in concert with other entrepreneurs, mutually restrict or conduct their business activities in such a manner as to fix, maintain, or increase prices, or to limit production, technology, products, facilities or counterparties, thereby causing, contrary or to the public interest, a substantial restraint of competition in any particular field of trade'.

A sub-plot: More dirty dealing in the marine products sector

The account of the Marine Hose Cartel may be set in the wider context of the production and supply of other related products. In particular, another cartel relating to foam-filled offenders and buoys was being dealt with by the US authorities at around the same time. In April 2009, two subsidiaries of Trelleborg – Virginia Harbor Services in the US and Trelleborg Industries SAS – entered guilty pleas in respect of alleged Sherman Act offences and agreed to pay a total of $11 million in criminal fines. The cartel activity in this market was proven to have taken place between 2002 and 2005. Two executives from Virginia Harbor Services, Robert D. Taylor and Donald L. Murray were convicted under the Sherman Act and received prison terms and fines.[56]

It is also important to note that Bridgestone's US guilty plea and fine of $28 million related not only to Sherman Act offending but also offences under the Foreign Corrupt Practice Act (FCPA) involving the making of corrupt payments to government officials in Latin American countries relating to the sale of marine hose and other industrial products.[57] An estimated 80 per cent of the total fine related to the FCPA conduct. This points to a not uncommon connection between bid-rigging activities and the bribery of officials.[58] In addition, Misao Hioki, the former general manager of Bridgestone's international engineered products department, had pleaded guilty in December 2008 to both Sherman Act and FCPA offences relating to the marine hose market, and was sentenced to a two year prison term and ordered to pay a $80,000 fine (see the sanction accumulation table in Appendix One to Chapter 3 above). To set this further in context: in the period April – September 2011, Japanese companies paid a total of $248 million in criminal fines for FCPA violations. Japan has equivalent legislation, but provides for no criminal liability for corporations for such activities.

Much of this would suggest an embedded cartel culture in this economic sector. Almost symbolically, Christian Calleca, one of the Trelleborg executives fined and imprisoned in the US for his involvement in the Marine Hose Cartel as President of the industrial fluids unit at Trelleborg, spoke at a dinner for cartel members in June 2001 and noted how the cartel had successfully raised the price for marine hose after the difficult years of 1998 and 1999.[59] It is more difficult to determine the more precise corporate location and specific gravity of cartel culture in such cases – at the level of individual executives, marketing departments, subsidiary companies, or parent companies. Certainly in the wake of the Marine Hose Cartel

---

56 DOJ Press Release 09–369, 20 April 2009.

57 DOJ Press Release 11–1193, 15 September 2011.

58 See for instance the OECD Policy Roundtable discussion paper, *Collusion and Corruption in Public Procurement*, 15 October 2010, DAF/COMP/GF (2010) 6.

59 *USA v Christian Calleca, Misao Hioki, Francesco Scaglia and Vanni Scodeggio*, US District Court, Southern District of Florida, Criminal Complaint, Case No 07-617-Snow.

proceedings, at the highest levels some of the parent companies acted to affirm their good citizen character and even express some public contrition. One of Bridgestone's first acts after it was penalised was to release a statement expressing both its regret and its plans for the immediate future. In part, that statement reads:

> We plan to proceed with the following actions in order to prevent future violations as soon as possible:
>
> 1. Withdrawal from the marine hose business. As a general principle, we will not take new orders. However, in order to minimize trouble to our customers, we will continue required services for those who continue to use our products and will do our best to assist such customers to change to other vendors.
>
> 2. Compliance education. We will enhance the compliance education program given to our employees. Simultaneously, we will emphasize to each employee that compliance is his or her responsibility that must be taken with the utmost seriousness by requiring each employee of the Bridgestone group to produce a declaration that he or she has a proper understanding of the compliance rules and that a violation will not only seriously damage corporate value but will result in relevant individuals being subject to severe punishment.
>
> 3. Strengthening future violation prevention. We will introduce a special decision-making system for bidding made through agents, which will prohibit sales departments making decisions on their own. Furthermore, we will structure an illegal action prevention system that includes, but is not limited to, a transaction monitoring system.[60]

Of the companies involved in the marine hose cartel, Bridgestone was the only one to leave the market entirely, although at the same time the supply of marine hose was a small proportion of its total business. Yokohama took a similarly apologetic stance, though it did so with a nod to the reason why it sought leniency.

> Yokohama Rubber has traditionally emphasized the importance of complying with antitrust laws and made efforts to eliminate its involvement in any bid-rigging or cartel by establishing a Corporate Compliance Committee and other programs within the company. In the court of an internal investigation conducted in the fall of 2006, the company's involvement in cartel behaviour in sale of the product was discovered. Yokohama Rubber therefore applied to the European Commission for immunity from a fine under the (leniency) Notice.[61]

---

60   http://www.bridgestone.com/corporate/news/2008021201.html.

61   *Plastics and Rubber Weekly* (PRW), 29 January 2009, 'EC Slaps Euro 131 Million Fine on Marine Hose Cartel': www.prw.com.

Swedish Trelleborg too was careful to reaffirm its commitment to upholding competition law, noting in a press release of 3 May 2007:

> Trelleborg takes a very serious view of infringements of competition legislation and already has a very clear and well-communicated set of rules and regulations to ensure conformity to applicable competition laws. However, as a result of these events, the Board and management have also decided to significantly reinforce the existing action program with the aim of further increasing knowledge of prevailing competition legislation and to strengthen the Group's internal processes and control system.[62]

Parker ITR likewise came out as committed to remaining within the boundaries of the law.[63]

At the same time, however, Bridgestone has been caught up in recidivist treatment. In February 2014 the company again pleaded guilty to further Sherman Act violations, this time for price-fixing in relation to automotive anti-vibrator rubber parts, a cartel in operation between 2001 and 2008.[64] A fine of $425 million was imposed on the company, and the Department of Justice stated that the fact that the company did not disclose its involvement in this cartel at the time of the investigation and its co-operation in relation to the Marine Hose Cartel was an aggravating feature which led to an increase in the amount of the present fine. At the highest level, the company expressed further contrition: in order to emphasise its 'sincere regret for this incident', board members would not receive bonus payments for March 2014 and would forfeit half their compensation for six months.[65]

Postscript: The Manuli acquittals

In this telling of the story of the Marine Hose Cartel, it may be tempting to conclude by pointing out eventual winners and losers. Such a judgment in the longer term might be difficult, if not impossible, and probably at least some way off, since first the dust has to settle. In the short term it might be thought that the particular corporate and individual cartelists dealt with in this case had by 2007 and the years immediately following lost a great deal. Sure enough, one Japanese company gained obviously through its successful application for immunity and one European company clawed back part of its EU fine, but for the most part this is a story of detection and considerable sanctioning.

---

62 http://feed.ne.cision.com/wpyfs/00/00/00/00/00/09/CA/4B/wkr0010.pdf.

63 Parker ITR's Global Code of Business Conduct.

64 Department of Justice Press Release 14-157, 13 February 2014. Thus far 26 companies – including Bridgestone – have entered guilty pleas in the US, a total fine of over $2 billion has been apportioned, and 28 individuals have been charged.

65 Reuters: www.reuters.com, 13 February 2014.

However, there is a small postscript concerning the perhaps unlikely escape of two individuals charged with Sherman Act offences under the US system. In the Florida trial in November 2008 of two of the Marine Hose Cartel defendants,[66] there resulted two acquittals following the defence attack on the prosecution evidence provided by other cartel members. Francesco Scaglia, a product manager, and Val M. Northcutt, a technician and installer of marine hose, were testified against by their former bosses, Robert L. Furness and Charles J. Gillespie, as part of an agreement that the latter pair had with the Department of Justice for reductions in their sentences. The master-organiser Peter Whittle, also returned to the US to testify against Scaglia and Northcutt under the same understanding However, the defence counsel convinced the jury that such evidence was untrustworthy, or perhaps exploited feelings of 'jury equity'.[67] This last point is expressed succinctly by some American commentators:

> This arms defense counsel to argue that the jury's sense of fair play and justice should be offended by the disparate treatment. It is not difficult to understand why juries simply do not like to rely on witnesses who have not had to accept responsibility for their own conduct and who have an obvious incentive to blame others in order to escape punishment.[68]

In such a way, one of the gains of leniency programmes – persuading a conspirator to cheat on the other conspirators – may eventually prove counter-productive in the legal process.

The Pre-Insulated Pipes Cartel: The cartel adventures of the dancing giant

The Pre-Insulated Pipes Cartel was a European (or regional) cartel and one of significance in economic and legal terms. It had classic features in terms of the strategies that were employed, but was also notable, as a matter of competition policy, for the aggressive manner of its operation. Beginning in Denmark in 1990, the Cartel extended first to Italy and Germany during 1991, and then, after a re-organisation, the entire European Union area by 1994. Its members shared the market, set prices, rigged bids and embarked on a campaign of coordinated

---

66   *United States v Val M. Northcutt, Francesco Scaglia*, US District Court, Southern District of Florida, 21 January 2008, Case No 07-60220-Cr-Hurley/Vitunac (s).

67   See: Michael S. Pasano, Paul A. Calli and Marissel Descalzo, 'An Antitrust Case History', www.cfjflaw.com.

68   F. Joseph Warin, David P. Burns and John W.F. Chesley, 'To Plead or Not to Plead?' *The Antitrust Source*, July 2006, p. 5. See further the discussion in K. Edghill, "Is the UK Cartel Offence Dead or is there a Problem with Immunity: The role of immunity as a prosecutorial tool in criminal cartel offences in the United Kingdom and Australia', Paper at UNISA Competition Law Workshop, 2011.

predation against a competitor they wanted to force out of the market. Although lacking some of the penal scope and drama reported above in relation to the Marine Hose Cartel, the legal proceeding resulted in a strong outcome in EU terms: the European Commission fined the 10 Cartel members over 92 million ECUs in 1998, and in 2005 four Danish municipalities successfully sued three of its members for a large amount of compensation. Reporting on the Commission's decision and fines in October 1998, EU Commissioner for Competition Karel Van Miert commented:

> In this particular instance, it is difficult to imagine a worse cartel. The main producers tried to bankrupt the only competitor who was willing to take them on. They deliberately flouted the EU public procurement rules. Bid-rigging is no better than fraud. They continued the violation for nine months after the Commission investigators had caught them red-handed. This violation calls for condign fines.[69]

ABB: THE DANCING GIANT

A reading of the narrative of the Pre-Insulated Pipes Cartel will make it clear that the main protagonist was ABB (Asea Brown Boveri), acting as the cartel ringleader. More exactly it was the Danish subsidiary, Asea Brown Boveri I C Møller, that was active in the pre-insulated pipes market and was the main cartel player, although it also needs to be asked to what extent the parent company, or individuals at that level of the corporate organisation, based in Zurich, were complicit in the cartel activity. ABB the international conglomerate is one of the largest engineering corporations in the world, specialising in robotics and power and automation technology. The company resulted from the merger of the Swedish ASEA and Swiss Brown Boveri companies in 1988. It experienced financial trouble in the early 2000s, mainly on account of debt and asbestos liability, but later returned to financial health. The conglomerate was well-known for its implementation of the matrix structure, which substituted dual reporting relationships for traditional linear management.[70] This may have worked well during the 1970s and 1980s but later led to problems of authority and in the chain of command, with increasing ambiguity and costs.[71]

---

69   Commission Press Release, IP/98/917, 21 October 1998. For detailed information on the Cartel, see the Commission's decision in 1998, OJ 1999, L24/1, and the judgment of the Court of First Instance in 2002, Case T-21/99, *Dansk Rorindustrie and others v Commission* (2002) ECR II-1681.

70   See Kevin Barham and Claudia Heimer, *ABB The Dancing Giant: Creating the Globally Connected Corporation* (Financial Times/Prentice Hall, 1998).

71   See 'ASEA Brown Boveri (ABB): What Went Wrong?', entry in H. Deresky, *International Management: Managing across Borders and Cultures* (5th edn, Pearson Education International, 2006), at pp. 304–7.

The market

Pre-insulated pipes connect district heating stations to households, and supply to the latter hot water from the former, and return cold water to the former from the households. They consist of an inner steel carrier pipe, an outer jacket made of dense plastic, and a layer of foam insulation – most often polyurethane – that separates the two pipes. The standard production method around 1990 was called discontinuous production, and involved filling the void between the inner pipe and the plastic jacket through injection points in tightly fitting caps at both ends.

Four Danish firms – Asea Brown Boveri IC Møller (ABB), Løgstør Rør, Dansk Rørindustri (a.k.a. Starpipe), and Tarco – formed the core of the cartel. These four firms controlled 50 per cent of production capacity in the EU. In addition, two German firms, Henss/Isoplus and Pan-Isovit, as well as the Finnish company KWH were significant members. Three companies only served their local markets and participated in the cartel for a short period: the German company Brugg Rohrsysteme, the Austrian company Ke Kelit Kunstoffwerk, and the Italian company Sigma Tecnologie.

Cartel origins

The cartel began in the later months of 1990 in Denmark after a long series of exchanges between ABB, Løgstør, Tarco and Starpipe that sought to find a solution to certain problems they felt were bedevilling their industry. The main one, according to ABB, was that it, as the largest manufacturer in the district heating market, had borne much of the financial burden that was incurred when this once profitable but by then mature, opportunity bare sector was restructured in the late 1980s. This, coupled with the supply by smaller producers of lower quality pipes (the poor durability of which 'undermined the economic case for district heating' and around 20 per cent less expensive than the higher quality stock produced by ABB and its counterparts), prompted the companies – acting through their senior executives – to make a 'peace agreement'. The first edict of this agreement was a coordinated price increase for Denmark of between 10 and 12 per cent, and on export markets to the tune of between 6 and 10 per cent.

Several further meetings were held – one of which on 16 January 1991 involved the managing directors of the participant companies, and established quota and customer allocation systems. It was also then agreed that a policy of 'established customer' relationships would be observed by all involved. Under this arrangement, each supplier was to keep its existing customers, and there was to be no aggressive targeting of another producer's customers.

As the Cartel's form solidified, a retired business executive who had formerly been on the Board of IC Møller and had close personal ties to ABB was brought in to coordinate its workings. This facilitator, along with the 'Contact Group', allocated the business amongst the Cartel members and maintained a database of projects and customers. The winner of each contract was decided in advance, and this company would then inform the other participants of the price it intended to quote. They then submitted higher priced tenders in order to ensure that the supplier designated by the cartel won through what would appear to outsiders as fair and rigorous competition.

These market-sharing arrangements were supported by a compensation scheme, the facilitation of which necessitated the exchange of individual price lists between the participant companies. At the end of a given year, the auditors of each producer certified the total sales of pipes based on the lists, and the certificates were then exchanged amongst those involved in the cartel. The first exchange occurred in 1991, ABB compiling the data into a single document in January of that year, and barely two months later the size of the discounts that were acceptable to give on the listed prices were agreed upon and implemented by the sales managers of each firm.[72]

Over and above the setting of quotas and customer allocations, price increases were also occasionally the subject of the cartelists' meetings. One such meeting was held in the autumn of 1991, in which the four Danish-based producers discussed their annual list price increases for both their home market and for export. By October of that year two German producers – Pan-Isovit, which is based in Speyer, and Henss/Isoplus which is based in Sondershausen – joined in on these talks, and an agreement was reached to raise prices outside Denmark by about 6 to 8 per cent with effect from 1 January 1992 as a result of their regular involvement.

The Cartel's first year saw a mixture of on target progress and significant, unplanned shifts in market share. ABB was meeting its commitments and projected outputs well, but Løgstør took large portions of market share from the Cartel's smaller Danish members, Tarco and Starpipe. If this action caused any dissatisfaction though, it was muted. Prices had risen in the interim, causing a substantial rise in earnings, and recourse to the compensation mechanism meant neither of the affected parties really suffered a loss they could not recoup.[73]

Løgstør the expansionist: Coping with dissension

In a series of meetings at the end of 1991 and beginning of 1992, a new market allocation was agreed to run for 1992 and 1993. This allocation became a matter of great consternation for Løgstør's, because the company felt its own increase in productivity entitled it to a higher quota than was apportioned to it in the revised

---

72   The managers did this by showing their sales personnel the scale of permitted rebates. The producers maintained internal consistency within the cartel and ensured compliance by exchanging copies of the instructions issued by their sales managers.

73   Though the precise mechanism used to apportion compensation is unclear, it was agreed between the participants that it would change in 1992. From then, surplus share would be rolled over and re-assigned to the producers who were below their given quota.

allocation.[74] Its dissatisfaction was such that it threatened to leave the cartel in late 1992 unless its demand for a quota of 34 per cent was met, but in the end decided not to exit, despite a severe bout of mudslinging between with ABB (claiming that ABB forced it to stay, while ABB accused *Løgstør* of 'dumping' the price level in Denmark and therefore breaking the agreement central to the cartel).

The fractious relations between the Danish producers at this time were complicated by two additional factors: a demand by ABB for a shareholding of up to 10 per cent in Løgstør, and increasingly insistent pressure from Henss/Isoplus and Pan-Isovit to be allocated a share of the Danish market.

Whatever disagreements may have arisen between the producers at the time, Løgstør itself admitted in evidence that 'the coordination in early 1993 was mainly based on an understanding of respect for traditional customer relationships'.[75] Even this though, after prices began to fall in Denmark in March and April 1993, began to disintegrate with time. During 1993 there were further mutual recriminations. According to Løgstør, ABB engineered the whole situation as a form of discipline for the other producers, to ensure commitment to the cartel.[76] ABB however saw Løgstør as a troublemaker in demanding an increase in its quota, a view apparently shared by Henss, which judged that Løgstør had taken a major 'traditional customer' from ABB at low prices in order to persuade ABB to give up some market share to Løgstør.

However the matter was viewed within the Cartel, the price fall in Denmark was the result of an internal trial of strength, and not a consequence of abandonment of Cartel aims. Indeed, as these frictions were developing and the Cartel tested, Løgstør and ABB were working towards an 'overall solution' to ensure the continued prosperity of the Cartel, and indeed agreements were being made regarding a planned expansion into Germany.

Expansion into Germany: The march south

The move to bring German producers into the fold had rather fragmented. ABB had taken over the German company Isolrohr in 1987 and so already had a toe-hold in the German market; it was then involved in bilateral discussions with Pan-Isovit between December 1990 and January 1991 in which it sought to form an 'informal strategic alliance'.[77,78] At that time there was little prospect of a formal

---

74   This led to ABB offering it 1.5 per cent from its own share and another 1 per cent to be divided between the two smaller producers, who predictably demurred.

75   Reply to Statement of Objections, p. 23.

76   It claimed that it was even told by ABB that the latter had allocated a credit line of 50 million Danish Krone in order to eliminate Løgstør in a price war (Løgstør Reply to Statement of Objections, pp. 22 to 24, 32, 40 and 42).

77   Appendices 30 and 31, ABB's Article 11 Reply, pp. 7–9.

78   These two producers together supplied the major part of the German market at the time: Isoplus, which had only recently bought Isolrohr's Austrian factory, was still in the

alliance between all four Danish producers and Pan-Isovit, as the German company plainly regarded Løgstør, Tarco and Starpipe as pirates who had attempted to seize a market share in Germany through posting artificially low prices. Thus ABB, as the owner of Isolrohr in Germany, was its natural partner. As well as covering technical co-operation, ABB's discussions with Pan-Isovit concerned the framework for a division of the market between them as the two largest suppliers in Germany. The underlying idea, as it had been in Denmark, was to divide client areas and maintain existing market shares. These activities would be coordinated by a 'Board Group' and a 'Strategy Group', which would work together to ensure joint domination of the German market for the two producers.[79] But by the autumn of 1991 institutionalised co-operation between the all the Danish companies was extended on a more formal basis to the German market, and from October of that year Pan-Isovit and Henss/Isoplus (the latter by this point well established in Germany) joined the main cartel. Henceforth, meetings were held between all six main suppliers to the German market on a regular basis.

In view of Pan-Isovit's earlier reservations regarding three of the Cartel's Danish participants, it is unsurprising that the arrangement's expansion into Germany encountered a number of teething problems before its flourishing in late 1993. From the outset Henss/Isoplus, like their compatriot, felt the Danish producers were using the profits generated by the well-established cartel in their local market to finance a price war designed to gain market share in Germany for themselves. Whether this was the case or not, each of the participant companies had markedly different objectives in seeking an overall arrangement of the market and these added to the initial friction.

ABB appears to have had a grand plan for securing near complete control over the industry, while Tarco's position was characterised by aggressive pricing in Germany that had provoked the German producers into retaliatory prospecting in the Danish market – much to the displeasure of Løgstør and Starpipe. This being so, the German companies were clearly interested in reaching a market share agreement in order to protect their position against the Danish producers. ABB saw only folly in the producers it was trying to organise fighting each other on price when the market was rapidly expanding and so regarded as vital some action at the top level to assist in making this a reality. Specifically, it sought an agreement on prices in Germany which would serve a dual purpose: reining in the activities of an exuberant Tarco, and allowing ABB to raise its price to its agents.

At a meeting in Frankfurt in October 1991, attended by all six producers, these goals were achieved to some extent. An increase of around 6 per cent in list prices was agreed, and was later confirmed at a meeting in Hamburg the following

---

process of being set up as a serious contender to enter the German market, with Henss as its commercial agents.

79   According to ABB, Pan-Isovit subsequently had reservations regarding the technical co-operation proposed and, after it had also declined an invitation to join EuHP, the bilateral discussions on market co-operation lapsed in April 1991.

December. This last meeting also brought about some additions and amendments to the overall working of the Cartel, principally that:

- all producers were to raise their prices by 6 per cent immediately;
- a 'hot line' was to be established between the participants;
- further meetings were to be held once a month; and,
- a minimum price list was to be prepared by 13 January 1992.

Over the next year meetings at senior level – the members of which going by the moniker 'The Popes' – were held regularly 'to discuss issues of common interest'. As further evidence of this turn towards organisation and away from mudslinging and distrust, the coordinator of the Danish cartel emerged as an 'honest broker' for the Germany group, while also coordinating its meetings and facilitating agreements in order to raise prices.

At this stage, no final agreement had been reached on market shares, and complex negotiations took place on the division of the German market between the two national groups. It was November 1992 before any real progress was made towards a resolution. At a meeting in Brussels, a table of the producers' sales and market shares in Germany for that year was drawn up, and the Danish producers Løgstør, Tarco and Starpipe demanded 40 per cent of the German market between them. This demand for distribution of market shares was based on each of the producers' achieved market shares in the preceding two years, 'together with consideration about the size of the market share company would be able to gain on their own'.

ABB's ambition and hegemony

With the successful – if rocky – expansion into Germany behind it, the major producers involved in the Cartel were looking, at the beginning of 1993, towards finding an overall settlement in the industry. ABB led the way in this, and was already outlining a 'European solution' that would cover Denmark, Sweden, Finland, Germany, Austria, the Netherlands, France and Italy, and would afford it a 42 per cent market share and Løgstør 25 per cent. With a combined market share of 67 per cent, this solution would allow these two dominant producers to effectively control the whole market.

Always leading from the front, ABB's tactics to secure agreement with its vision for the Cartel were described by Løgstør as a 'carrot and stick' strategy,[80] holding out inducements while making threats if its proposals were not accepted. Its policy was to consolidate its position as market leader through the Cartel, in combination with a strategic alliance with at least one of its competitors. Apart from its demanding a shareholding in Løgstør (and offering it an increased quota within the Cartel) ABB also attempted – unsuccessfully – via agents to buy out

---

80 Reply to Statement of Objections, p. 37.

Isoplus, and later warned the German company to stay out of the Danish market.[81] Nonetheless by mid-1993 Pan-Isovit and Isoplus, in order to obtain more leverage, decided defiantly to enter the Danish market. But, despite such dissension and chafing under ABB hegemony, the six producers were still working towards resolving their differences and reaching a settlement – representatives again met in Hamburg later in April 1993 to restart progress towards a common price list and to agree a common price increase for Germany.[82] In the ensuing months, discussion of this concept evolved through a number of meetings, underpinned by the realisation that attempts to raise prices without a market-sharing or quota agreement would inevitably fail, into talk of making a 'more structured attempt at market-sharing'.[83] ABB predicted in preparatory note for a meeting between its senior executives and those from Løgstør in Zurich in early July with a degree of well-placed confidence that a comprehensive European solution would soon be reached.

The Europe-wide cartel begins

Further meetings during 1994 resulted in the autumn of that year in an overall agreement on how to share the European market. Quotas for the total market were agreed for each producer; the value of the total market (in Danish Kroner) was calculated and the percentage Europe-wide quotas of each producer were translated into money terms; and individual national markets were then divided accordingly with the producers having different quotas in each – this covered not only the European Community countries, but also Switzerland, the non-member Nordic countries, the Baltic republics and several Eastern Europe countries. The fundamental aim was to raise price levels. In September, two other producers, Finnish KWH and German Brugg, were formally into the Cartel. Also at that time, an agreement was reached on an overall quota system for Scandinavia, and the remainder of Western and Eastern Europe, with detailed figures for each national market to be set by the Popes and then passed on to the lower level marketing meetings for implementation.

The principle underlying the quota system was that, in future, market share could only be 'bought' – a change resulting from, according to Løgstør, ABB's insistence on a 'deadlock' or freezing of market shares. Under this system, if a producer wanted its overall share to increase, it would be necessary to acquire one of its competitors. Those producers whose market share in certain countries was considered too low were either encouraged or required to withdraw from those markets, so that their marginal commercial presence would cease to push down price levels, a common feature of markets populated by numerous small producers.

---

81   Isoplus Statement of 10 October 1996, p. 23.
82   ABB's Article 11 Reply, pp. 32 and 33.
83   ABB's Article 11 Reply, p. 35.

Compensation in the form of an increase of their quota allocation in other markets in which they were already present was given to the companies that took this step.

The European Cartel's structure

The pan-European cartel had a two-tier structure that was largely based on that of its Danish predecessor. The supervisory body, consisting of the chairman or managing directors (those once known as 'Popes' in the Danish cartel) of the participating producers was known variously as the 'directors' club' and the 'elephant group'. Its members were: ABB; Løgstør; Starpipe; Tarco; Henss/Isoplus; Pan-Isovit and, as of May 1995, KWH.

The tier below the directors was occupied by 'marketing' or 'contact' groups that consisted of local sales managers. They were set up in each important national market and were given the task of administering the cartel arrangements under the overall supervision of the directors. The national contact groups did not decide quotas: these were fixed for each country at the more senior level. Their task was to assign individual projects and coordinate the collusive bidding procedure – the 'established customer' principle that had been used successfully in the Danish cartel.

For most projects the traditional supplier was designated the favourite and the other producers were required to either decline to bid, or to give a higher 'protect' quote so as to ensure that the favourite received the contract. In the case of major projects where there may have been several suppliers, the producers which normally supplied the customer were expected to share the contract between them. Where there were new tenders for large projects and no pre-existing customer relationship, the contract was allocated in accordance with the remainder of the companies' agreed annual quotas. Any project which was worth more than a specified amount had to be registered with the coordinator appointed by the Cartel for the market in question. In Germany for example this threshold was DM50,000.

Contact groups were set up in Germany, Denmark, Italy (where Sigma Tecnologie became a member of the Cartel from around April of 1995), Sweden, the Netherlands, the United Kingdom, Austria (a key member of the Cartel there was, from January 1995, Ke Kelit Kunstoffwerk), and Finland, ans also in some non-EU countries. For the most part their members were the local sales managers or directors of the participant companies, but on occasions more senior executives got involved. Meetings were held frequently – the German group met either weekly or every fortnight depending on how much business it had to discuss – and complex internal mechanisms were present in, though not standardised across, all of them. These groups continued meeting long after Powerpipe's complaint brought the Commission in to investigate the cartel.

The dispute with Powerpipe

Formed in 1986 by former employees of the Swedish producer Ecopipe after the company acquired the Finnish firm Uponor, Powerpipe AB was one of the first producers in its field to develop CFC-free insulation foam for pre-insulated pipes. After a composition with creditors and financial restructuring that was initiated and guaranteed by Birka Business Development AB in 1988, Powerpipe was taken over and became a wholly owned subsidiary of that company.

POWERPIPE ENTERS THE MARKET: DAVID VERSUS GOLIATH

'Unlike some other smaller producers, Powerpipe not only rejected pressure to join the club; it incurred the wrath of the cartel by systematically underbidding the favourite and winning a series of major projects in Germany. The most egregious example was the Leipzig-Lippendorf project, one so big that no single cartel member could meet it; a "consortium" of three German producers – including ABB – was therefore secretly nominated to "win" the tendering procedure. When the news broke in March 1995, the cartel met in a Dusseldorf hotel and decided an immediate boycott: a meeting note reads succinctly: 'no producer to supply at all to L-L ... none of our subcontractors can work for Powerpipe; if they do, further co-operation will be stopped. We shall try to prevent Powerpipe from obtaining supplies of (for example) plastic'.

Julian Joshua, Commission *Competition Policy Newsletter* (1999),
No 1, February 1999, 'Cartel Enforcement, p. 27, at p. 28.

From about 1993, Powerpipe began to expand its business into other European markets, including Germany. One of its many reasons for doing this was to counteract the inexplicably low price levels it was encountering in Sweden – where ABB was the market leader. The company believed – not entirely inaccurately – that the larger producers were deliberately depressing the prices in Sweden in order to damage its business. In Powerpipe's point of view, the larger, better established producers had sought to eliminate or neutralise it as a competitive threat since its inception. From 1991 onwards the other companies made persistent approaches to Birka with a view to acquiring Powerpipe, but the negotiations were never successful.

Much as Powerpipe suspected, its elimination as a competitor had been an essential part of ABB's long-term strategy of market control from at least 1992. The maintenance and use of an artificially low level of pricing for district heating pipes in order to damage Powerpipe's business was part of this plan. The report of ABB's Swedish management group meeting of 10 February 1992 corroborates this:

> Everyone was of the opinion that it was an action against Powerpipe that should be undertaken (instead of a September campaign against Løgstør because Løgstør has the financial strength to withstand it). Backing from the Board of Directors is requested for ABB, Ecopipe and Løgstør to attempt to price out Powerpipe. Were Powerpipe to be forced into bankruptcy, then ABB would

be the only company producing on that market and a powerful sales argument could be built up, and we can go after Løgstør in Phase 2.

The Cartel's own 'Strategic Plan' for 1992–1996 – authored by ABB – is also very specific regarding the threat from Powerpipe: 'Powerpipe (Sweden) is dumping prices in Sweden very severely and now also in Finland and "Neue Bundesländer". ABB and Løgstør will try to squeeze him out of the market'.

In July 1992 Powerpipe's foray into the German market led to Birka, as the company's owner, being invited by ABB to a meeting in Billund. Together with Løgstør and the coordinator of the Danish cartel, the cartelist participants of this meeting proposed that their Swedish counterpart should confine its activities to its home market and stay out of the German market in particular. In exchange for this, they would raise price levels in Sweden to an acceptable level and apportion to Powerpipe a guaranteed quota. This offer was rejected, and in response Løgstør (according to Powerpipe's testimony to the Commission) offered to purchase Birka's shares in the company. This was one of a number of occasions when different members of the Cartel fruitlessly attempted to take over Powerpipe in this way. In the following year, ABB employed another strategy, by embarking on a systematic campaign of luring away key employees from the company, including its then managing director, by offering lucrative salaries and conditions. According to Powerpipe, the prime purpose of this tactic was to obtain internal information regarding its manufacturing, strategies and markets, and then adversely affect its relations with customers. This tactic was regarded by ABB as part of the overall European settlement which it had foreseen and explored with its fellow conspirators in mid-1993:

> The situation in Denmark, Germany and Poland will probably be settled by a reduction of ABB's market-share in Denmark by 1.5% and acceptance of an increase in Løgstør's market-share in Poland in the long term, as well as the fact that we have employed. (Powerpipe's Managing Director)

It was agreed between the architects of this plot that Løgstør was to pay 40 per cent and ABB 60 per cent of the cost of employing the Director in question, and in late 1993 the former Powerpipe employee relocated to ABB. Subsequently at least part of his work for the company was to provide intelligence to ABB on Powerpipe's activities. Two other important Powerpipe employees were also hired by ABB within the year, and talk of damaging Powerpipe in this manner was still taking place in early 1995.

The battle for the German market and showdown

Powerpipe feistily continued its efforts to enter the German market as a serious contender by setting up a German sales subsidiary in April 1994. In October of that year Powerpipe Fernwärmetechnik GmbH was then involved in the bidding for an important contract that went by the name of *Neubrandenburg*. Following the meeting of the Cartel's German contact group on 7 October, when it became known that Powerpipe was bidding for the project, the company's German subsidiary was telephoned on 10 October by Henss, which demanded that Powerpipe should position its bid at such a level that Isoplus was awarded the contract.

Following this call, according to Powerpipe, a whole series of threats were made and various inducements offered in an attempt to persuade it to abandon the *Neubrandenburg* bid. When it proceeded with its bid – one that was substantially lower the prices agreed between the cartelist companies – the matter was taken up by senior executives at Henss and Løgstør. They telephoned both Powerpipe's Managing Director and its then owner on numerous occasions, telling them that were they to abandon the *Neubrandenburg* contract in favour of Isoplus (which had been allocated the contract by the Cartel), and Isoplus would arrange for Powerpipe's 'admission' to the Cartel. If it did not comply, however, it would bring itself into a price war with the other producers that, given its size and market share, it simply would not win. When Powerpipe did not comply, it was accused of bad faith and a proposed crisis meeting between Powepipe, ABB, Løgstør and Henss was called off. Powerpipe had also informed a manager at Neubrandenburg of the Cartel's activities, and the company was instructed to change its report so as to exonerate the cartelists.

During 1994 Birka, as the owner of Powerpipe, made two approaches to ABB regarding its manoeuvres against the company – first to the chairman of the transportation segment of ABB in Zurich, who refused to meet with Birka on the matter, and then to a member of ABB's board of directors, with a request that the board act to stop the illegal activities. This prompted an internal inquiry by ABB's general counsel and a meeting with Powqerpipe's lawyers, but in December of that year the ABB head office emphatically denied that any infringements of the competition rules (that is, cartel activity and the boycott measures) had taken place, and threatening legal action against any further allegations of this kind: 'ABB will fiercely defend any improper action or interference with its business and seek indemnification for any damages it may suffer'. Following this, Powerpipe lodged a complaint with the Commission at the start of 1995. The Commission carried out dawn raids of the offices of the alleged members of the Cartel in June of that year. Only a few days after the Commission's investigation, the managing directors of the Cartel companies met and decided to continue their collusion with the proviso that extra security measures should be were used to conceal the Cartel's operation. Their meetings were all to be held outside the EU for example; mainly in Zurich, where ABB's headquarters are located. The Danish participants were also not to travel to and from meetings with a commercial airline, but in Løgstør's private plane. As late as October of that year ABB faxed through tables showing the adjusted quotas for 1995 to KWH. On one, collected by the Commission in evidence, the following annotation appears: 'Pekka: to be destroyed completely … EU case looks bad. Be careful for Christ's sake'. Even as the companies were realising that this particular game was up, and some approached the Commission with cooperative evidence, meetings were still held to discuss how the cartel could continue by other means.

The legal resolution: Penalties and appeals

After signalling their wish to cooperate, some of the companies (Løgstør, Tarco, and KWH) provided cartel documents to the Commission which had not been found in the June investigations. ABB, now also expressing a desire to cooperate, supplied a full historical account of the Cartel's activities to the Commission. The fine imposed on ABB reflects the fact that the violation represented corporate policy at the highest level.

A PROFILE OF LEADERSHIP AND DOMINATION: THE RINGLEADER'S STORY

'There can be no doubt that ABB was the ringleader and main instigator of the cartel. Domination of the market via a cartel in which it played a leading role was a clearly stated strategic objective of the company. The whole enterprise was conceived, authorised, approved and guided at the most senior corporate level. Throughout the whole five-year period, the initiatives to consolidate, reinforce and extend the cartel came from ABB ... Both the cartel and the measures to deny and conceal its existence were conceived, directed and actively supported at a high level in ABB group management.'

Commission decision 1999/60, 21 October 1998,
OJ 1999, L24/1 (at paras 121 and 155)

The Commission decided[84] to impose fines totalling €92.21 million on the 10 members of the Cartel. In March 2002, the Court of First Instance upheld the decision of the EU Commission in broad terms.[85] The companies had complained of misapplication of Community competition law, infringement of the rights of defence,[86] and the procedure for setting the fines. These actions were almost wholly dismissed by the Court, but the fines imposed on two undertakings were reduced – in particular the €70 million penalty imposed on ABB was cut to €65 million. The Court's reason for doing this was that the company (contrary to its earlier aggressive denial of wrongdoing) eventually did not dispute its participation in the cartel and had cooperated in providing the Commission with evidence after receiving the statement of objections. Sigma too received a reduction of its fine of €400,000, to €300,000, because the company only operated in the Italian market.

---

84 OJ 1999, L24/1 note 69 above.

85 Case T-21/99, note 69 above.

86 Interestingly, this included a complaint that a Commission official had in public suggested that the title ABB should be read as an acronym for 'A bad business' – the Court found that, though regrettable, this statement had not in fact prejudiced the Commission's evaluation of the case.

Seven of the undertakings subsequently appealed to the Court of Justice, requesting it set aside the judgments of the Court of First Instance. The main pleas concerned certain alleged breaches of the Rules of Procedure of the Court of First Instance, the liability of an undertaking for the anti-competitive conduct of another undertaking, the determination of the amount of fines and also the breach of the right to be heard and of the obligations to state reasons. The Court of Justice, in its ruling in 2005,[87] dismissed the appeals and fully upheld the judgments of the Court of First Instance. As part of this appeal, Løgstør, by then transformed into LR af 1998 A/S,[88] argued without success that account should have been taken in setting its fine of the fact that it had been coerced by ABB into involvement in the Cartel. Both Courts observed that, even if this was the case, it had been open to the company to report the matter to competition authorities (which indeed, proved to be Powerpipe's final option).

More than 10 years after the dawn raid, in one of the first serious suits for damages connected to an EU cartel case, four Danish municipalities succeeded in retrieving €21 million in damages. The case was litigated at the High Court of Western Denmark during 2004/5 and resulted in an award of damages that amounted to 25 per cent of the fine imposed upon the companies, then a significant sum compared with previous European experience. This took the total 'penal cost' for the cartel to well over €100 million.

After-life

Of the main protagonists in this narrative, Powerpipe has continued to trade from Sweden, as Powerpipe Systems AB, describing itself as 'a medium sized producer of pre-insulated district heating pipes'.

ABB, as the only multinational firm involved in the Cartel, has been involved in a number of other major cartels dealt with by the competition authorities, but in two of these cases has acted as the whistle blower and gained immunity under the EU rules. ABB reported the cartel relating to gas insulated switchgear (GIS) to the European Commission and thereby gained total immunity from what otherwise would have been a fine set at €215 million.[89] The GIS Cartel was a long-standing and sophisticated arrangement, operating from 1988 until 2004 and comprising 11 European and Japanese companies, and eventually employing carefully worked out strategies to ensure secrecy. ABB's cancelled fine was set to take into account its status as a repeat offender, and was second only to the fine

---

87   28 June 2005, Joined Cases C-189/02 P, *Dansk Rorindustrie v Commission, et al.* (2005) ECR I-5495.

88   By 2014, Løgstør, still trading energetically under that name and describing itself as a 'global energy company', was owned by Triton Fund III.

89   *Gas Insulated Switchgear*, decision of 24 January 2007, OJ 2007, C5/7, Press Release IP/07/80.

of over €300 million imposed on Siemens among the cartel participants.[90] ABB
had itself announced that in May 2004, following an internal investigation, cartel
activities on the part of some of its employees had been uncovered and were duly
reported to the relevant competition authorities, including the EU Commission.
The company said that it was also cooperating with other authorities in a number
of jurisdictions, including Brazil. The GIS Cartel's activities in due course gave
rise to further legal proceedings. The Czech Republic's Office for Competition
had also investigated the cartel and imposed fines amounting to €37 million, and
this fine was upheld subsequently by the European Court of Justice in so far as it
related to the Cartel's activities prior to Czech membership of the EU in 2004, since
that did not infringe the *ne bis in idem* (double jeopardy) principle.[91] There were
also civil claims brought by aggrieved major customers. A claim for compensation
against ABB was brought in the Dutch courts by one of its customers, TenneT. In
January 2013 the East Netherlands District Court confirmed ABB's liability and
rejected the latter's argument that TenneT would have passed on the overcharge
from the cartel to its own customers, and held that the overcharge in itself was
damage suffered by TenneT.[92] This part of the Court's ruling was subsequently
overturned by the Arnhem Court of Appeal, but otherwise the liability in damages
was confirmed, the exact amount of compensation to be worked out in a separate
proceeding.[93] Proceedings have also been started in the UK courts, where another
major customer, National Grid, has brought a claim for damages against ABB.[94]

In February 2007 dawn raids were carried out in relation to a suspected cartel
in the market for power transformers, and two of the companies investigated were
again ABB and the German company Siemens. In October 2009, the Commission
imposed fines totalling over €67 million on seven European and Japanese companies
in relation to the operation of the cartel between 1999 and 2003. The cartel was
reported by the German company Siemens, who then received immunity; ABB's
fine of €33,750,000 was based upon an increase for its repeat offending.[95]

Most recently the Commission has established the existence of a cartel in the
market for high voltage cables and in a decision in June 2014[96] imposed fines
on a number of European and East Asian companies, totalling €302 million for
operating the cartel from 1999 to 2009. Once again, ABB had reported the cartel
and thereby gained immunity, so avoiding what would otherwise have been a fine
of €33 million. But, again civil claims may follow in the wake of this proceeding.

---

90 Ibid.
91 Judgment of the European Court of Justice, 14 February 2012, Case C-17/10, *Toshiba and others* (2012) ECR 72.
92 District Court judgment, September 2013.
93 Leon Korsten and Sophie Gilliam, 'Dutch appeal court allows passing-on defence in follow-on cartel damages litigation', *Lexology*, 21 November 2013.
94 *National Grid Electricity Transmission v ABB* (2012) EWHC 869 (Ch).
95 Commission Press Release, 7 October 2009, IP/09/1432.
96 Commission Press Release, 2 April 2014, IP/14/358.

Cartel Criminality

For a summary of the EU proceedings, see Table 5.2.

Table 5.2   ABB after Pre-Insuated Pipes: Legal fate under the EU regime

Cartel	Participants	Period	Total fines (€)	Immunity	ABB sanction
Gas Insulated Switchgear (GIS) 24/1/2007 IP/07/80	ABB, Alstom, Areva, Fuji, Hitachi, Mitsubishi, Siemens, Schneider, Toshiba, VAT Tech	1988–2004 (14 years)	750,712,500	ABB	€215,156,250 Fine cancelled
Power Transformers 7/10/2009 IP/09/1432	ABB, Alstom, Fuji, Hitachi, Siemens, Toshiba	1999–2003 (4 years)	67,644,000	Siemens	€33,750,00
High Voltage Cables 2/4/2014	ABB, Brugg, Nexans, NKT, Prysmann, Safran, Silec, VISCAT, Sumitomo, Hitachi, J-Power, Furukawa, SWCC Showa, Mitsubishi, EXSYM, Taihan Electric, LS Cable and Wire Systems	1999–2009 (10 years)	302,000,000	ABB	€33,000,000 Fine cancelled

The company has also been involved in legal proceedings in the US in relation to its activities in other markets, particularly in relation to procurement processes. In April 2001 ABB Middle East was convicted of bid-rigging in the Egyptian market between 1989 and 1996, and ordered to pay a criminal fine of $53 million.[97] In July 2004 the company incurred a civil penalty of $10.5 million in respect of the bribing by its British and American subsidiaries of a Nigerian oil company, in order to secure a $12 million contract.[98] The ABB parent company had disclosed these suspicious payments to the authorities in 2003. And then in September 2010, a criminal fine of $19 million was imposed on the company under the Federal Corrupt Payments Act (FCPA), in relation to bribes paid by an ABB subsidiary company to a Mexican utility company, during the period 1997–2004.[99]

Much of this later narrative relating to Asea Brown Boveri suggests the story of a large international conglomerate coming to terms with a pervasive culture of anti-competitive activity among its subsidiaries and employees in different parts

---

97   Department of Justice Press Release 01-170, 12 April 2001.
98   Department of Justice Press Release 04-465, 6 July 2004.
99   Department of Justice Press Release 10-1096, 29 September 2010.

of the world, in a sector of business where the potential rewards of bid-rigging, price-fixing and market sharing are all too tempting.

The Lysine (amino acid) Cartel: The American Mid-West intrudes upon the Asian market

The Lysine Cartel[100] is another major international cartel employing classic strategies, but also possessing a high notoriety, arising from the much vaunted Department of Justice infiltration of meetings and subsequent release to the public of the evidence used against the Cartel, the 'Lysine Tapes' (see the box below), and the subsequent feature film based on the Cartel's activity, *The Informant*.[101] It is sometimes referred to as a Department of Justice 'first' – as the first successful busting of a major international cartel, although not relying so much on the new leniency programme as on covert surveillance via an opportunistic infiltration by a maverick inside informant. Leniency, in the US, the EU and Canada, enters the story at a later stage, as the cartel, and an associated cartel in citric acids, began to unravel.

On one reading, a narrative of the Cartel is a story of cartel publicisation – through the Department of Justice's enthusiastic dissemination of evidence and crusading speeches, through journalists' accounts, and through cinematic depiction of the subject. On another, more economics-based reading, it is a story of trans-Pacific trade rivalry, of American intrusion into East Asian trade hegemony.

BUSINESS, LIES AND VIDEOTAPE (I)

'This was a monumental case for the Division's criminal enforcement efforts because it grabbed the attention of so many groups that we were urgently trying to reach – including the media, US consumers, the business community and foreign governments ...

... I know that I had friends ... call me about the case and say "Oh, now I finally get what you do for a living – go and nail the crooks!" When the public viewed the tapes, they saw with their own eyes an unmitigated, undeniable crime of fraud and deceit. One could not have asked for a better introductory lesson for the US public as to why price fixing is a crime and why those who commit it are criminals ...'

Scott D. Hammond, 'From Hollywood to Hong Kong', 2001.[102]

100　As elsewhere, an important source of information is the official EU documentation, comprising the Commission's decision on the Cartel in June 2000, OJ 3001, L152.24, and the judgments of the Court of First Instance and Court of Justice on appeal: respectively, Case T-224/000, *Archer Daniel Midland v Commission* (2003) ECR II-2597, and Case C-397/03P, *Archer Daniel Midland v Commission* (2006) ECR 1-4429.

101　See 'Cartel Cinema', Appendix Two to Chapter 4, and the discussion further below.

102　Scott D. Hammond, 'From Hollywood to Hong Kong – Criminal Antitrust Enforcement is Coming to a City near You', Department of Justice paper, presented in Chicago 2001.

BUSINESS, LIES AND VIDEOTAPE (2)

'Tape Segment One: January 18, 1995 Cartel Meeting in Atlanta Georgia – The Lysine Cartel Members Show disdain for Customers and Antitrust Enforcement.

The knock at the door heard at the very end of the tape segment, in fact, was an FBI agent, disguised as a hotel employee returning to a cooperating witness the briefcase containing a hidden audio recorder he had mistakenly left in a hotel restaurant. In another tape, played at the lysine trial, ADM's president summed up the company's attitude towards its customers in a single phrase, when he told a senior executive from his largest competitor that ADM had a corporate slogan that "penetrated the whole company". "Our competitors are our friends. Our customers are the enemy". Imagine, one of the world's largest companies, which bills itself as 'the supermarket to the world', having such a disdainful slogan as its internal corporate trademark. Not only are the cartel members disdainful of their customers and law enforcement authorities, some are even defiant of their own company's rules ...'

James M. Griffin, 'An Inside Look at a Cartel at Work: Common Characteristics of International Cartels'[103]

'AN AUDACIOUS TRUE STORY OF CORPORATE GREED, CRIMINAL CONSPIRACY AND A LONE MAVERICK WHISTLEBLOWER'

'To ensure accuracy in a story involving so many people who have lied, I established a "pyramid of credibility". Tapes and transcripts were at the base: they trumped all other recollections or documents. Second were contemporaneous documents – teletypes, expense records and travel documents, contemporaneous diaries, notes and memos, schedule books, phone logs. Just above that were 302s, but only for establishing what was said at an interview, not necessarily for the underlying truth of the statements. Third were sworn statements and testimony. Last were interviews. In essence the story was built on a foundation of documents, then fleshed out with information from interviews that was corroborated by those records.'

Kurt Eichenwald, *The Informant*.[104]

The Cartel involved five companies – the American company Archer Daniels Midland (ADM), two from Japan, Ajinomoto and Kyowa Hakko Kogyo, and two from Korea, Miwon (later renamed and hereinafter referred to as Sewon), and Cheil Jedang – and aimed, during the mid-1990s, to raise the price of the animal feed additive and essential amino acid lysine. The Lysine machinations resulted in one of the best documented corporates crime of the twentieth century, thanks to the presence of a markedly duplicitous inside agent. The Department of Justice's investigations resulted in fines and prison terms for three executives of ADM who colluded with the other companies to fix prices. The Korean and Japanese firms

---

103   Department of Justice Address, American Bar Association Annual Meeting, April 2000, Washington.

104   Kurt Eichenwald, *The Informant: A True Story* (George Allen & Unwin, 2009), pp. 569–70.

entered into a plea bargain, and each of them, along with four executives, were heavily fined.

The lysine market

Lysine is an α-amino acid, and is both an essential part of the human diet (since the human body cannot produce it by itself), and important for those of animals that are reared for their meat because it promotes growth.[105] It is produced through a fermentation method in which enzymes feed off of a sugar supply, sourced for example from starchy crops like cane or beet, and makes the acid as the sugar is digested. For all its importance, however, relatively few companies produce lysine because of the costs inherent in joining the market. Of the actual producers, Ajinomoto was, during the late 1980s and early 1990s, the industry leader by a large margin – along with its subsidiaries, Eurolysine in Paris, and Heartland Lysine of Chicago, it commanded between some 50 per cent of the total lysine sales worldwide. At that time the remaining 50 per cent was shared between two companies, both Asian, and their subsidiaries:[106] the South Korean Sewon company and the Japanese Kyowa Hakko, the first company in the world to make fermented lysine in 1978.

In the Department of Justice's analysis, lysine, much like oil, is 'a highly fungible commodity and sold almost entirely on the basis of price'.[107] Of many variables that can affect a product's overall price, two affect lysine particularly: the cost of organic substitutes, soy or fish meal for example, from which the substance is made, and the prices charged by other lysine producers. Being that the market was so concentrated, the Asian companies that monopolised the world lysine market until the early 1990s took every opportunity to collude and coordinate their prices for mutual gain – continuing a decades-old practice until, in 1989, ADM announced that it was building what would be the world's largest lysine plant. Based in Illinois, the facility would cost $100 million to operationalise and would, if targets were met, could supply upwards of half of the world's demand for lysine, two to three times more than any other plant that was then in operation. This, along with the emergence, in 1990, of another small Korean lysine producer named Cheil Jedang, caused waves in the once settled lysine market, and the ensuing price war brought the cost of the product down three fold – from around $3 per pound to ¢70.

The lysine market is part of a larger economic sector comprising biotechnology and animal feedstuff, which has been subject to increasing regulatory attention

---

105   Lysine supplementation is also cost effective as it allows for the use of lower-cost plant protein (maize, for example, in place of soy) while maintaining high growth rates, and limiting the pollution caused by nitrogen excretion.

106   Miwon owned a New Jersey-based subsidiary called Sewon America, and Kyowa owned the Missouri-based Biokyowa, company.

107   http://www.justice.gov/atr/cases/f220000/220009.htm.

over the past 20 years or so. Alongside the Lysine Cartel, the same companies were involved a Citric Acid Cartel, which was also investigated and sanctioned in both North America and the EU[108] (see further below). Another related cartel, dealing in choline chloride, was also dealt with in the EU and in Canada.[109] For a summary account of this regulatory intervention in this sector, written at the time, see the article by Gregory Parlast published in *The Guardian* in October 1998.[110]

The emergence of the Cartel

Deeply concerned by the downturn in profitability facing this once lucrative market, Kyowa arranged a meeting between market leader Ajinomoto and ADM in the June of 1992. Held in Mexico to avoid American antitrust laws, the gathering was attended by Kanji Mimoto and Hirokazu Ikeda from Ajinomoto's Tokyo headquarters, and Alain Crouy from its European subsidiary. Masaru Yamamoto represented Kyowa; and from ADM came Terrance Wilson and Mark Whitacre.

To open the meeting, price agreements and sales allocations were discussed at length. Consensus on these issues was reached quickly – Sewon and Cheil's absence left Ajinomoto and Kyowa for ADM to deal with – and a two-stage price rise, which sought to increase the cost of a pound of lysine first to $1.05 by October 1992 and up again to $1.20 by December of that year, was met with general approval from those attending. But on the allocation of sales volumes though there was great dissent. Wilson, speaking for ADM, argued that his company should be apportioned a clear third of the world's lysine market. Ajinomoto and its subsidiaries, he said, should have a third as well, and the remaining third should be split by Kyowa and the smaller Korean firms. Ajinomoto, the industry leader prior to ADM's emergence, disagreed with Wilson's assessment of his company's potential, and the meeting ended in stalemate. Despite this setback, and at Whitacre's suggestion, the mooted two stage price increase went ahead – raising the price of a pound of lysine from ¢70 to the agreed $1.05.

Whitacre's influence was once more felt shortly after at a Mexico meeting. He knew that without a sales volume allocation to work from, the cartel arrangement would be dogged with uncertainty as its participants might be drawn to cheat – posting lower prices in order to poach sales while its competitors continued to abide by the agreed price. This activity would cause prices to drop, undermining the Cartel was formed to accomplish. Thus, as a gesture of good faith, Whitacre opened ADM's Illinois lysine facility to, amongst others, the representatives Mimoto, Ikeda and Fujiwara of Ajinomoto. It was his hope that a thorough inspection would offer proof of ADM's production capacity, and that the tensions that were the legacy of the Mexico meeting might be put to rest. That the price

---

108   Commission Press Release, 5 December 2001, IP/01/1743.

109   Commission Press Release, 9 December 2004, IP/04/1454.

110   Gregory Parlast, 'How a few little piggies tried to rig the market', *The Guardian*, 25 October 1998.

schedule mooted at that meeting was confirmed between Whitacre and Mimoto before this inspection testified to the seeming success of the latter's plan.

It was October when the Cartel met again – representatives from all five participants, Whitacre and Wilson representing ADM – this time in Paris. In an effort to disguise the purpose of the gathering, those attending produced both a fake agenda, and a fictitious lysine producers trade association, so that they could more easily meet without seeming suspicious to either sharp eyed customers or law enforcement officials. Though they were slated, on their agenda, to be discussing animal rights and the environment, their true aim was to, '1, confirm (the) present price level and reaction of the market, and 2, (discuss the) future price schedule'.

Tensions and fractiousness

Despite the best efforts of Whitacre and his cartelist associates, the lack of an agreement on sales volume came back to haunt them in 1993. Underbidding on the agreed price, and the consequent need for the other companies to match that lower bid or lose business, forced the price of lysine down sharply, and it was June 1993 before the companies met once more, having picked up the monikers 'G-5' and 'the clue', and sought to set, at the insistence of the Asian firms, an allocation that limited each company to a prescribed annual tonnage. But ADM was not happy with its allotted share, and rejected this suggestion. The tension between that company and Ajinomoto, who viewed the fledgling producer as greedy and overreaching, endured and led to another failed meeting in Paris, and then to the convening of a meeting between the top management at ADM and Ajinomoto: Mick Andreas and Kazutoshi Yamada.

The top management meeting, attended by Andreas, Whitacre, Yamada and Ikeda, was held in Irvine California in October of 1993 and began confrontationally. Andreas made it clear that in the absence of a sales volume allocation that met ADM's specifications, the company would flood the market and therefore, because of the over-supply, force the price for lysine down further than it had fallen at any point during the Cartel's existence. This initial rancour was tempered though as the participants pontificated on the dangers of competition, and moved on to discuss Andreas' concerns about the ability of his Asian counterparts to maintain the price levels agreed to in previous meetings.

Unlike ADM, which had a highly centralised sales system that worked with third parties very little, Ajinomoto and the other Asian companies employed agents to make deals with customers. These agents had some discretion on price that simply did not feature in ADM's sales plans, and Andreas suggested that his fellow cartelists might emulate this more western, ADM-like model for themselves in order to reduce the risk of prices being bargained down by industrious customers. The meeting closed with a brief discussion of a quick-response system that would allow for the verification between producers of the prices being offered to specific customers, and with the striking of a deal that, while not apportioning ADM its desired third of the market, would allow the company to make steady gains in market share over the coming years.

The next meeting of the cartelists was held in Tokyo, and had as its aim the finalisation of the plans made in the bilateral meeting between Yamada and Andreas. With the expectation that the lysine market would resurge in 1994, the participants – but for Cheil, whose volume demand was felt but the others to be unreasonable given its size – agreed to split a market of an estimated 245,000 tons between them as follows: Ajinomoto, as market leader, would sell 84,000 tons; ADM 67,000 tons; Kyowa 46,000 tons, Miwon 34,000 tons, and Cheil, if it ever accepted the deal, 14,000 tons. Once these figures were settled, Wilson, who was again attending for ADM with Whitacre as his second, suggested and had agreed amongst his fellows the institution of a monthly habit – the reporting of monthly sales figures by telephone to Mimoto. Should any single producer go beyond its allocated tonnage in sales, it would be for that company to compensate the others by buying enough from them to balance out the allocations. Mimoto said of this idea:

> Since there is an agreement on the quantity allocation, our sales quantity is guaranteed by other manufacturers of the lysine. So by matching the price, to us, lowering the price is very silly. We can just keep the price.

In keeping with Mimoto's mention there of price, a new standard for the US market – $1.20 per pound – was also agreed at this meeting, and this remained in place until February of 1994. On 10 March of that year, the participant companies met, on Whitacre and Wilson's behest, in Hawaii. Three main points were raised at this gathering: the volume allocation agreement's progress, each participant's sales figures, and, importantly, the introduction of the once truculent Cheil into the Cartel with a share of 17,000 tons – a gain for that company of 3,000 tons compared to the Cartel's previous offer. Cheil accepted these new terms and joined its fellows in both discussing prices for Europe, South America, Asia and the rest of the world, and in exploring how the allocation scheme would work regionally.

Following the meeting in Hawaii, the cartelists next met in Sapporo, Japan. Here, Sewon agitated for a larger market share in the coming year; a move that caused serious problems within the Cartel. Amid the arguments engendered by this, Whitacre, now representing ADM alone, managed to arrange another meeting between Ajinomoto's Yamada and ADM's Andreas, that was subsequently held in a private dining room at the Four Seasons Hotel in Chicago. Whitacre, Wilson and Mimoto were also in attendance, and at the beginning of January 1995 the decisions made at this meeting were put into effect. Sewon, in reprisal for its unrealistic demands, was excluded from the Cartel for 1995, though rejoined its fellows in discussing the end of year sales figures for 1994, and the new allotments for the coming year.

One further meeting was held between the cartelists, in Hong Kong, before dawn raids were made by the FBI on the offices of ADM and Heartland Lysine,

Ajinomoto's American subsidiary. Ajinomoto was informed immediately of this occurrence and began purging its Tokyo offices of evidence. At that point, the companies were not aware of how the Cartel had attracted the attention of the American authorities.

The Mark Whitacre sub-plot

Mark Whitacre, a high-ranking executive within ADM had in many respects been responsible for turning around the fortunes of the massive bioproducts division of the company, for which he was the head. Prior to his employment it was haemorrhaging profits, losing close to $7 million per month due to mismanagement and improper utilisation of capacity, but following his appointment these losses became gains of roughly the same amount. Well-liked, expert in his field and charismatic, he was perfectly positioned to exploit the illegal cartel activities that ADM was engaging in, and, seizing the opportunity for himself, he opened a dialogue with the FBI. The way he did this, however, was typical of his character in ways that, at the time, misled the authorities.

Having embezzled, through the use of fake invoices and other means,$9 million from ADM, he planned to cover up his wrongdoing by accusing Ajinomoto of planting a saboteur in ADM's Illinois plant. The teething problems the plant was experiencing at the time, in early 1992, would seemingly corroborate this ruse, and he would then go on, and went on, to inform the company vice chairman Michael 'Mick" Andreas that an engineer from Ajinomoto by the name of Fujiwara had contacted him at his home and offered to sell him the saboteur's name for $10 million. But this proved a fatal miscalculation for Whitacre.

Dwayne Andreas, the father of Mick Andreas, took Whitacres' claims to the CIA, which in turn passed the case to the FBI. When an FBI agent enquired about the possibility of tapping his landline to record any subsequent extortion demands, Whitacre responded with hastily conceived half-truths. He confessed to having lied about the extortion, but not to his embezzlement, and sought to avoid prosecution for the former by revealing ADM's price-fixing activities[111] and procuring evidence enough for the FBI to bust the cartel. From that point on Whitacre was the consummate double-agent. For the ensuring three years, and at an enormous amount of personal risk, he recorded hundreds of hours of incriminating conversations at 237 meetings, photocopied innumerable documents and, perhaps

---

111   Interestingly, it was apparently Whitacre's wife who persuaded him to inform on the price-fixing, actually threatening to report it herself if he did not agree: 'I became a whistleblower and informant because my wife insisted I come forward and report what I knew' – 'Interview: Mark Whitacre – Lysine Cartel Whistleblower on Price Fixing and Rebuilding his Life After Prison', *FeedInfo News Service*, 13 January 2009. This prompts some reflection on the impact of such business activity on personal lives, something which is prominent in the narrative of the Australian Competition Authority's film, *The Marker* (see 'Cartel Cinema', Appendix Three to Chapter 4).

most impressive of all, was able to convince his wary and historically cautious co-conspirators to relocate one of their price-fixing summits from Japan to Hawaii – an achievement that allowed the FBI to secretly record the cartel's proceedings directly for the first time.

Despite the many small victories he gave the authorities through the investigation, however, Whitacre was to say the least an erratic and delusional agent. He failed numerous polygraph tests, bragged to his gardener about his role in the investigation, continued, throughout said investigation, to embezzle millions of dollars from ADM and, ludicrously seemed to harbour the belief that by exposing ADM's illegal activities, the company's shareholders and board of directors would promote him to CEO once the current executives were convicted.

On 27th June 1995, with the FBI case against the cartelist companies now strong on the back of Whitacre's work, a move was made to bust the arrangement. Even then, the case was threatened by Whitacre's scheming – attempts were made by ADM's defence counsel to discredit Whitacre's testimony, but his duplicity and dealings were all too clearly evidenced at the subsequent trial Because of his lies and attempts at fraud, he received a longer prison sentence than the executives he helped to incriminate, and also lost his immunity in the price-fixing case. Whitacre was ultimately convicted of the same Sherman Act offences as his superiors at ADM, but was allowed to serve his antitrust sentence and his nine-year fraud sentence simultaneously.

Legal sanctions against the Cartel

Proceedings in the US
For the companies involved in the cartel, a then record Sherman Act fine of $105 million was apportioned between them – the bulk ($70 million) falling on ADM for its leading role. ADM was also in due course fined $30 million for its participation in the related cartel in the citric acid market – and thus paid a total of $100 million in corporate fines. Furthermore, three once high-ranking executives in ADM (Mick Andreas, the vice chairman, Terry Wilson, the vice president, and Whitacre) were convicted under the Sherman Act in 1998, and sentenced to between 24 and 30 months prison terms, and fines of up to $350,000. The company paid out $38 million in order to settle numerous mismanagement suits that were brought by its shareholders, and buyers of lysine in the US and Canada sued for and recovered sums between $80 million and $100 million in damages from the Cartel's five members.

The comparatively light treatment of the Japanese and Korean companies is attributable to their co-operation, through the latter months of 1996, with the DOJ's investigations. The fines imposed upon them totalled $21.25 million, and three executives – Mimoto (of Ajinomoto), Yamamoto (of Kyowa) and Kim (from Sewon) – each entered guilty pleas and paid heavy fines as part of the bargain. A fourth Asian executive, Yamada, was indicted but remains, to date, a fugitive.

Proceedings in the EU

The leading players in the cartel, ADM and Ajinomoto were fined €47.3 million and €28.3 million respectively. The other three cartel participants, Cheil, Kyowa and Sewon were fined €12.2 million, €13.2 million and €8.9 million respectively.

Although Ajinomoto was the first to come in and give decisive evidence of the Cartel to the Commission, it was also a ringleader and failed to inform the Commission of an earlier cartel involving the three Asian producers Ajinomoto, Kyowa and Sewon. In these circumstances the Leniency Notice allowed for a 50 per cent reduction in fines, which the Commission granted. The Commission also granted a 50 per cent reduction to Sewon, as it informed the Commission about the earlier cartel while also producing further evidence of the present one. Cheil and Kyowa also provided the Commission with further evidence confirming the existence of the infringements. They received reductions of 30 per cent each. ADM on the other hand did not cooperate with the Commission during its investigation. It did not contest the facts set out in the Commission's Statement of Objections however, and for this the company was awarded a 10 per cent reduction in its fine.

In subsequent appeals against the fines, the Court of First Instance decided on some small reduction of the amount,[112] but the Court of Justice confirmed the fines thereafter.[113]

Proceedings elsewhere

ADM was fined $125,000 by Mexico's Federal Competition Commission in 1999. The Canadian competition authorities also imposed penalties upon the companies: ADM, having entered a guilty plea, was fined $16 million, Ajinomoto received a $3.5 million penalty, and Sewon a fine of $70,000. Kyowa was granted immunity under Canada's leniency policy, being the first to report there.

The Cartel adventures of Archer Daniels Midland: Recidivist or cartel leader of the time?

ADM's involvement in the Lysine Cartel may be set in the context of a wider participation in such activities at that time, as revealed in a number of American and European investigations in relation to the food additives and animal feedstuff market. The company was subject to proceedings in both the US and the EU relating to the Citric Acid and Sodium Gluconate Cartels. In relation to the former, whose operations extended from 1991 until 1995, ADM received in the EU a fine of €39.69 million in 2001, which took into account both its leadership role but also a certain amount of later co-operation.[114] This was also judged to be a serious and injurious cartel, highly organised in a secretive way, using strategic

---

112 Note 1 above.
113 Note 1 above.
114 Commission Press Release, 5 December 2001, IP/01/1743.

'Masters' meetings and technical 'Sherpas' meetings. In this case the Cartel had to deal with new competition from China, and part of its purpose was to take concerted action against that new competitive force and recover customers lost to the Chinese suppliers (referred to within the Cartel as customers on the 'Serbian List'). As in the case of the Lysine Cartel, the companies involved also pleaded guilty and paid fines in the US and in Canada. In relation to the Sodium Gluconates Cartel, ADM paid an EU fine of €10.3 million,[115] as well as pleading guilty and paying fines in the US and Canada. There was also a further cartel established as operating in the market for choline chloride (animal feed vitamins), penalised by the EU Commission in 2004.[116] ADM was not active in this market, but a number of American companies who had been involved in the cartel left the arrangement in 1994, when it was agreed between the European and American producers to a market sharing arrangement across the Atlantic, respecting each other's reserved regional markets. The five year limitation period prevented the Commission from imposing fines on the American companies, although the decision was still addressed to those companies as a warning to their future conduct.

ADM's 'criminal record' in Europe is summarised in Table 5.3. As such, it is perhaps indicative of 'contemporaneous' rather than 'repeat' offending (see the discussion in Chapter 6 below). But it is certainly evidence of widespread participation in the early 1990s and of a 'leadership role' at that time.

Table 5.3   Archer Daniel Midlands: EU sanctions

Cartel	Period of operation	Commission decision	Participants	ADM fine
Lysine	1990–1995	7 June 2000	ADM, Ajinomoto, Kyowa, Sewon, Cheil Jedang	€47.3 million
Citric Acid	1991–1995	5 December 2001	ADM, Jungbunz Lauer, Haarmann and Reimer, Cerestar Bioproducts	€39.69 million
Sodium Gluconate	1987–1995	19 March 2002	ADM, Akzo Nobel, Roquettes Freres, Avebe, Fujisawa	€10.3 million

---

115   Commission Press Release, 19 March 2002, IP/01/1355.
116   Commission Press Release, 9 December 2004, IP/04/1454.

After-life

By the Department of Justice's own admission, the Lysine case had an energising and transformative effect on its and achievement in the field of antitrust enforcement, a veritable tipping point in that respect. From the mid-1990s the DOJ has undisputedly been a leading force in global anti-cartel enforcement. That is one line of narrative, which elevates the impact of the exposure of ADM and Mark Whitacre to seminal significance, although there are of course other possible explanatory narratives in the history of the subject.

Of the companies involved, mention has been made of ADM's contemporaneous and significant cartel activity in related markets, and subsequent small success in gaining some reduction of its EU fine from the Court of First Instance. But since the 1990s it has not appeared as a detected antitrust offender, although it has been embroiled in other kinds of legal proceeding, notably in relation to alleged environmental offending and infractions of the US Foreign Corrupt Payments Act (FCPA), the latter in relation to business in Ukraine. Nor have the Japanese or Korean companies been detected in further cartel offending, although Ajinomoto, one of the world's larger corporations, has been involved in legal and political argument regarding the quality and content of some of its products.

One of the main outcomes at ADM, was the loosening of the grip of the Andreas family on the firm. The powerful and influential Dwayne Andreas resigned as CEO in 1997, and his son Michael served his prison term and on his release in 2002 did not return to the company. From 2007, there were no members of the family involved in the management of ADM. Whitacre on the other hand achieved celebrity status, despite his criminal convictions and prison term. The case had attracted literary attention, and there were two books published on the subject of the cartel and its business context: James Lieber's *Rats in the Grain*[117] and Kurt Eichenwald's *The Informant*.[118] Lieber's treatment of the subject was more critical of ADM and the FBI's role in the matter, and has some sympathy with Whitacre. Eichenwald's detailed reporting of the ADM and Whitacre story provided the basis for the feature film *The Informant!* which was released by Warner Brothers in 2009,[119] with actor Matt Damon taking on Whitacre's role, in what was described as a 'comedy/drama'. As perhaps the single most important individual protagonist, Whitacre has, since his release from prison, recovered his career, or rather established a new career. Fully repentant in his public statements, Whitacre was able to take up a new role, leading to a senior position as a manager of operations with a California based biotechnology company, Cypress Systems. There had also been a campaign to earn Whitacre a presidential pardon, initiated by supporters within the DOJ and FBI, who had subsequently become friends with

---

117   James Lieber, *Rats in the Grain: The Dirty Tricks and Trials of Archer Daniels Midland, the Supermarket to the World* (Basic Books, 2002).

118   Note 5 above.

119   Directed by Steven Soderbergh.

the whistleblower.[120] Some 20 years on, Whitacre had acquired something of a 'national treasure' status, opining: '... no matter what view you have, price fixing is a criminal act ... The short-term gain is not worth the long-term consequence. I can tell you this fact from first-hand experience'.[121]

Competing narratives of explanation

Mark Whitacre's 'born again' autobiographical account of his role at ADM is based on a resolutely individualistic understanding of human action, almost a classic advertisement for methodological individualism.

A CARTELIST AUTOBIOGRAPHY: DAMASCENE CONVERSION?

'I made some horrific decisions and broke some serious federal laws. In fact, ego and greed were behind many of these poorly made decisions. Others have said that ultimately the corporate culture of ADM played a primary role in my decision making at the time. Also, not true. These were decisions of my own making. When trying to win so hard that truth and ethics do not matter anymore, then one is in a bad place in his or her life. That is exactly where I was in the early and mid-1990s. I cannot explain how I lost my way, but I did.'

Mark Whitacre, interview transcript, 2009.[122]

This reading of motivation and events may be set alongside that gained from the transcript of the 'Lysine Tapes', containing as they do a rich body of corporate-individual statements and views, as presented above, of the 'customer is the enemy' kind. The Whitacre autobiographical account can also be set alongside the following account, presented as part of anthropological explanation of events in the Lysine Cartel story:

> The ADM culture seems to have lacked countervailing forces that might have provoked resistance. Resistance would have been an act of disloyalty to the company as well as to the family that personified it, and disloyalty is a cardinal sin in an autocratic institution. A putative whistle-blower would have been most reluctant to seek allies, and very unlikely to find any. Moreover, disloyalty probably seemed irrational. Whatever the Andreas family was doing, it worked. The company got bigger and richer and more powerful. Anyone contemplating resistance would have been plagued by self-doubt. Who am I to question ADM?

---

120 'Interview: Mark Whitacre – Lysine Cartel Whistleblower on Price Fixing and Rebuilding his Life after Prison', *FeedInfo News Service*, 13 January 2009.
121 Ibid.
122 Ibid.

In hindsight, it seems almost inevitable that the whistle-blower turned out to be an emotionally unstable person.[123]

These are very different narratives, each very dependent on a particular view of the world and understanding of human action and relations.

The Art House Auctions Cartel: A maverick and elite conspiracy

The Art House Auctions Cartel (sometimes referred to as 'Sotheby's/Christie's', reflecting its high profile corporate participation and small membership) again provides an example of classic cartelist strategies, but also has distinctive features, not least the amount of media attention that it garnered, but perhaps most significantly the fact that this was an activity driven clearly by a small number of individuals rather than the corporate entities concerned, almost qualifying then as an executive frolic. Following this as a story of participation, focusing on the actors, this is a tale of four powerful executives (the two chairpersons and the two CEOs) and of individual ambition and hubris, and the adjective 'maverick' may well be appropriate in this situation. In contrast to the three preceding narratives, it is not so easy to set this account in a context of established and pervasive business collusion, and art house auctions is an economic sector far removed in market terms from industrial raw material such as soda ash or high technology engineering such as marine hose and district heating systems. There is also, in relation to the art house auction story, a flavour of celebrity, and – in the context of business cartels – a gender point, since it provides a rare example of significant female participation. Finally, this case provides a rarer example of an American proceeding which went to trial, and in this way opened up to external view some of the more detailed working and motivation of the cartel – as Ashenfelter and Graddy comment, 'because it ended in a public, criminal trial, this lawsuit provides an extraordinary window for viewing the operation of successful price conspirators'.[124]

---

123   John M. Conley and William M. O'Barr, 'Crime and Custom in Corporate Society: A Cultural Perspective on Corporate Misconduct', 60 (1997) *Law and Contemporary Problems* 5, at pp. 13–14.

124   Orley Ashenfelter and Kathryn Graddy, 'Anatomy of the Rise and Fall of a Price-Fixing Conspiracy: Auctions at Sotheby's and Christie's', 1 (2005) *Journal of Competition Law and Economics* 3, at p. 4. See the comments of these authors on the value of the evidence provided by such a trial to researchers, whether in law or economics.

The cartel in brief[125]

For seven years between 1993 and 2000, Sotheby's Holdings and Christie's International, the world's leading fine arts auction houses, agreed to fix seller's commissions, publish non-negotiable sellers' commission rate schedules and exchange customer information to enforce adherence to non-negotiable seller's commission rates with a view to increasing fees in the auction house services market. This stratagem was discussed and managed at the most senior levels of the companies – their chairmen making a habit of meeting at each other's private residences – and was maintained through regular meetings between the companies' two chief executive officers.

A joint investigation was launched by the European Commission and the US Department of Justice after Christie's approached both agencies with information it sought to exchange for leniency.

The market context

Sotheby's and Christie's qualify as the world's two leading multinational arts businesses, clear leaders in the field of art dealing. They have similar histories – both founded in London, Sotheby's in 1744, and Christie's in 1766. By the later twentieth century they had both become Anglo-American in character, Christie's with headquarter offices in both London and New York, and Sotheby's reincorporated as an American company in 1983 and now a company registered since 2006 in Delaware. Since 1998 Christie's has been owned by the French company Groupe Artémis SA.

At an earlier stage, as the two dominant firms in the field, competition between Sotheby's and Christie's had sometimes been fierce, in relation to the amount of commission charged, the payment of guarantees (a minimum payment to the seller by the auction house, even if no sale took place at auction), cash advances to sellers, and financial contributions to charities of the sellers' choice.[126] But rumours and allegations regarding price-fixing between the two firms had also existed from the time that both auction houses, in 1975, implemented buyers' premiums of 10 per cent within days of each other. Legal counsel was hired by the Society of London Art Dealers and the British Antique Dealers Association to try to stop this imposition, but by 1981 the dealers' legal expenses had risen so sharply – to around £150,000 – that the maximum penalty Sotheby's and Christie's would have to pay under UK competition law was outweighed 75 fold. Consequently the case

---

125   Two full and informative sources in relation to this cartel are: Christopher Mason, *The Art of the Steal: Inside the Sotheby's – Christie's Auction House Scandal* (Putnam Publishing, 2004), reviewed by Christopher R. Leslie in *The Antitrust Source*, November 2004; and Orley Ashenfelter and Kathryn Graddy, 'Anatomy of the Rise and Fall of a Price-Fixing Conspiracy', note 25 above.

126   See generally, *The Art of the Steal*, note 26 above.

was dropped, and the auction houses settled for £75,000.[127] This settlement, as a buying-off of troublesome legal allegations, may have encouraged some later complacency within the firms regarding the risks of competition enforcement.

Though there was a boom in the art auction industry in the late 1980s, a sharp economic downturn, resulting in part from the disappearance of many Japanese clients, took place during the early and mid-1990s. Because of this, in the three years between 1989 and 1991 Sotheby's net profit shrank from $113 million to $3.9 million, and Christie's fared little better. Panicked by this turn of events, the auction houses began competing furiously for consignments; each variously extending what amounted to financial guarantees in the form of non-recourse loans to clients, making drastic cuts to the commission rates it expected from clients, and also making charitable donations to organisations of sellers' choosing when given items had been sold.

The collusion

After four years of intense rivalry, however, there was an abrupt change in the spring of 1995. Christie's announced in a press release that as of the 1 September, it would charge sellers a fixed non-negotiable sliding-scale commission – a sharp departure from its past behaviour. Although Sotheby's did not respond immediately, it fell into step with Christie's in the middle of April, announcing changes of a like kind in its commission apportionment policies. This alignment, though it seemed merely coincidental to most observers at the time – forgivable perhaps as a shift in industry-wide behaviours – was in fact the first publicly visible result of a price-fixing conspiracy, the seeds of which had been sown around 1993 through the discussions and meetings of four top executives within the auction houses: Christie's CEO Christopher Davidge, Diana (better known as Dede) Brooks, CEO of Sotheby's, and Sir Anthony Tennant and A. Alfred Taubman, respectively the chairmen of Christie's and Sotheby's.

The Cartel, in its workings, was for all intents and purposes quite typical of a price-fixing scheme. Tennant and Taubman took the initiative, agreeing first in principle to rein in competition in relation to a number of strategies, but left the specifics of any collusive arrangement to be worked out by the two CEOs. Meetings between the latter began at the end of 1993, shortly after Brooks' appointment as Sotheby's CEO. While Taubman and Tennant met at each other's residences in London and New York for 'breakfast meetings', a total of 12 times over the arrangement's course, Davidge and Brooks engaged in a number of clandestine meetings of their own. On one notable occasion, Davidge flew from London to New York on Concorde. He arrived at 9.25 p.m., met Brooks and conducted their business in a two hour meeting in her private car, and then caught the 12.30 p.m. flight on Concord back to London.[128] After several further discussions with

---

127 Ashenfelter and Graddy, note 25 above, at p. 5.
128 Aschenfelter and Graddy, note 25 above, at p. 6.

**THE FOUR INDIVIDUAL PROTAGONISTS:
A MATTER OF PERSONAL CHEMISTRY**

'Alfred Taubman rose from modest beginnings to become a multimillionaire who would serve as a white knight to buy the struggling Sotheby's and save it from a hostile takeover by two carpet manufacturers from New Jersey. After he became the chairman of Sotheby's, Taubman elevated Dede Brooks to the position of CEO of Sotheby's, the first woman to lead a major auction house. Born into a world of privilege Brooks would nevertheless have to work her way to the top, leaving her position in the financial sector to begin life at Sotheby's, initially without any salary at all.

The two key players from Christie's also presented a tale of two different paths to power. While Anthony Tennant came from the privileged classes to head Christie's as its chairman, Christopher Davidge took a different route. After Christie's lost its chairman following a scandal (he lied to the press about the money fetched by two paintings at auction), Christie's did the unthinkable and hired Christopher Davidge, a man from England's lower middle class who was raised in a government housing project in North London and had been running the catalog printing division at Christie's immediately prior to being tapped for the top position.

... The introduction of new blood can revitalize competition in the marketplace. Until the early 1980s, both Christie's and Sotheby's were relatively staid, conservative institutions run by establishment Englishmen bred from the upper classes who attended the proper schools. After Sotheby's hired Alfred Taubman, the American businessman introduced a new competitive spirit into the market that forced Christie's to respond. Davidge took over the day-to-day operations at Christie's at a time when Sotheby's new aggressive competitive approach was putting pressures on Christie's executives.'

Christopher R. Leslie, Review of Christopher Mason's *Art of the Steal*, in *The Antitrust Source* (November 2004).

Davidge, not all of which necessitated brisk transatlantic jaunts, Sotheby's quietly abandoned two of the tactics it had long employed to maintain a competitive edge over Christie's – its habit of offering interest-free advances to sellers, and that of donating to charities in order to win business – in 1994. The CEOs' discussions covered a range of collusive strategies, even some peripheral issues such as the waiving of charges for catalogue illustrations, shipping or insurance, as a means of ensuring that neither secretly cheated on the cartel in relation to less obvious matters.[129] But the cosiness of these meetings and arrangements also to some extent masked a fragility of trust – Davidge in particular was careful to keep his own written records of what was taking place, which eventually served him well when the cartel was being revealed. The cartel was also operating in a conscious climate of subterfuge and suspicion. While both Davidge and Brooks were clearly aware of the illegality of their actions through their own secretiveness, both were increasingly bare-faced in their denials in response to any concerned enquiries from general counsel within both firms.

---

129   Ashenfelter and Graddy, note 1 above, at pp. 5–7.

It would be a full three years before the auction houses would negotiate with sellers again, the reinvigoration of their market through the availability for auction of several major art collections prompting Sotheby's to break ranks with an offer to waive its commission on the sale of Impressionist pictures from the estate of John Langeloth Loeb, and his wife, Francis Lehman Loeb.[130] Seeking a better deal, representatives of the Loeb estate approached Christie's, and thus inadvertently alerted the other firm to its cartel-mate's duplicity. In retaliation for this, Christie's agreed to contribute a large sum to the Loeb family foundation, and thereby restarted fully the competitive practices that had been abandoned in favour of co-operation when times were harder.

Despite their apparent return to competition, the auction houses could not escape the suspicion wrought by the near identical commission tables they had published during their collusive period. In early 1996 the UK's Office of Fair Trading began making informal inquiries regarding the tables as possible evidence of anti-competitive behaviour that was contrary to both the Competition Act 1980 and the Fair Trading Act 1973. Following on, the US Department of Justice (DOJ) started, in 1996, to investigate both Sotheby's and Christie's, along with a number of smaller art houses, and sought to collect through subpoenas all documents that concerned sellers' commissions, buyers' premiums and other conditions of sale at auction since 1992. Interviews with each company's top executives, at which the latter roundly professed their innocence, were held by their respective outside counsel; it was concluded by the counsel that there were no admissions of contacts of an inappropriate nature between Christie's and Sotheby's, nor did any documents appear, either in the US or the UK, which contained references suggesting inappropriate contacts.

There the matter lay until April 1999.

The busting of the cartel[131]

The convincing revelation of the cartel activity had its origin in the happenstance of particular personal disaffection on the part of a Christie's employee, Patricia Hambrecht, as an act of reprisal following her forced resignation.

Shortly afterwards Hambrecht approached Christie's lawyers and stated that she had evidence, sourced directly from Christopher Davidge, of what appeared to be antitrust collusion at the top of the firm. This prompted an internal investigation by Christie's. Although Davidge remained as tight-lipped about any such activity as when he had been interviewed before, his secretary was more forthcoming. She recalled several meetings between Davidge and Sotheby's Dede Brooks at about the time of the 1995 sellers' commissions, and remarked upon his seeming

---

130   Ibid., at p. 6.

131   See generally on the criminal proceeding: J.B. Stewart, 'Bidding War: How an Antitrust Investigation into Christie's and Sotheby's Became a Race to See Who Could Betray Whom', *The New Yorker*, 15 October 2001, 158.

THE HAMBRECHT SUB-PLOT: AN INTERNAL WHISTLEBLOWER
The decisive reporting of the cartel had its beginnings in the mid-1990s with the appraisal by Christie's of the worth of the estate of the acclaimed photographer Robert Mapplethorpe, estimated at $228 million. This valuation was overseen by the president of Christie's North and South America, Patricia Hambrecht, a Harvard graduate who was described in a 1997 *Town and Country* article as 'petite, dark-haired and very soignée', and was known colloquially as Christie's answer to Dede Brooks. In response to questions regarding her valuation of the Mapplethorpe estate, Hambrecht claimed that its executor Michael Ward Stout had lied to her about its contents. Stout then sued her for defamation and, in the ensuing case, it was found that Hambrecht's claims and representations were fatally flawed. Hambrecht eventually lost in the action and, as part of the settlement of the case, she was forced to resign in 1999. But she did not do this quietly.

confidence that their rival would follow their example. When the investigation moved on to interview Tennant's successor as Christie's chairman, Lord Hindlip, further light was shed on Davidge's suspiciously cosy relationship with Sotheby's CEO. According to Hindlip, Davidge had confided in him that he had discussed the commission rates with Brooks, and had also included the names of clients that were to be exempt from these rates on what he called 'grandfather lists'.

With the evidential noose clearly tightening, Christie's counsel sought again to interview Davidge himself, but were repeated informed that he was unavailable. Sensing the growing necessity for his own counsel, Davidge hired a criminal lawyer based in Chicago, who was then alarmed at the extent of the documentary evidence of collusion, such as the 'grandfather list'. Sharing his concerns with other lawyers at Christie's was sufficient to provoke a 'scramble for amnesty'. Christie's became increasingly convinced of the need for it to win the race for leniency, but had to negotiate a tricky accommodation with Davidge regarding his own personal position.

The first move was to contact the US prosecutor in charge of the case and hand over the incriminating evidence. This was the first step towards a leniency application for Christie's, but the prospects were uncertain, given that the DOJ investigation was well underway and that one of their employees was obviously guilty. According to the DOJ's guidelines, it would need to be shown that Christie's had not initiated the collusion, and in order to do that it would be necessary for Davidge, who had resigned on Christmas Eve 1999 as Christie's CEO, to testify that it had been Tennant and Taubman at Sotheby's who had masterminded the arrangement. Davidge, as a UK national based in London, was not extraditable – price-fixing at that time in the UK was not a criminal offence – but Christie's had a certain degree of financial leverage over him so that eventually his co-operation was secured. The company had awarded Davidge a £5 million severance package upon his resignation, a large proportion of which it then threatened to withhold if he refused to assist. This incentive proved successful, and with Davidge on board counsel for Christie's simultaneously sought leniency in both the US and the EU. Both applications were successful.

In the US Sherman Act proceedings, Davidge testified, having received immunity from prosecution, as did Christie's. Tennant, as a UK national and resident, could not be extradited and remained out of reach. Dede Brooks, having tendered her resignation as Sotheby's CEO, entered a guilty plea to one count of price-fixing and promised her full co-operation in the investigation. Taubman did not cooperate nor appear in court to defend himself. The Cartel, already over in economic terms, was now fully busted in legal terms. The legal sanctions resulting from the proceedings in the US and elsewhere are laid out for the corporate and individual parties in Table 5.4.

Table 5.4   Art House Auctions Cartel: Legal sanctions

Alfred Taubman	Convicted under the Sherman Act in the US. Sentenced to a prison term of one year and one day. Fine of $7.5 million.
Diana Brooks	Convicted under the Sherman Act in the US. Following co-operation, sentenced to three years' probation, including six months home detention and tagging, 1000 hours of community service. Fine of $350,000.
Christopher Davidge	Not prosecuted (awarded immunity under US law).
Anthony Tennant	Not prosecuted (outside US jurisdiction and not extraditable).
Sotheby's	Convicted under the Sherman Act in the US. Fine of $45 million in the US. In the EU, a fine of €20.4 million. In Canada, a prohibition order requiring Sotheby's Holdings and Sotheby's (Canada) to refrain from future violations of the Canadian Competition Act, to pay $800,000 for the Competition Bureau's investigation costs, and a requirement to carry out compliance training. In the US, along with Christie's settlement of a class action in 2001 brought by 130,000 buyers and sellers: $512 million approved by the District Court for the Southern District of New York.
Christie's	Not prosecuted in the US (awarded immunity under US law). No penalty under EU (awarded immunity under the EU leniency programme). Under US law, along with Sotheby's, settlement of a class action: $512,000.

Apart from the investigation and fine imposed by the EU Commission (itself a sizeable sanction on Sotheby's), the bulk of legal proceeding was sited in North America and is notable for its sanctions-focus on the two American executives involved. But there is a further legal sub-plot involving the subsequent civil claim, brought as a class action.

THE FOLLOW-ON CIVIL CLAIM: THE BIGGER PRIZE?

'Immediately after the news of Christie's admission of price-fixing, Christie's customers began filing civil suits. In April 2000, Judge Lewis A. Kaplan agreed to class-action status for the suits, and furthermore announced that the lead counsel would be decided by auction. The law firms were asked to name a dollar amount that was the minimum sum they expected they could win for the plaintiffs, excluding fees or expenses. The law firm with the highest bid would then win the position of lead counsel and would receive 25 per cent of any settlement in excess of their dollar amount. The remaining 75 per cent of the excess would go to the class members.

In September 2001, the civil suit was settled when Sotheby's and Christie's agreed each to pay $256 million to the plaintiffs. The class in this law suit comprised anyone who had bought items through Christie's or Sotheby's in the United States between 1 January 1993 and 7 February 2000, and those who had sold through either of the two companies between 1 September 1995, and 7 February 2000.

... The lead counsel received $26.75 million, which was only about 5 per cent of the total recovery ... the action designed by Judge Kaplan appears to be very successful in that the lawyers received what are generally perceived to be quite low fees.'

Ashenfelt and Graddy, 'Anatomy of the Rise and Fall of a Price-Fixing Conspiracy'.[132]

The successful civil claim and settlement in purely economic terms was much larger than the value of the criminal sanctions.[133] In fact, neither firm had admitted to fixing buyers' premiums in the criminal proceedings, yet this became an important part of the basis for the civil settlement. The latter was also the one area of sanctioning which Christie's did not avoid as a result of its winning the race for leniency.

The other more distinctive legal outcome, moving beyond the financial penalties, involved the degree of future monitoring in the North American context: the home confinement and tagging of Brooks, and the Canadian imposition of corporate probation and requirement of compliance training on Sotheby's. Again this illustrates what may be more feasible, in terms of sanctions, in the North American context.

---

132   See note 25 above.

133   For a critical evaluation of the civil proceeding and its outcome, see the main part of Ashenfelter and Graddy's discussion, note 25 above.

The after-life of celebrity cartelists

As organisations both Sotheby's and Christie's were keen to distance themselves from the misdeeds of their high-ranking executives and there is clear evidence that their legal departments were genuinely dismayed throughout most of the time at what had been happening in relation to the cartel. While it would be untrue to claim that the firms and that economic sector had previously not been prone to anti-competitive activity, it would now be more convincing to believe in corporate clean hands after the event. Given the publicity arising from the case, and the fact that, as the two dominant players in that market, they are more easily open to future scrutiny, it would not be surprising if both firms felt thereafter well within the antitrust radar and a consequent need to be legally more scrupulous.

Of the individuals who played such a prominent role, there appear to have somewhat mixed fates, but nothing fatal.[134]

Tennant had the fortune to be a British citizen based in Britain at a time which pre-dated the cartel offence under UK law, and was therefore able to say nothing secure in the knowledge that there would be no attempt at extradition. Keeping his head down, it was for him very much business as before. Davidge, who had been more deeply implicated in the detail of the cartel, had played a deft game, preserving documentary evidence which would eventually secure his immunity and also that of Christie's, in both the US and Europe. Known in the British tabloid press as 'the Golden Hamster', he took away from Christie's a large severance package and, married to an expert in South East Asian art, was reputedly five years later speculating in contemporary Asian paintings.

Of the American protagonists, first the whistle blower Hambrecht, having been eased out of Christie's, went on to form Jaspar LCC, a company advising clients, particularly from Russia, Asia and the Middle East, on jewelry investments. Dede Brook perhaps experienced the most dramatic fall from grace, which attracted a great deal of media attention and interest at the time; while she avoided a prison term, she nonetheless lost her position (and others, such as that of a Yale trustee) and suffered the humiliation of house confinement, tagging and community service, and also had to fight off the enquiries of actor Sigourney Weaver, who was interested in making a biopic film about Brooks. Godfrey Barker's article in *The Telegraph* in January 2001, presents a very dramatic picture of Brook's experience at the time of the trial:

---

134   This after-life summary draws upon a number of sources, in particular: Godfrey Barker, 'The Fall of Dede Brooks', *The Telegraph*, 6 January 2001; Alexandra Peers, 'Five Years Après le Sotheby's vs. Christie's Scandale', *New York Magazine* 2007; Arthur Austin, 'A Price-Fixer's Memoir – Exculpation and Revenge While Confronting the Antitrust Abyss: An Essay on *Threshold Resistance* by Alfred Taubman', *The Antitrust Source*, October 2008; Alfred Taubman, *Threshold Resistance: The Extraordinary Career of a Luxury Retailing Pioneer* (Harper Business, 2007); Christopher Mason, *The Art of the Steal*, note 26 above.

preppy, well-bred, short skirts; star of stage, screen and radio; heroine of
Sotheby's Duchess of Windsor and Jackie Kennedy Onassis auctions; darling
of American millionaires – has suffered anguish in court over nine months and
may have run up $3 million-plus in law fees. She has been sacked by Sotheby's
and has resigned from the board of Yale University. She has brought Sotheby's
close to financial ruin.[135]

Unsurprisingly, Brooks appears to have retreated into a quieter lifestyle, living
in a mansion in Florida, and occasionally seen at New York auctions, but as a
customer. And finally, Alfred Taubman, already immensely wealthy and successful
as a businessman, fell victim to Brook's testimony in court, presenting him as
the cartel mastermind, and misjudged his defence tactics by refusing to appear
in court to defend himself. Convicted under the Sherman Act, he was both fined
and sentenced to a year's prison term, of which he served nine months. But he
emerged, even then almost 80 years old, unrepentant, as is clear from his later
autobiography, *Threshold Resistance*:

Hey, I wasn't guilty. And I wasn't about to beg for mercy.[136]

Regarding his present reputation, his conviction under the Sherman Act is fading
into little significance – biographical summaries describe him as an entrepreneur
and philanthropist, mainly remembered for pioneering the concept of the shopping
mall and as the 'white knight' rescuer of Sotheby's, while the prison term has been
reduced to a footnote, if mentioned at all.

Overall, it may be said that these main protagonists have negotiated the risks
of cartel involvement in a very business-like way.

The LCD Panels Cartel: A Far Eastern conspiracy in Western courts

The offence was no regulatory violation, nor a momentary lapse soon
regretted. Rather, fully conscious of the wrongdoing of their actions, AUO
and its executives conspired with the major makers of TFT-LCD panels to
systematically fix prices.[137]

Foreign companies, like European ones, need to understand that if they want
to do business in Europe they must play fair. The companies concerned knew
they were breaking competition rules and took steps to conceal their illegal

---

135   Godfrey Barker, 'The Fall of Dede Brooks', note 35 above.
136   Alfred Taubman, *Threshold Resistance*, note 35 above, at p. 170. See further in
Chapter 7.
137   Department of Justice observation in support of 10-year prison terms for
convicted AU Optronics executives, DOJ Press Release, 18 December 2012.

behaviour. The only understanding we will show is for those that come forward to denounce a cartel and help prove its existence.[138]

Industry background[139]

LCD panels or screens, as a marketable product, are relatively new. Most often used as the main component in computer screens, televisions, digital watches, pocket calculators and countless other devices, they consist of a lower glass plate (a thin-film transistor or 'TFT') an upper glass plate, and an injected liquid crystal which is inserted between these plates – hence *liquid crystal* display. LCD panels are more energy efficient and can be disposed of more easily than cathode ray tube (CRT) displays and by 2008 LCD screen sales had overtaken those of CRT units, and have now virtually replaced the latter. This relatively young but fast developing industry and market had its technological origins in the US in the 1960s, but production quickly moved to Japan, Korea, Taiwan and, most recently, China. Manufacture of the screens is now almost entirely centred in east Asia. This fact is reflected in the identity of the companies involved in the LCD Cartel: Samsung Electronics and LG Display are based in Korea; and Chunghwa Picture Tubes, AU Optronics (AUO), Chimei InnoLux, and HannStar Display in Taiwan.

The coming together of these companies as a cartel was spurred by a change in the market for LCD screens. The opening of two new, large production facilities in Taiwan in or around the year 2000 saw the prices drop dramatically in the following year, and in response to this crisis talks were held between the companies most directly affected – Chimei, AU and HannStar, leading to the formation of a cartel.[140] The following sections, based on the EU Commission's account of the Cartel in its decision of October 2011, provides a detailed view of internal cartel organisation and management.

The cartel's operation

The cartel operated from 2001 until 2006. During that time the companies agreed prices, including price ranges and minimum prices, exchanged information on

---

138   EU Commissioner for Competition, Joaquin Almunia, commenting on the decision establishing and fining violations of the EU competition rules by members of the LCD Panels Cartel, Press Release, 8 December 2010, IP/10/1683.

139   Once again the EU documentation provides a detailed source of information regarding the cartel's context and operation, in particular the text of the Commission's decision against the cartel in 2010 (see OJ 2010, C295/8 and more especially the non-confidential published version of this decision, of 8 December 2010, C (2010) 8761 final) and the judgment of the General Court in the appeal against the Commission's decision: Case T-91/11, *InnoLux v Commission* (2014) ECR. 27 February 2014.

140   Quoting evidence from the European Commission's decision on the case: '[T] here [was] an oversupply situation in the LCD industry throughout 2001, due to the large number of new factories that had been built in Taiwan.'

future production planning, capacity utilisation, pricing and other commercial conditions. The cartel members held monthly multilateral meetings and further bilateral meetings, meeting around 60 times mainly in hotels in Taiwan, aptly referred to by the participants as 'the Crystal meetings'.

For its duration, the cartel participants held monthly meetings to track their arrangements' progress. This practice was institutionalised in 2001 at the October meeting at the Westin Taipei Hotel, Taiwan. Representatives from AUO, Chimei, HannStar, LG Display and Chunghwa were present and, amongst sundry business-related matters, made formal both the cartel itself and the 'Crystal Meetings' that, when the arrangement came to the attention of the authorities, made it particularly memorable. These meetings came in two forms – high level, which were occasionally referred to as 'Green Meetings' and were populated by high-ranking members of each company's management team, and working level or commercial meetings. All the meetings were multilateral, and were held in Taiwan.[141]

The general workings of the cartel, and the need for secrecy – and thus the awareness of the parties involved of the illegality of what they were doing – are apparent in the following extract from the minutes of the 2001 meeting:

> Principal for pricing: the list prices are net prices. Each maker can adjust according to situation, but the prices cannot be lower than the net price. The upper limit for discount on intra-group sales is [*] and can be offered using after-sale rebates, in order to avoid disturbing the order of market prices ... Principals [*sic*] for meetings: Each maker takes turn organising each quarter. The order is HannStar, Chunghwa, Chimei and AU. Established Commercial Meetings will be done by vice presidents of sales set at each month to discuss how to stabilize prices and exchange necessary supply and demand information ... Others: Do not talk about this meeting, not even to colleagues – keep a low profile.

Added to this, the prices for the remaining period of 2001 were agreed upon, as was a plan to for the reduction of capacity as a way of ensuring favourable market conditions for the price increase decided upon. Again, quoting from the meeting's minutes:

> ... price for December 2001 – March 2002: considering that after December the arrival of low season will cause price drop, it would be difficult to raise the price again once it slides. Therefore, decided to maintain the November price of 15" until the first quarter of next year.

---

141   Out of 58 Crystal Meetings which are proved to have been held, actual participants can be identified in 52 cases. At those 52 meetings Hannstar was absent twice, namely on 4 November 2004 and 8 December 2004. Samsung was absent twice, namely on 5 October 2001 and 6 April 2005. AUO was absent twice, namely on 5 or 6 May 2005 and 4 November 2005 (Commission's decision).

To achieve this target, every maker must review how to maintain an optimum loading rate, lowering production capacity.

Finally, to assist in the dissemination of information, the creation of a 'hotline' was mooted and agreed upon as this meeting, its purpose being the exchange of information on a real time basis, as was the inclusion of Samsung, Chunghwa and LG Display within the cartel. The potential for new entrants first came to the Taiwanese cartelists' attention when representatives from Chunghwa requested that LP attend meetings that had already been organised among the Taiwanese LCD panel manufacturers. Behind this request was a mixture of pragmatism and necessity. Quoting again from the EU Commission's report:

> TFT-LCD is a complex business to manage. Constant updates are required in order to monitor how the market develops and what the other suppliers are doing ... As a result of these market conditions, TFT-LCD suppliers undertook significant efforts to ascertain how the market was developing, what components were available in the market, which volumes, and at what price. This included regular interaction between competitors.

The October 2001 Green meeting is a prime example of this regular interaction. Like the meeting on 5 October that preceded it, this second meeting took place in Taiwan – at the Howard Plaza Hotel specifically – and involved representatives from AUO, Samsung, Chunghwa, HannStar, LG Display and Chimei. The meeting concerned future pricing, supply and demand forecasts and a loading adjustment plan. An agreement on minimum prices was also reached, and an analysis of the companies' output situation was undertaken to determine whether a reduction in production capacity was needed to maintain a workable balance between supply and demand. On this point, the minutes of the meeting noted:

> Loading adjustment: Taiwanese companies plan shutdown for 8 days during Chinese New Year holidays, asked plans for Korean companies ... no shut down plan – will not affect Taiwanese companies' market.→ consensus: if demand/ supply is balanced, no reason to reduce production – let's wait and see.

Dealing with internal dissension

Internal frictions were apparent from an early stage. An email sent on 24 October 2001 – most likely relating to prices quoted by two members for 14" panels – makes clear a process of bilateral monitoring within the arrangement – one member making a complaint about another members' conduct. The email notes, in part:

> '(I would like to) report this price issue and formally complain to [*] and [*]. Please report back on the result'. The mail's recipient replies that he has, 'already raised about the problem relating to this matter with both companies'.

Furthermore, he reports: 'Even though both companies admitted to it, they have asked for our understanding as they had already committed to it early October. Therefore, it will be corrected from December ...'

This issue was revisited in the next CEO or 'Green' meeting held between AU, Chimei, Chunghwa, HannStar, LG Displays and Samsung at the Sherwood Hotel on 30 October 2001. The representative of the accuser-company made his thoughts on the matter clear, but those he accused denied their involvement in any wrongdoing – one saying that the firm he represented, '... will do everything to keep the price over (the agreed amount), including giving away a part of its market share'. Clearly, at least at this point, the stabilisation of prices was more important than enlarging or earning further shares in the market. The next meetings were scheduled for 13 and 15 November – the former concerning operations and the latter business for the participant companies' CEOs.

A second meeting was also conducted on the 13th – a Suppliers' Working Level Meeting that was held in the Holiday Inn Rebar Crowne Plaza. The agenda of the meeting included a discussion of the state of demand and supply until the third quarter of 2002, along with a review of the competitors' estimates and their production plans for that period. Much as they had been in the meeting on 30 October, deviations from the agreed pricing levels were discussed; one company in particular going as far to say that it could no longer do business with the alleged perpetrator of this non-compliance because its prices were disproportionately low. The same perpetrator was also said to have failed to raise its prices for monitors to the level agreed upon in the October meeting.

The 15 November Green meeting also took place at the Crowne Plaza Hotel in Taipei. In attendance were representatives from AUO, Chunghwa, Chimei, HannStar and LG Display; the representatives discussed, amongst other things, the November price review, the prospective demand and supply situation for 2002, the optimal loading rate, ideas on pricing for December and 2002, the issue of co-operation with certain Japanese competitors and a schedule for forthcoming meetings.

The general feeling of the attendees is expressed nicely in the following excerpt from a presentation made at this meeting – provided to the Commission in evidence upon Samsung's application for leniency: 'In general, we have raised price successfully, but there's still exceptional case!!!' This exceptional case is a reference to the continued bouts of deviation that were reported earlier in the year; something that was becoming such a recurrent issue that guidance notes were produced with suggestions as to how to combat it. They read:

'To avoid vicious price competition, several suggestions as follows:

1) Must follow target price for new orders.

2) Use Hot Line to contact other makers in the industry, to prevent being tricked by customers into cutting price.

3) Even though each maker has strategic clients, internal clients and commitments that are exceptional case, try to gradually decrease these exceptional cases.

4) With the same client, makers can each control price with supply.

5) Sufficiently remind Monitor makers not to grab orders with low price and never support such conduct'.

At the meeting's close the parties agreed that their current loading rate needed no adjustment, due to an existing shortage of their products on the market. In order to be able to regulate the market it was suggested to keep inventories instead of reducing price.

The next working level or operational meeting convened on 7 December at the Howard Plaza Hotel in Taipei. Representatives from Chimei, Samsung, Chunghwa, LG Philips and HannStar were in attendance, and their discussion was chiefly based on how the increases in price the cartel had caused were being received by their customers. They noted that, '... even though the market selling price rose by (the amount agreed) at the end of November, channel dealers continue to pull-in' and that, 'OEM/PC customers can accept paying a premium to secure allocation'. The parties reached an agreement on the price difference that should be maintained between certain product categories. The final meeting of 2001 was held on 11 December. It was attended by representatives of all six participants, and concerned, amongst other things, channel inventory, expected patterns of demand for 2002, the pricing for December and January ('we decide to raise ... price(s) in January'), and the price difference to be maintained between different products. The parties also reviewed the price increases achieved as from October and the targeted price increase ('we have to reach (a given amount) in Jan'.). A tentative price projection for the whole year of 2002 was also discussed, and it was agreed that, 'meeting attendees (will) cancel any rebate from January next year'. Finally it was decided that:

> ... the CEO meetings will no longer be held on a monthly basis. It will only be scheduled if any specific issues occur. As a basic principle, it will be held every quarter. (Green Meeting is fine)

The modalities of cartel operation

During the second year of activity, a number of behavioural trends and distinct preoccupations emerge from the evidence submitted to and gathered by the Commission: the need for confidentiality; a watchfulness of the market – particularly the extent to which the over-supply that had prompted the formation of the Cartel was either rising or falling; the need to manage customer reactions to the price increases; and the need to avoid of a price war – this being the cornerstone of competition and therefore the anathema of a cartel.

In order to avoid a price war, '… production should be adjusted since the companies might force themselves into a price war in case large amount of products are accumulated in stock'. Concerns about avoiding competition were raised just over a month later at a meeting towards the end of July. Representatives stated as the meeting opened that they, 'will do their best to avoid a price war'. On top of this expression of solidarity they discussed capacity issues, and it was concluded

---

SECRECY
Explicit instructions to maintain secrecy were included in numerous documents. Most obviously, in relation to activities during 2002, the records for a 'Crystal Operation Meeting' on 6 February in the Howard Plaza Hotel, Taipei, with all six companies in attendance, contain a note, perhaps intended for secretarial staff who may encounter documentation, which reads: 'Please do not copy and release to anyone!!!' And after a meeting in 2004, quoting from an employee's email:
   '(The participants were reminded) that DRAM makers were subject to Anti-trust law charges two years ago, requested everybody to take care of security/confidentiality matters and to limit written communication.'

KEEPING AN EYE ON OVER-SUPPLY
During March 2002, oversupply was the Cartel's focus. In a meeting held on 13 March, it was projected that this would still be a major issue in coming years, and therefore necessitate structured, coordinated action to combat it. The participants noted:
   'Combined data from all sources predicts that oversupply in 2004 is inevitable, and with larger amount and for a longer period than during 2000–2001, which in turn would cause deeper price decline. It is suggested that included at the next CEO meeting's agenda be a discussion on whether to set up a preparatory response or pre-control production capacity in order to react to the next oversupply wave.'

MANAGING KICKBACK FROM CUSTOMERS
Though secret, the publicly visible consequences of cartel activity are felt by and reacted to by consumers – often negatively. Managing this reaction was the subject of the June meeting held in Korea and attended by representatives of all of the Cartel's participants: the manner in which they should 'respond to customers' requests for decrease in prices'. Along with this, prices, capacity, demand issues, cost levels, and new output and sales plans were discussed, and it was decided that the participants '… must prevent any decrease in prices within the LCD industry …' despite the rancour such practices was causing amongst consumers. It was repeated in the meeting's minutes that the participants '… must … not lower their prices'. Going against this edict, it was warned, could incite a price war – where each company competitively lowers prices and therefore *competes* for custom – and that would be the undoing of the cartel.

that since '… monitoring every company's production status is not possible', they would 'determine whether or not to adjust production through a meeting among company CEOs sometime in late July'.

The Cartel survived continuing concerns about over-supply, and reported a generally positive mood after the first meeting in 2005. At this meeting, at operational level, it was noted by the author of its minutes to have had a generally positive 'good mood', despite depressed profits from the December just past. This good feeling was not to last, however. Of the 2005 meetings, that held on 5 May has the distinction of being the only one in which the presence of a woman

---

FRACTIOUSNESS AND THREATS TO LEAVE THE CARTEL

On 13 September 2002, a 'Crystal Operation Meeting' took place at the Evergreen Hotel, Taipei. In the discussions a complaint was raised: '(The aggrieved company) could no longer comply with (the current) price rules (because of the threat of) … oversupply (that came from sources outside of the cartel) …' It was suggested in response to this that a CEO Meeting be held, 'to discuss possibilities of production reduction or other measures to stabilize the situation', and that at this meeting an overall production and sales policy be created to try and solve the problems faced by the Cartel's aggrieved member:

'… if upstream sources (the cartelising companies) cannot reduce production capacity, and downstream (the non-cartelist whose trading activities were causing the complaining cartelist concern) inventory increases, it would be impossible (for us – the cartelists) not to cut prices.'

One of the other companies noted that it might be cheating. Specifically, in an internal communiqué, the suspicious cartelist wrote: '(more order-taking, obviously!!) Quoting low price behind the back?'

The outcomes of this meeting were summarised in an email dated 17 September 2002:

'Limited market visibility and pricing chaos. No meeting conclusion for price guideline and/or capacity utilisation hold. Need upcoming CEO meeting for further decision and progress: How to control market? How to control price? How to control output? Percentage production loading?' The email recalls the upcoming Crystal CEO meeting scheduled for 19 September 2002 and its major topics, namely, 'Pricing Control & Capacity Utilisation …'

These difficulties were surmounted however and after moving through, '… a great deal of external pressure … top management … decided to increase price(s) again'. This policy endured throughout the remainder of 2002 and 2003; a report from a meeting on 20 March in the latter year evidencing this, and the cartelist's continual monitoring of the market:

'Even though (one of the participant companies) has been insisting on an increase in price by itself, the other companies have been carefully considering an increase in price … Price for April will be stayed for all companies, except for (that which insisted). Prices (will be increased). The atmosphere was to carefully prepare for increases in the future … Must continue to monitor cost of competitors to adjust prices.'

was both noted in its minutes and seemingly regretted by the minutes' author in an email:

> (From one particular company) ... only working-level female employee ... attended, resulting in an atmosphere that was difficult to promote active discussion. Later, the attendees decided to ... meet (at a later date) at a 'private' location among working-level employees – however, I'm not certain whether I should attend. I will determine whether I should continue to attend after attending the June meeting ...

Though it cannot be concluded with certainty, an email that concerned a Crystal Meeting that took place on the 4 August may shed further light on the identity of this sole female participant in the cartel:

> For your information, attached is the industry meeting report that Vera drafted. The size of the meetings is being cut down and the meeting is being conducted with a focus on working level employees. Due to the characteristic of the meeting, as before, will continue to keep the existence of the meeting confidential.

The final operational meeting took place on 6 January 2006 at the Tsun-Shue Tang Teahouse in Taipei, and the last multilateral meeting between the parties took place in the following February. During 2006 Samsung broke ranks within the Cartel and approached the US Department of Justice for immunity, which was granted, leading to coordinated investigations into the Cartel's operation across a number of jurisdictions (the US, the EU, Brazil, China, Japan and Korea). Samsung also succeeded in gaining immunity under the EU leniency programme towards the end of 2006. By 2007 investigation of the Cartel and the consequent legal proceedings were well under way.

Legal sanctions across jurisdictions

Although the Cartel's planning and discussion was confined to the two main countries of corporate location, the market impact of the Cartel's activities was global and both the legal investigations and the legal proceedings against the Cartel participants was spread across a number of jurisdictions. Although Samsung avoided a number of the criminal and other penal sanctions through its successful applications for immunity, it has been caught up in the follow-on claims for damages (see below). The other five companies and some of their executives have been subject to sanctions in the US, in the EU and in China.

By the spring of 2013, and following a number of guilty pleas, 10 companies (including some US subsidiaries) had been fined a total of $1.39 billion in the US and 13 individuals had been convicted of Sherman Act offences (although six executives charged with offences remained fugitive). The criminal trial of

AUO in California in 2012 was notable: this resulted in a fine for the company of $500 million and conviction and prison sentences for two senior executives – former president of the company, Hsuan Bin Chen, and former vice president, Hui Hsiung, both of whom were fined £200,000 and sentenced to terms of 36 months in prison. A third individual was convicted after a re-trial in December of that year,[142] but two other lower-ranking executives were acquitted. The San Francisco Court also ordered the company to publish advertisements in three major trade publications in the US and Taiwan, acknowledging the convictions and penalties and announcing remedial steps to be taken by the company.[143] By February 2013 the tally of individuals dealt with was 22 charged and 12 jailed for a total of 160 months.

AUO IN THE DOCK: THE SAN FRANCISCO TRIAL

'The AUO trial lasted eight weeks. During the course of the trial, the Antitrust Division called a variety of witnesses, including co-conspirators who pled guilty and served prison terms in the US, representatives of US companies that were victims of the alleged cartel (such as Hewlett-Packard), and an economist who testified on the monetary impact of the conspiracy. Defence attorneys – lawyers representing AUO, lawyers representing its US subsidiary and lawyers representing each of the individual defendants – cross-examined the government's witnesses aggressively. They did not, however, call any fact witnesses of their own. And none of the individual defendants took the stand. In fact, the only AOU witness was an economist who attempted to rebut the government's damages evidence.'

GCR Antitrust Review of the Americas, 2013.[144]

In the EU, the Commission imposed fines on five of the companies in December 2010,[145] totalling €648,925,000, as detailed in Table 5.5.

---

142 Department of Justice, Antitrust Division, *Update on Criminal Enforcement*, Spring 2013.

143 Department of Justice, Press Release, 20 September 2012.

144 Ray Hartwell and Djordje Petkoski, 'US: Anti-Cartel Enforcement, *Global Competition Review, Antitrust Review of the Americas 2013*.

145 Decision of 8 December 2010, note 40 above.

Table 5.5   LCD Panels Cartel: EU sanctions

Company	Fine	Leniency
Samsung	0	100%
LG Display	215,000,000	50% partial immunity
AU Optronics	116,800,000	20%
Chimei Innolux Corporation	300,000,000	0%
Chunghwa Picture Tubes	9,025,000	5%
HannStar Display Corporation	8,100,000	0%

There were subsequent appeals to the General Court, achieving very small reductions in the fines imposed on LG Display and InnoLux, on the basis of how the fines had been calculated.[146] Further appeals have been lodged in July 2014, against the judgment of the General Court, to the Court of Justice.

In a further, interesting development, all six companies (including Samsung) were fined in total the equivalent of $56 million by the Chinese National Development and Reform Commission in August 2013 in its first decision relating to a global cartel, for manipulating the price of LCD panels in the Chinese market.

Returning to the US jurisdiction, the LCD panel manufacturers face numerous claims for damages from direct and indirect purchasers, and class actions by direct customers and end-consumers. These claims have led to complex economic argument in the US courts regarding the amount of anti-competitive overcharge during the operation of the Cartel, with a considerable amount of expert testimony being offered by economists.[147]

Finally, it may be noted that, in a wider context, the LCD Panels Cartel investigation was accompanied by or led to other investigations into price-fixing by some of the same companies in relation to the products in the cathode ray tubes and dynamic random access memory (DRAM) markets. Three cartels were established by the European Commission in the cathode ray tubes (CRT) market: one in relation to CRT glass, in operation from 1999 until 2004 and for which Samsung Corning Precision Metals gained immunity,[148] and two cartels relating to colour picture tubes and colour display tubes – Samsung being involved in both was fined by the Commission a total of €150,842 million, while Chunghwa gained immunity.[149] In relation to the DRAM cartel, the Commission imposed fines on a number of companies in 2010, including once again Samsung, whose fine was fixed at €145,728, 000.[150] There can be little doubt, therefore that this is a heavily cartelised economic sector, especially involving the participation of East Asian companies.

---

146   Case T-91/11, *InnoLux v Commission*, note 40 above.

147   See Oxera, 'Flat Screens, Raised Prices: Pursuing the Global LCD Cartel', *Agenda*, March 2013.

148   Commission decision of 19 October 2011, Press Release IP/11/1214.

149   Commission decision of 5 December 2012, Press Release IP/12/1317.

150   Commission decision of 19 May 2010, Press Release IP/10/586.

Chapter 6
Measuring Impact:
Conceptual and Methodological Problems

First thoughts

At first sight, it may seem that the exercise of measuring or assessing the impact of legal sanctions, once the relevant factual data has been collected, would be a fairly straightforward matter. There are a number of clear objectives underlying the application of the sanctions in question: to impose a retributively appropriate penalty or measure of restoration of illegal gain, and to achieve an appropriate dissuasive effect, both generally and individually, either through a process of deterrence or internally motivated alteration of future conduct (what might be termed 'reform' of the offending party). The first main goal – retributive, restorative and compensatory – may be tested in a backward-looking way, by reference to evidence of the offending conduct and circumstances of the offending parties. The second main goal – consequentialist and dissuasive in character – may be assessed with reference to evidence of subsequent conduct, on the part of the offender or others who may be tempted to engage in similar conduct. All of this is a standard exercise of criminology and penology.

The cartel biographies, as presented in this study, provide a certain body of data, some of it full and rich, for such purposes of assessment. That relating to the nature and circumstances of cartel offending enables some judgment on the question of restoring the balance and depriving the offending parties of ill-gotten, illegal gain, through a sanctioning process that is punitive and restorative. That relating to the later conduct of the companies and individuals dealt with by the sanctions, and other parties operating in the same market, will enable some judgment on dissuasive impact, whether through deterrence or change of disposition. There is much factual data to be drawn upon, but some further reflection will quickly reveal that how this may be done, in order to arrive at convincing and reliable conclusions as to effect or impact of the measures applied, may not be such a straightforward process of measurement. As Margaret Drabble has argued, the construction of narrative is based on a selection of memories, anecdotes and telling moments, and that selection may determine the meaning and the denouement of the narrative.[1]

There would seem, in this particular context, to be three major problems in measuring such impact:

---

1   Margaret Drabble, *The Sea Lady* (Penguin Books, 2006), p. 40.

- First, one of agency – whose conduct, more exactly, is being examined for this purpose?
- Secondly, following on the question of the relevant actor, what circumstantial and character evidence in relation to the actors is then relevant?
- And thirdly, and again partly connected to the above questions, the relevant data of surrounding and subsequent conduct – how far and for how long should be net be cast for that purpose?

Moreover, measurement and assessment is also a matter of interpretation and selection – the facts are there, but how should they be read and how much more data should be sought to understand fully the facts already known? There will always be some risk of premature, over-simplified conclusion drawn from a limited amount of data which may be imperfectly understood. But such risks may be greater in the particular context of cartel activity.

A limited exercise

It may be useful at this point to attempt a limited reading of some of the material presented in the narratives in Chapter 5, to show how some sense of impact may be gained, but also lead to new questions and the need to read and interpret the data further. For purposes of this exercise, a single major protagonist may be selected from the six cartels described in Chapter 5 and a crude quantification of the sanctions imposed on that actor used as a measure of retributive or restorative impact, while a simple report of any further involvement in antitrust proceedings could be taken as some measure of dissuasive impact. The limited value of the exercise in that form will be quickly apparent.

In each of the boxes below there is a simple record of the sanctions imposed and of any further involvement in legal proceedings relating to competition violations. Without trespassing too far into the further discussion of these examples in Chapter 7, a few points may be made briefly regarding these 'impact reports'.

To begin – a first attempt to provide an 'enforcement impact score', for both retributive/restorative and dissuasive impact, would suggest a low enforcement score in relation to Solvay (perhaps even a minus score in view of the cost of 20 years of legal process) and a high enforcement score in relation to Sotheby's. But would this be an accurate comparative reading? The range of sanctions depends to some extent on the jurisdictions involved (the EU is limited to corporate fines) and the happenstance of leniency applications, while further involvement may include contemporaneous as well as subsequent offending (as discussed below), and depend on the happenstance of detection and prosecution. It may then be misleading to conclude too much regarding appropriate retributive or dissuasive impact from such a limited reading. It would also be instructive to map the outcomes listed above on to an 'antitrust delinquency ranking' for each of the

Table 6.1   A first impact report on six cartels

Solvay (Soda Ash Cartel)

Sanctions: zero fines in the EU (after successful appeals on procedural defects leading to removal of the fine)

Further involvement: yes

Dunlop Oil and Marine (Marine Hose Cartel)

Sanctions: corporate and individual fines in US, EU, Korea, Australia; three prison terms for individuals (US and UK); class action liability (US)

Further involvement: no

Asea Brown Boveri (ABB) (Pre-insulated Pipes Cartel)

Sanctions: corporate fine (EU); damages from civil proceeding in Denmark

Further involvement: yes

Sotheby's (Art House Auctions Cartel)

Sanctions: corporate and individuals fines (US, EU); costs (Canada); prison term and probation (US); class action liability (US)

Further involvement: no

Archer Daniels Midland (ADM) (Lysine Cartel)

Sanctions: Corporate fines (US, EU, Mexico, Canada); three prison terms (US); settlement of civil claims (US, Canada)

Further involvement: yes

Samsung (LCD Panels Cartel)

Sanctions: zero fines in the US and EU following successful applications for immunity, but a fine imposed in China; class action liability and share of settlement in US

Further involvement: yes

---

companies[2] – an assessment of their delinquency as competition violators, based upon the market impact, illegal profit and duration of the violation; the degree of cartel leadership; anti-competitive strategies used and commitment to the cartel; and engagement in obstruction of justice and subterfuge. Although the application of such criteria would not be wholly unproblematic in itself (indeed a ranking of the six might not prove easy),[3] there would at least be some ground for rating Solvay as more delinquent than Sotheby's.

Secondly, this presentation of data and report on outcomes is reductive in relation to the question of agency, by missing the corporate complexity of some of the protagonists (for instance in the case of ABB by not disaggregating the roles of the Danish subsidiary company (clearly a main player) and the parent company based in Zurich) or the diversity of behaviour within a single company (for instance, in the case of Sotheby's, the separation between the Taubman/Brooks elite conspiracy and much of the rest of the company as represented by the General Counsel's view of the matter).

Thirdly, it is clear that the happenstance of the geographical location and scope of the cartel, and hence the question of jurisdiction can lead to a major difference in legal outcome. In particular, a cartel which is confined to the European market may find itself dealt with very differently from one which traverses the Atlantic or Pacific Oceans so as to include the North American market. Once the US is involved the range of sanctions becomes much extended and the legal culture is transformed. As will be discussed below, while Europe is a legal playground for would-be corporate appellants, the US in contrast is hazardous for individuals who may then encounter the force of a powerful and sophisticated plea bargaining system, while companies need then to contemplate the longer-term cost of large civil claims.

Finally, regarding dissuasive impact, a finding of either some or no 'further involvement' will mask a number of ambiguities and obscurities: contemporaneous as well as subsequent rule-breaking, action known or unknown in different but often related markets, the fortuity of detection and prosecution effort, the capacity and attention of competition authorities, and the difficulty of identifying and distinguishing between deterrent fear and spontaneous reform.

It is clear therefore that the above reading of outcomes from the six cartel narratives may take the discussion and understanding of the impact of sanctions only so far. At this point and before moving to some conclusions on the impact of

---

2   'Delinquency ranking' would serve as a kind of sentencing exercise, especially regarding the evaluation of some aggravating and mitigating features and how these should be taken into account in deciding on the quantum of any penalty. See the Glossary of Explanatory and Analytical Concepts and Metaphors, above, under 'cartel delinquency'.

3   Indeed it may be questioned whether an absolute ranking, in order from one to six, would be a useful exercise (although perhaps enjoyable as a dinner party game), whereas a relative ranking (X appears to be more delinquent than Y) would have more value.

sanctions from the above evidence, it would be helpful to explore further some of the methodology to be employed in reading and analysing this kind of data.

This can be done in the remainder of this chapter under the following main headings, relating first to the conditions for impact to occur, and then some possible measures of impact, as summarised in the tables below.

Table 6.2   Conditions for impact

Period of time	The amount of time after the adoption or application of the sanction necessary to judge its impact.
Awareness	The degree of awareness on the part of the subjects of the sanction of the system of regulation, of the possible sanctions and their likely consequences, and of the risk of sanctions being applied.
Agency	The actors to whom the sanctions are addressed and applicable: corporate and/or human actors, changing identity of such actors – individuals may come and go, corporate forms may change (restructuring and merger).

Table 6.3   Measures of impact

Actor sensitivity	The degree to which the subject of the sanction is aware of its possible application and may be affected by its possible or actual application.
Repeat offending	An indication of recalcitrance or desistance as a measure of dissuasion – the problem of what counts as repetition and what constitutes the same offence.
Market diversion	The offender continues to offend, but in other markets (clear up in one market but push the delinquency elsewhere).
Enforcement gaming	The offender with a high degree of awareness and expertise manipulates and exploits the process of enforcement as a business practice and with an eye to profit.

The period of time

This is an essential matter to decide upon, yet not obvious in its resolution, especially in the present context, while the decision on what kind of time frame to apply may make a considerable difference to the outcome. It may then be sensible to talk more accurately about short-term or long-term effects, and there will be a number of issues to take into account in working out a reasonable time within which certain impacts may take place. The short answer is that much will depend on the kind of possible effect being investigated and then the kind of actor subject to the sanction in any particular case. For example, it is a reasonable hypothesis that an individual being arrested and charged in relation to a Sherman Act offence will experience both immediate and longer-term effects in a palpable fashion, whereas the impact of that legal action on the individual's company may be less immediate and more difficult to gauge. Or to provide another example: what period of time should be used to assess the impact of the fine imposed on Solvay for its participation in the Soda Ash Cartel, when that fine was not legally confirmed and operational for a period of 20 or more years, and indeed was eventually annulled? The relevant question then has to be reframed: what is a reasonable period within which to judge the impact of a prospective sanction, rather than one actually applied and experienced, or the impact of being apprehended, and subject to and tied up in legal proceedings?

Thus the relevant time period will depend on what more precisely is being measured – the impact of what upon whom, and then, more pragmatically, of the position of the questioner and researcher in relation to the activity, and (a more banal consideration) the time and resources of the researcher. But the question of time frame cannot be avoided. For instance, as will be made clear below, it is an essential component of any judgment about repeat offending.

Awareness and dissuasion

It is self-evident that the impact of any sanction will assume some kind of awareness of the sanction and its provenance on the part of the actor subject to that measure, and that the degree of such awareness is an important component of any dissuasive effect. Even an assessment of retributive justification of a penal measure, for instance whether a certain quantum of penalty was deserved, will hit this issue of awareness, in the form of the argument that penalisation of an unknowing and unaware actor is not morally appropriate, since there is no responsibility in a crucial sense, and may undermine both the legitimacy of the normative system in question and any motivation to conform to those norms. This is an issue which has come to the forefront recently in the European context, as regulators and courts have become more determined to impose liability on parent companies, successor companies and investor companies in relation to competition infringements perpetrated by subsidiaries and investee companies.[4] The European

---

4   There has been an increasing amount of legal argument on this issue before the EU Courts, first in relation to the liability of parent companies, but more recently also in relation to investment companies. In April 2014 the European Commission fined investment bank Goldman Sachs in relation to the involvement of its investee company Prysmian in the High Voltage Power Cables Cartel (Commission Press Release IP/14/358, 2 April 2014), and

Court of Justice in 2009 confirmed a rebuttable presumption of such liability, based on a theory of decisive influence within a single economic entity or 'undertaking', in the face of vigorous arguments by AKZO Nobel that this amounted to a form of strict liability, contrary to the basic principle of personal responsibility.[5] But certainly, any assessment of dissuasive impact necessarily should take on board the issue of awareness. There can be no deterrence in any meaningful sense without awareness of the relevant rules and prohibition, of the sanctions which may follow from infringement, and also of the probability of being subject to those sanctions.

A social scientific or criminological assessment of how sanctions are operating and with what effect will therefore have to confront this issue of actor awareness. In this way, for instance, it was natural enough for Michael O'Kane in his interrogation of cartelist Bryan Allison,[6] to ask: were you aware of the illegality of your conduct, how did you view this illegality, did you believe that you would be apprehended and dealt with in a certain way, and do you now have a different awareness and feeling about the conduct in question? In another example, when a number of British schools were accused of fee-rigging, a first response was that the parties in question did not think that they were covered by the legal prohibition.[7] Whatever the credibility of this defensive statement, it was raised as a relevant issue of awareness, which then had to be legally addressed in dealing with the case, and should give rise to reflection on the effectiveness of the system of legal control.

There is evidence that enforcement agencies are increasingly concerned to ensure and enhance awareness and recognise that this may be a valuable strategy in itself, since it may in fact reduce the need for either the threat or application of sanctions. Scott Hammond's comments on the effect of publicising the 'Lysine tapes'[8] acknowledge the need to engage a more informed public awareness of the nature of anti-competitive conduct and of the objectives of antitrust regulation, as a way of inculcating a stronger culture of compliance in this area of policy and law. The recent output of educational films by competition authorities also provides evidence of the need and the value of promoting awareness on the part of both the wider public and the business community. Revealingly, both the Australian film,

---

Goldman Sachs has appealed to the General Court against this imposition of joint and several liability. At the end of 2014, the Dutch competition authority similarly imposed fines on three investment firms, in relation to their investee firms' involvement in a cartel in the flour market, even though the investment companies had no direct involvement in the cartel.

5   Case C-97/08, *AKZO Nobel and others v Commission* (2009) ECR 1–8237. See in particular the opinion of Advocate General Kokott.

6   Michael O'Kane, 'Does Prison Work for Cartelists?: The View from behind Bars', 56 (2011) *The Antitrust Bulletin* 483.

7   Office of Fair Trading, *Exchange of Information on Future Fees by Certain Independent Fee-Paying Schools*, CA 98/05/2006, 20 November 2006.

8   Scott D. Hammond, 'From Hollywood to Hong Kong: Criminal Antitrust Enforcement is Coming to a City near You', Address, 9 November 2001, Chicago.

The Marker,[9] and the Swedish film, *Kom Furst*,[10] present a narrative of a relatively innocent and unaware individual business actor being drawn into antitrust conspiracy, and then escaping through leniency programme whistle blowing. As Martin's friend advises in *The Marker*: 'It sounds like you've got yourself into a cartel, mate – you need to get out of it!' And both films almost trade upon an assumption of innocence and low awareness, concluding with the message to report anything suspicious or legally doubtful to the competition authority 'if you find yourself caught up in it'. The Swedish film was also shown repeatedly on the train service between Stockholm and Arlanda Airport, clearly in an attempt to convey the message and inform individual business persons regularly using that train service.

Agency

In the context of cartel activity, this is a crucial aspect of the subject. Any enforcement involving the application of sanctions needs to ensure that sanctions are appropriately addressed to the responsible actors, and it will be clear from the present study that in the case at least of large international cartels the identification of the responsible actor may be a matter of real uncertainty. In the case of small, more local businesses this may not be so much of a problem. But large businesses, operating at an international level, will comprise a large number of human individuals, carrying out different roles, and complex corporate structures, involving perhaps a number of different companies as distinct legal persons, and again performing different roles. Penetrating the corporate form and following the maze-like route of action and decision-making within such structures may prove difficult for purposes of both evidence and legal attribution. Sufficient has already been said concerning the problems of disentangling human and corporate action and decision-making, and making sense of corporate shape-shifting over time – after subsequent merger or sale of assets or take-over, is it the same actor for purposes of any legal attribution of liability? To take just one or two examples from the biographies presented in the previous chapter – does the delinquency in the Art House Auctions Cartel reside with Taubman and Brooks or with Sotheby's, with both or one more than the other, and in the case of the Pre-Insulated Pipes Cartel, does the core delinquency reside with the Danish ABB subsidiary, or ABB the parent company, or some of the individuals working for the Danish company at that time?

The evidence from the studies is that it is difficult to provide a consistent answer, since from one case to another the significance of individual involvement and the nature of corporate structures and roles will vary. To that extent, the answer will lie in the ability of enforcement agencies to penetrate the record of action – to

---

9   See Appendix Two to Chapter 4 above.
10   Ibid.

find sufficient evidence and to be able to use that evidence in a legally expert way so as to allocate responsibility and liability to sanctions in an appropriate manner. On the other hand, such a task may be fine as a matter of legal theory, but much less feasible in practice. Would it be practically possible to uncover fully all such relevant evidence, and do competition authorities have the time and resources to do so? Moreover, the passage of time compounds such problems of agency – individuals come and go, and to some extent the same is true of companies. In what sense, for example, was the Solvay company which was finally dealt with by the European Court of Justice in 2011 the same legal person, the same actor or actors, as the company involved in the cartel in the 1980s? This is surely a pertinent question to be posed in relation to any sensible and effective process of enforcement.

It is the daunting practical prospect of carrying out such investigation and evidence collection that helps to explain certain outcomes of legal doctrine and practice in this context – such as the American pragmatism of bundling together individuals and companies in single Sherman Act conspiracies and settling as many cases as possible without going to trial; or opting for a kind of vicarious responsibility which makes parent, successor or investment companies liable for the actions of subsidiaries, acquired and investee companies, as discussed above. The enforcement gains of such principles and practice are considerable. But, as has been pointed out, this comes at the cost of hearing the full story, and in more legal terms the sacrifice of procedural rigour, of the exercise of rights, of the clarification of law, and of the fullest working out of policy.

Ultimately, this requires a difficult balancing of policy and principle, between what is feasible, possible and sustainable as a matter of resources, and on the other hand, a transparent and fully worked out enforcement process. In that sense, it may be seen that the European model of process, with its highly developed rights culture and full accommodation of appeals, tends to tip the balance in the latter direction, with the kind of outcome that may be seen in the Soda Ash Cartel litigation: over 20 years of litigation, and then the complete removal of the sanction imposed for a clear violation.

Actor sensitivity

Turning now to what may be regarded as a significant measure of enforcement and sanction impact, the issue of how the subject of any sanction receives the measure is self-evidently at the heart of the discussion. Depending on the enforcement objective in making use of any particular sanction, this may more specifically be a matter of deterrent effect, retributive 'suffering', or alteration in the habit of compliance or attitude towards the values informing the underlying norms of prohibition. In order to address and estimate such possible outcomes, the following would be the most obvious and more specific questions to pose:

- Has the subject of the sanction thereby (by the threat or actual application of the sanction) been deterred from engaging further in such conduct?
- Are other potential offenders deterred in that way by the example of the sanction being threatened or applied in this case?
- Has the sanction effectively removed the illegitimate benefit or gain arising from the infringement, by imposing an appropriate quantum of penalty and compensatory mechanism for restoring the loss or injury suffered by victims of the infringement?
- Has the sanction achieved a change in the subject's habit of compliance and acceptance of the policy and values embodied in the rules which have been infringed, or in other words, brought about a 'reform' of the offending party?

In order to answer any of those key penological questions, it is necessary to probe what is being referred to here as the actor's sensitivity to the sanction, in the sense of how the measure may be experienced or is actually experienced. 'Sensitivity', then, is a shorthand term or concept, used to convey evidence of actual dissuasion, actual penal or compensatory loss, or actual change in habit and attitude.

In such penological research evidence may be found which can be used to attest or not to such outcomes, and some such evidence has been proffered in the biographical narratives presented above. The problem, of course, relates to the extent that such evidence is convincing and final. In some cases, although probably rarely, it may be convincing and virtually final. If, for instance, after a period of 20 years and a thorough and close examination of conduct, there is no indication whatsoever of further engagement in the prohibited activity, then there *may* be a convincing conclusion of dissuasive effect, although the reasons for that outcome are likely to remain uncertain – deterred, or attitude changed in some way as a result of that sanction (or of that and other sanctions), or through 'spontaneous reform'? But research experience and the existing literature suggest that it will often be difficult to find such convincing or unequivocal evidence, since the successful penetration of the actor's penal sensitivity is in itself so problematic.

It may be noted in passing, however, that nonetheless research claims may be made to assert convincing evidence and conclusions, but should then be treated with some caution. An example of such a research claim in the present context is provided by the two studies commissioned by the UK Office of Fair Trading concerning the general deterrent effect of that authority's enforcement activities. These two reports, by Deloitte in 2007[11] and by London Economics in 2011,[12] have been used to assert that each investigation carried out by the OFT has the effect of deterring at least five prospective infringements. This positive 'performance

---

11   Deloitte and Touche for the Office of Fair Trading, 'The Deterrent Effect of Competition Enforcement by the OFT', Office of Fair Trading, OFT 962, 2007.

12   London Economics, 'The Impact of Competition Interventions on Compliance and Deterrence – Final Report', OFT 1391, December 2011.

indicator', coinciding with the OFT's 'value for money' agreement with the UK Government Treasury to demonstrate that its enforcement activity generated at least five time its taxpayer funded costs,[13] was then enthusiastically taken up and generalised by EU Competition Commissioner Neelie Kroes,[14] and uncritically accepted by some other researchers – Davies and Ormosi asserting for instance that 'it is widely acknowledged that the beneficial effects of competition enforcement are likely to be considerable, far outweighing the measurable benefits of the actual caseloads' of competition authorities.[15] A UK Government Consultation Paper in 2012 was prompted to claim that recent research carried out by the OFT 'suggest that for every case that it investigates, 12–40 potentially anticompetitive occasions of anticompetitive behaviour are stopped' [*sic*].[16] But the methodology and rigour of the two pieces of research has also been questioned.[17] Veljanovski has provided a detailed critical account of the methodological and statistical flaws in the two surveys,[18] arguing for instance that:

> the interviewees [senior competition lawyers and some business persons] were asked whether they had abandoned or modified their conduct as the result of a 'risk of an OFT investigation'. They were not given any information on the number and likelihood of an investigation. Thus their responses to the questions were wholly impressionistic. It is unclear both from the perspectives of the interviewees and the OFT what the risk of an OFT investigation amounted to in practical terms, An investigation is a vague and unreliable measure of OFT enforcement activity ... tangible risk from an investigation was in reality miniscule ... But the real problem was that the risk of an investigation was not defined, revealed or quantified by the interviewer or interviewee.[19]

This illustrates the emergence of a research 'mythology', a quickly accepted and retailed account of enforcement activity and its impact, despite strongly expressed reservations regarding the conclusions of the research. And this demonstrates the challenge in probing the real sensitivity of businesses to an idea of enforcement,

---

13   UK Office of Fair Trading, *OFT Annual Plan*, 2008-9, HC 374, at p. 25.

14   Neelie Kroes, remarks at the Anti-Cartel Enforcement: Criminal and Administrative Policy Panel Session, 8 October 2009.

15   Stephen Davies and Peter Ormosi, 'A Comparative Assessment of Methodologies Used to Evaluate Competition Policy', 8 (2012) *Journal of Competition Law and Economics*, at p. 769.

16   UK Department of Business, Innovation and Skills, *Private Actions in Competition Law: A Consultation on Options for Reform – Impact Assessment*, April 2012.

17   See Christopher Harding, 'Cartel Deterrence: The Search for Evidence and Argument', 56 (2011) *The Antitrust Bulletin* 345, at p. 361 *et seq.*

18   Cento Veljanovski, 'A Statistical Analysis of UK Antitrust Enforcement', 10 (2014) *Journal of Competition Law and Economics* 1.

19   Ibid., at p. 23.

the research in question having limited itself to eliciting impressionistic answers from a small sample of lawyers and businesses.

It is indeed uncertain how the real penal sensitivity of businesses may be probed in this way. Admittedly, individuals directly involved in cartel activity may be questioned after the event regarding their own personal experience of enforcement and the application of sanctions, but such a sample is always likely to be small and by its nature perhaps of the more extrovert kind and not very representative.[20] Moreover, the results of such enquiry may comprise an intriguing but also confusing mixture of very different responses, ranging from continuing declaration of innocence and contempt for legal process (Alfred Taubman in Art House Auctions), to strongly expressed contrition and born-again vision (Mark Whitacre in Lysine), to a pragmatic acceptance of the sanction but remaining much the same as before (Bryan Allison in Marine Hose), as will be evident from some further discussion of these examples in the next chapter.[21]

But approaching companies and especially large transnational corporate conglomerates, to gain an idea of *their* perception, feeling and reaction in relation to potential or actual enforcement and sanctions is even more problematic: who to approach, who to talk to, who may speak on behalf of companies such as Solvay, Asea Brown Boveri, AKZO Nobel, or Samsung about the *corporate* experience of sanctions over a period of 20 or 30 years? Moreover, what kind of corporate feeling might be expected in relation to a single matter such as antitrust sanctions? A large international firm will have 'on its mind' at any one time a large range of commercial and legal issues, and competition regulation may only be a small part of the picture – would there be very much in the way of a corporate policy, strategy or reaction, sustained over time, which could be tapped into to judge the company's sensitivity to one particular kind of sanction which may in most cases be rarely experienced? In short, how much would such corporate actors care about competition regulation and possible sanctions? The answer to that question may require a more careful disaggregation of internal corporate actors – general counsel, CEO, board of directors, shareholders, heads of marketing and production, regional and area sales managers – and again the experience and perceptions of each may not be consistent, either within the same organisation, or across different firms. That much is suggested by the biographies – for instance that there were very different business cultures as between Archer Daniels Midland on the one hand and Sotheby's (Taubman apart) and Christie's on the other hand, so that a consistent and easily generalisable picture should not be expected.

---

20   But see also the discussion of anecdote and its value in Chapter 4 above.
21   See pp. 220–25 in Chapter 7.

Cartel recidivism or repeat offending

In discussing the impact of sanctions applied to cartels and cartelists, and taking into account any evidence that such sanctions appear to have little or no effect, it may be tempting to then refer to a pattern of repeat offending or (to use a more criminological term) recidivism: the actors continue to behave in the prescribed manner or commit further similar offences, despite the application or prospect of sanctions relating to the prohibited conduct. The concept of recidivism may then be used as a measure of failure of regulation or legal control – in short, that the system of control is not working as hoped or intended. A notable rate of what is identified as recidivist cartel activity may in particular indicate a poor deterrent impact of the rules against cartels and of the strategies and sanctions associated with those rules. Therefore, probing any apparent pattern of repeat offending is an important part of the assessment of effectiveness and achievement of the effort of cartel regulation.

Assertions regarding the existence or otherwise of cartel recidivism appear in the literature. For instance, Harding and Gibbs in 2005 refer to 'an awesome level of recidivism on the part of major companies who appear as usual suspects in the world of business cartels',[22] and Connor in 2010 has claimed that 'recidivism appears to be increasing rapidly, both in number and relative to all corporate cartelists'.[23] On the other hand Wils in 2012 has asserted that 'looking at the recent cartel decisions adopted by the European Commission, there does indeed not appear to be a continuing trend of increased recidivism',[24] and Werden, Hammond and Barnett in 2011 have argued that a search of US enforcement records for instances of cartel recidivism have found none at all since 1999.[25] This sample of quotations signals first of all the way in which repeat offending has become part of the debate regarding the legal control of cartel activity and its effectiveness, but secondly that this is also a contested discussion involving some different interpretations and conclusions in relation to the evidence of repeat offending. It may be asked then whether these authors and commentators are using the vocabulary and concept of recidivism consistently and how in fact assessments and arguments concerning recidivist outcomes are being worked out. Some further reflection on the application of the concept to cartel activity and its legal control suggests that this may not be at all a straightforward matter. Indeed, it may be questioned whether

---

22   Christopher Harding and Alun Gibbs, 'Why Go to Court in Europe? An Analysis of Cartel Appeals, 1995–2004' 30 (2005) *European Law Review* 349.

23   John M. Connor, 'Recidivism Revealed: Private International Cartels 1990–2009' (2010) *Competition Policy International* 101.

24   Wouter P.J. Wils, 'Recidivism in EU Antitrust Enforcement: A Legal and Economic Analysis' 35 (2012) *World Competition* 5.

25   Gregory J. Werden, Scott D. Hammond and Belinda A. Barnett, 'Recidivism Eliminated: Cartel Enforcement in the United States since 1999' (Department of Justice, September 2011).

the concept can be comfortably transferred from its original criminological homeland (the commission of 'core' criminal offences by human individuals) to the complex organisational and corporate context of cartel delinquency. Nonetheless, regulators are now willing to take into account a perception of recidivist behaviour in calculating the quantum of sanction to be applied to cartelists – for instance, the European Commission in its *Fining Guidelines*.[26]

Evidence of cartel (or cartelist?) repeat offending is largely drawn from the record of formal proceedings brought by competition authorities. In some respects this is a real enough and reliable record of delinquency that undoubtedly attests well-established serious breaches of competition law on the part of certain actors. But both the definition of recidivism and the way in which that record has been constructed require some further consideration. First it may be asked what counts as recidivism in this context in terms of the quantity and defined scope of the offending behaviour (counts of infringements), its frequency, and how it may be spread over different sectors of economic activity. Secondly, it may be asked how strategies and patterns of investigation and enforcement affect the outcome of cases – or indeed, their very existence as cases – which then provide the official account and statistics of detection and established infringement. For instance, is there a tendency on the part of enforcement agencies to focus attention on particular sectors of economic activity? Or is there a domino effect, whereby evidence in relation to one cartel leads easily to evidence of involvement in another, so confining enforcers' attention to familiar actors and familiar markets ('usual suspects')?

Underlying the whole discussion is the fundamental question of how the terms 'repeat offending' and 'recidivism' are understood and being used. What counts as an offence and when is it repeated, so that recidivism has occurred? There is surprisingly little discussion in standard criminological literature of this definitional issue. Indeed, there is some imprecision of language, which slips in an interchangeable way between 'repeat', 'persistent' and 'habitual' offending, and dictionaries and handbooks of criminology have little under the heading 'recidivism'. The idea seems largely taken for granted. And it may be that in certain contexts there is less need to agonise over definition. An individual house burglar carrying out the same kind of burglary sequentially on a number of separate occasions might seem self-evidently a recidivist house burglar. But in the context of cartel offending the matter is complicated by issues of agency and actor identity, diversity of role, temporal measurement, market definition, and continuity and discontinuity – all partly associated as well with the problem of cartel definition referred to already in Chapter 2.

Some of these complications may be represented and ordered in the following tabular scheme. In Table 6.4 below the first column lists a number of crucial *elements* of a recidivist situation: (a) an action (b) repeated a number of times

---

26   European Commission, *Guidelines on the Method for Setting Fines* (2006) OJ C210/2.

(c) within a particular period (d) described or qualified in a particular way (e) by a particular actor (or more generically, the elements of act, number, time frame, offence description, and agency).

The second column provides some idea of the *function* of each element within the overall concept of recidivism, for instance the act as an indicator of actor resistance or recalcitrance, or the time frame as a meaningful 'window' for the measurement of recidivist behaviour.

The third column lists possible facts as *evidence* of each element. For instance, in relation to the act, whether a reported act would suffice, or whether it is necessary to have a formally alleged act (a 'charge') or legally established

Table 6.4   How to identify an instance of cartel recidivism (corporate)

Act	Measure of sanction failure? measure of actor's fall from grace? measure of actor recalcitrance? measure of actor resilience?	Report of act? Initiation of formal process (charge)? Infringement formally established (conviction)? Admission of act but no formal action taken?	Probative value of evidence associated with the act
Repetition number	Measure of confirmed recalcitrance? Occasional, opportunistic but not determined repetition?	Two or more? Frequency and regularity (pattern)?	Significance of number of repeated act and spread of the number over time
Time frame	Length of time for measurement as a 'window' of recidivism?	Start date / close date	Relation to changing market circumstances, and evolving regulatory environment?
Offence definition	Same offence?	Market definition (related or distinct cartel)? Type of cartel strategy? Continuous or stuttering cartel? Site of legal enforcement (jurisdiction)?	Specificity of offence definition
Identity of actor (agency)	Same actor?	Conglomerates and groups of companies? Mergers? Successor companies and lost companies?	Existential questions of identity, legal personality, vicarious role, representation, and agency

202   *Cartel Criminality*

and proven act ('conviction'). Or in relation to the time frame, it needs to be determined what may be taken as the starting and finishing dates of the period of survey and measurement.

Finally, the fourth column provides some idea of the *factors to be taken into account* in deciding on a definition or choice of act, number, time frame, offence and actor.

The table demonstrates a range of variable factors which may occur in an alleged cartel recidivism situation, which may then bedevil a discussion of whether there is a convincing claim of repeat offending as distinct from a complex pattern of different offending. Such discussion may then lead to the question of whether it is possible to talk about degrees of recidivism, based on some scale or calculation of the *intensity of the recidivist activity*. Alternatively, a closer examination of actual further anti-competitive behaviour may demonstrate such a diversity of activity and circumstances as to render any description of the activity *as repetition* meaningless.

Take the following three examples as possible instances of recidivist behaviour.

Example One: Intense Repetition

Ten legally established and proven violations of the same law within the same jurisdiction by the same one company over a period of 10 years in the same market and employing the same anti-competitive strategies.

Example Two: Oblique Repetition

One further legally established violation after an interval of 10 years in another jurisdiction in a related market by a successor company following a merger five years previously, using different anti-competitive strategies.

Example Three: Doubtful Repetition

One reported but not legally proven anti-competitive act using a different strategy in a different jurisdiction within a period of one year in a different market carried out by a subsidiary company of the original actor.

Each of the above examples could qualify as some kind of repeat offending, but it is clear from of a reading of each in turn that they tell different stories of continuing cartel behaviour. At the least, it should become clear that it is not easy to talk in terms of a single, monolithic concept of cartel recidivism. This point should be borne in mind when engaging in any critical or evaluative discussion of cartel activity and dealing with any assertion of 'recidivist' behaviour. What does it mean, more precisely to make such an assertion and are those involved in such discussion using the terminology in the same or a consistent way? A glance at the existing literature and legal practice would suggest that there is much imprecision and lack of clarity and consistency in cartel recidivist discussion and readers therefore need to be careful in their understanding of such discussion. For example, in their recent paper 'Recidivism Eliminated',[27] Werden, Hammond and Barnett open their argument by quoting the Compact OED definition: 'in ordinary usage, 'recidivism' means 'relapsing into crime'' (a broad definition). They then comment that Connor[28] changes his definition quickly in his same paper from 'having been sanctioned previously for the same offence' to 'being convicted a second time no matter when or where the earlier violation took place' (i.e. to include contemporaneous violations). Or, to take another example, the European Commission's 2006 Fining Guidelines[29] defines 'repeated infringement' (for purposes of quantifying sanctions) as continuing or repeating 'the same or a similar infringement' after a finding has been made that the undertaking in question violated the same rule. There the concepts of 'continuing or repeating', and 'same or similar' raise issues of precise understanding and interpretation. And Wils notes that the Commission does not use the term 'recidivism', perhaps out of caution regarding the use of criminal law vocabulary in the context of an administrative procedure.[30]

Market diversion

Another relevant feature of cartel activity and cartel regulation is the fact that many larger companies will be acting in a number of markets and so may be involved in cartel activities in different markets, either contemporaneously or sequentially. This is particularly true in the context of significant international cartels, as has been illustrated in some of the biographies presented in Chapter 5 above. Also, international cartels will operate in a number of geographical markets and may over the course of time extend or retract their operations geographically, for either business or legal reasons, and this again is evident from some of the biographies. Companies therefore may enter or withdraw from both product markets and geographical markets, and cartel operations may similarly expand and contract in that way.

'Market diversion' is used here as a term to indicate the removal of cartel operations or a company's activity from certain geographical or product markets, and may in certain circumstances be considered as evidence of the impact, actual or potential, of anti-cartel sanctions. For instance, it may be remembered that the Japanese company Bridgestone announced, after being sanctioned for its

---

27 Note 25 above.
28 Note 23 above.
29 Note 26 above.
30 Note 24 above.

involvement in the Marine Hose Cartel, that it would withdraw from the marine hose market, as an act of contrition.[31] It is also evident that apprehensive cartelists may avoid, or 'carve out', the American market or at least ensure that they do not have any meetings on US territory,[32] being aware of the higher enforcement risks within the US jurisdiction. Or, again, it may be reasonable to assume that once a cartel has been apprehended and sanctioned in a particular market that companies would be wary of repeating their behaviour there since that market would now be well within the regulatory 'radar'. In such ways, diversion of cartel activity from particular markets may be seen as an indicator of the impact of sanctions.

Clarke and Evenett carried out an interesting study[33] of possible diversion of this kind in relation to the international Vitamins Cartel dealt with by the Department of Justice and the European Commission in the 1990s. Drawing upon the legally established evidence of the Cartel's activities, they examined a possible correlation between trade flow and sales within the Cartel's overall operation and the legal jurisdictions covered by the cartel activity, according to whether such jurisdictions were perceived to have stronger or weaker competition enforcement regimes, according to evidence of 'active' anti-cartel enforcement. They concluded that, after the formation of the Cartel, 'exports from countries where the cartel conspirators' headquarters were located to those nations in Asia, Western Europe, and Latin America that did not have active cartel enforcement regimes tended to rise in value more than in those nations that had such regimes'.[34] Their overall conclusion then was that 'strong cartel enforcement regimes have a deterrent value'.[35] But it has to be remembered that the deterrent impact then results in diversion rather than eradication of the activity, and such relocation of criminal business is a familiar phenomenon of crime control.[36] Moreover, as Harding has commented: 'in the final analysis such research findings also say something about the resilience of cartelists and their canny and adaptive strategies in the face of legal control'.[37] According to that argument, enforcement and sanctions do have a certain kind of impact, but the latter will include some intelligent and informed

---

31 See Chapter 5, p. 137. Bridgestone's action here is open to interpretation. This was a small part of its total business and there may have been other economic incentives for this move.

32 This was evident for instance from the 'Lysine Tapes', when preference was expressed for cartel meetings in 'safe' jurisdictions. Nonetheless, even with such awareness, risks of this kind may still be taken, as is evident from the examples of both the Marine Hose Cartel, meeting in Houston, and the Lysine Cartel, meeting in Florida and Hawaii.

33 Julian L. Clarke and Simon J. Evenett, 'The Deterrent Effects of National Antitrust Laws: Evidence from the International Vitamins Cartel', 48 (2003) *The Antitrust Bulletin* 689.

34 Ibid., at p. 692.

35 Ibid., at p. 718.

36 See Nicole Stelle Garnett, 'Relocating Disorder', 91 (2005) *Virginia Law Review* 1075.

37 Harding, 'Cartel Deterrence', note 17 above, at p. 367.

offender reaction, which is as much, or more, a matter of business exploitation rather than being awed by the prospect of even criminal law sanctions.

That last observation leads naturally in the final area of this discussion – the phenomenon of 'enforcement gaming' and business 'capture' of the regulatory process.

Enforcement gaming

There is a growing perception that experienced, aware and sophisticated business actors, rather than being very apprehensive or deterred by the prospect of legal sanctions in relation to cartel activities, may recognise some profit-making and business opportunities in the process of legal enforcement, especially through the exploitation of leniency programmes which have become such a widespread and significant feature of anti-cartel law enforcement. For instance, Wils has commented:

> Successful cartels tend to be sophisticated organisations, capable of learning. It is thus safe to assume that cartel participants will try to adapt their organisation to leniency policies, not only so as to minimise the destabilising effect, but also, where possible, to exploit leniency policies to facilitate the creation and maintenance of cartels. This raises the question whether there could be features of leniency programmes that risk being exploited to perverse effects.[38]

Moreover, Sokol's research carried out in the US, and drawing upon a practitioner survey, confirms the reality of some strategic use of leniency programmes by firms engaged in cartel activity. Sokol reports from his survey that:

> Nearly all practitioners stated that the strategic use of leniency (strategic in the sense that the leniency program may be used to punish rivals and in some cases even help to enforce collusion) is a reality and the only issue was the frequency and severity of the strategic gaming. Over half of the interviewees found that strategic leniency was significant.[39]

It may be, then, that another aspect of the impact of regulation and the use of sanctions in this context, is an unintended and unwelcome (from a regulatory perspective) 'reverse exploitation' or capture of the process of enforcement by firms subject to the regulatory process as a kind of business opportunity. Beaton-

---

38 Wouter P.J. Wils, *Efficiency and Justice in European Antitrust Enforcement* (Hart Publishing, 2008), at p. 137. The term 'perverse' here is used from a legal perspective; this may not be the business view of the matter.

39 Daniel Sokol, 'Cartels, Corporate Compliance, and What Practitioners Really Think about Enforcement', 78 (2012) *Antitrust Law Journal* 201, at p. 212.

Wells, Edwards and Harding[40] have listed a number of possible strategies in relation to leniency programmes which may be used in this way:

1. Enter the cartel in the full knowledge of the legal risks but also of the possible availability of immunity from most legal sanctions through a leniency application, and log this as a future business calculation.
2. The cartel is not working well and an important factor is the lukewarm or untrustworthy attitude of other participants – the latter need to be 'disciplined'. The lesson is given, or may be understood as a threat, by ending the cartel through reporting the other members, who then stand to be sanctioned by the competition authority.[41]
3. The cartel is not working well for economic or market factor reasons and might just as well be terminated. If this is done by reporting the cartel, then the whistle blowing member gains an economic advantage at the expense of the other erstwhile participants.
4. A variant of such strategic internal cartel busting – the cartel defector first cheats on the cartel, for instance by expanding production or sales beyond the agreed quota, and then reports the cartel and gains immunity, and so a double business gain (in American parlance, 'cheat and squeal').
5. In the context of firms operating in a number of cartels in related ('multiple') markets, the decision is taken to report the cartel in one less significant market as a sacrifice, with the intention of diverting the regulators' attention from the other markets and perhaps also tying up the regulatory resources ('jam the process') in that one reported case.[42]
6. In those situations in which a leniency programme provides substantial discounts on fines for later co-operation, when additional valuable evidence is provided by cartel members other than the successful immunity applicant ('also-rans'), there may be an incentive not to report the cartel and forgo the immunity prize, but with the consolation that, if the cartel is reported, there may be the opportunity to gain from later fine

40   Caron Beaton-Wells, Jennifer Edwards and Christopher Harding, 'Leniency and Criminal Sanctions in Anti-Cartel Enforcement: Happily Married or Uneasy Bedfollows?', in Caron Beaton-Wells (ed.), *The Leniency Religion: Anti-Cartel Enforcement in a Contemporary Age* (Hart Publishing, 2015).

41   As Neyrinck explains: 'In the most classic example, the ringleader harbouring evidence of the participation of other cartel members, will use it to threaten reluctant firms that have no other choice than complying with the cartel rule or suffer the administrative sanction triggered by the ringleader that has applied for leniency in the meantime'. Norman Neyrinck, 'Granting Incentives, Deterring Collusion: The Leniency Policy', Working Paper 2/2009, Institut D'Etudes Juridiques Européennes (IEJE), p. 15.

42   Leslie M. Marx et al., 'Antitrust Leniency with Multi-Product Colluders', Working Paper, March 2014, at p. 26: 'Firms might create sacrificial cartels in minor products in order to protect cartels in more valuable products from the threat that a cartel member might apply for leniency'.

discounts or fine reductions on appeal.[43] Keep the cartel going, and bank on a later discount as an also-ran.[44]

7. The cartel is formed on the understanding that it may well be sensible to close it down at a future point for economic reasons. The cartel members are co-cartelists in a number of related markets. It may be agreed at the outset that reporting the matter can be a profitable way to end the arrangement, provided that each party is able to take its turn in being the whistle blower in different markets. In this way leniency programmes become a kind of market, and in advance the market may be rigged or divided out in a kind of sharing arrangement, when each participant is allocated a place on a kind of leniency application rota. This would be a kind of cartel within the cartel.

8. A final option may be to play at being an old-school secretive cartelist and guard the evidence of own involvement well enough to feel secure that, whatever is reported by others elsewhere, it will be insufficient to implicate that company's participation.[45]

As those authors note, actual evidence of cartel recidivism and of serial leniency applications, although circumstantial, would tend to corroborate a significant possibility of such strategic exploitation of leniency programmes.

A short survey of EU legal proceedings against cartels over the past 30 years reveals an interesting profile of corporate repeat players as defendants and successful immunity applicants. Consider, for instance, the record of the following companies over the period 2001–2012, and all broadly speaking operating in the chemicals/pharmaceutical markets in Table 6.5:

---

43   This would be a good possibility in the EU system for instance, where the leniency programme provides for a number of discounts in return for later co-operation and also a good prospect of fine reduction on appeal when the sufficiency of evidence is legally challenged.

44   Neyrinck, note 41 above, at p. 13, describes this as 'an ex-ante pro-collusive effect': 'The danger is that enterprises may not apply for leniency if they know that a substantial reduction in fines would still be available later, in the hope that the cartel will not collapse at all'.

45   A tactic which served a number of the companies implicated in the Air Cargo Cartel well, when they decided to sit tight, admit nothing, and eventually it was not possible to prove the case against them, while other companies paid to some extent through their own discount-inspired admissions. The Commission dropped the charges against 11 carriers and a consultancy firm for insufficient evidence – see Press Release IP/10/1487, 9 November 2010.

Table 6.5   Serial cartelists and leniency applicants[46]

AKZO Nobel (Netherlands): dealt with in relation to nine cartels, complete immunity in three and fine reductions in four of these (a 'gain' in seven out of nine)

Aventis (France): dealt with in relation to five cartels, complete immunity in three and fine reductions in two of these (a 'gain' in five out of five)

Bayer (Germany): dealt with in relation to four cartels, complete immunity in two and fine reductions in two of these (a 'gain' in four out of four)

Degussa (Germany): dealt with in relation to three cartels, complete immunity in two and fine reduction in one of these (a 'gain' in three out of three)

Chemtura (US): dealt with in relation to two cartels, complete immunity in two (a 'gain' in two out of two)

Hoffmann-La Roche (Switzerland): dealt with in relation to thirteen cartels, fine reductions in nine of these (a 'gain' in nine out of thirteen)

BASF (Germany): dealt with in relation to eleven cartels, fine reductions in nine of these (a 'gain' in nine out of eleven)

Source: Commission cartel decisions, *Official Journal of the EU*; European Court Reports

At the very least this data suggests a cohort of experienced corporate cartelists in a position to respond to and even manipulate the regulatory system, as evidenced in a successful track record in gaining the benefits of leniency and 'co-operative' fine reduction. Such strategic behaviour is unlikely to be characteristic of all cartels everywhere, but may well be feasible in the case of larger firms, operating in international markets, attuned to the risks of regulation, and able to draw upon expert legal guidance within or without their organisation.

A summary on method

Any exercise of measuring or assessing the impact or effect of sanctions therefore has to be set within a considered frame of time and awareness, and to decide upon the relevant responsible actors as the subject of enforcement. Then account should be taken, in this context, of certain crucial modalities of reception of the sanctions by these subjects: the sensitivity or susceptibility of the actor; any repetition of the conduct; diversion into other areas or markets; and any responsive exploitation.

---

46   Beaton-Wells, Edwards and Harding, note 40 above.

Chapter 7
Desistance, Recalcitrance and Cartelist After-Life

ADM [Archer Daniels Midland] actually appears to fit a model of culture as a relatively homogeneous, top-down determinant of individual behaviour. In anthropology, that model has rarely proved useful in analyzing elements of complex industrial societies (such as corporate culture ...) and its utility in dealing with even small-scale, face-to-face societies has also been called into question. The fact that it does work here is unusual, so legal reformers should draw no general inferences about their ability to repair other dysfunctional corporate cultures by making discrete structural changes.[1]

'Hey, I wasn't guilty. And I wasn't about to beg for mercy. Sure, I was sorry all this happened. Sorry that I had ever met with Sir Anthony Tennant. Sorry that I hadn't listened to my closest partners when they warned me about Dede Brooks. Sorry that Judge Daniels and the Justice Department had made it impossible for me to get a fair trial.'[2]

'How has the experience affected you? Do you think it has changed you'?

I don't actually think it's changed me that all that much because I came to terms with it very quickly ... I hope it hasn't affected me too much. It's probably made me much more aware of areas of the world that I knew nothing about ... I hope I'm more tolerant of other peoples' foibles and mistakes and I do believe that there's always two sides to a story, nearly always, and I try not to rush the judgment on anything I read or see. So I hope it's made me more tolerant and I hope it hasn't affected me too much, I hope I haven't changed too much. I was reasonably happy with the bloke I was before ...[3]

Whether time really does heal all wounds, as the old saying goes, may seriously be called into question in the light of present dispute. This case has been occupying the European administrative and judicial authorities for over twenty years now. Generations of lawyers have worked on it. Documents have disappeared and the court proceedings have dragged on for years.[4]

---

1 John M. Conley and William M. O'Barr, 'Crime and Custom in Corporate Society: A Cultural Perspective on Corporate Misconduct', 60 (1997) *Law and Contemporary Problems* 5, at p. 15.

2 Alfred Taubman, *Threshold Resistance: The Extraordinary Career of a Luxury Retailer Pioneer* (Harper Business, 2007), at p. 170.

3 Bryan Allison: An interview of Bryan Allison by Michael O'Kane, 'Does Prison Work for Cartelists?: The View from behind Bars', 56 (2011) *The Antitrust Bulletin* 483, at p. 499.

4 Opinion of Advocate General Kokott in Case C-109/10 P, *Solvay v Commission* (2011) ECR I-1044, at point 1.

Discrete changes and dysfunctional corporate cultures

What may be gleaned, then, from a biographical reading of a number of legal proceedings taken against significant international cartels,[5] regarding the effect of those proceedings and the impact of sanctions which had been imposed on companies and on individuals? As the quotations above will show, the evidence is varied. Is there strong evidence of dissuasion and desistance, or is there strong evidence of cartel resilience and recalcitrance? The answer, based upon the material used in this study, is surely that there is strong evidence of neither and that it is difficult to generalise one way or another. In short, the outcomes are ambivalent, and the message to be drawn from analysis of this material is that ready and quick assumptions that sanctions generally work as intended, or do not do so, are unwarranted. The effects of enforcement and the impact of sanctions are variable, and it is the need to appreciate and understand such variables that is the main lesson for policy-makers, enforcement agencies and lawyers. As Conley and O'Barr argue: general inferences should not be drawn regarding the ability to repair dysfunctional corporate culture through discrete remedial action.

To open the discussion: taking a broad comparative view of the international landscape of enforcement, it may be seen that much depends upon jurisdiction, and consequently on the policy and culture of legal enforcement across jurisdictions. If it is asked, assuming some degree of apprehension and prosecution of cartel activity, what would be the main consequences of enforcement action in different countries and jurisdictions, the following observations may be confidently made:

- In the US, companies and individuals may expect to confront a powerful and persuasive process of negotiation and being steered towards a 'settlement' and a deal, which would involve possible prison terms for individuals, large criminal fines and later, a significant pay-out to settle civil claims for damages – in other words, a determined, well-developed and hard-hitting process of law enforcement where the agenda is set by the enforcer.
- In Europe, companies may expect lengthy investigation and the possibility of large financial penalties, but not to be treated as criminal, and at the same time the opportunity to engage in lengthy appeals and rights-based arguments, so that in the end, the day (or more exactly days) in court may provide the most notable outcome, while individuals tend to fade from the picture.
- In those east Asian countries with active competition law enforcement, companies may expect to suffer financial penalties, but not to be treated as criminals, and to be able to shrug off the enforcement action with a feeling of 'business as before'.

---

5   In much of the following discussion in this chapter there will be frequent reference to material and facts reported in the accounts presented in Chapter 5 above.

Taking briefly for the moment some of the examples from the biographical accounts presented in Chapter 5, a comparison of the eventual fate of Solvay in the EU system regarding its involvement in the Soda Ash Cartel (no sanction despite a clear and significant infringement) is very different from the that of a number of the East Asian companies subject to the US jurisdiction in relation to their involvement in the Marine Hose, Lysine and LCD Panels Cartels (large fines, some prison terms, and civil claims for compensation); or the outcome for the individuals involved in the Art House Auctions Cartel, which was very different for the two Americans, Taubman and Brooks, on the one hand, and the two British executives, Tennant and Davidge, on the other hand, the latter benefiting from both their extra-territorial location and the immunity which had been exploited under the leniency programme. Another comparison: despite the evident aggressive and bullying behaviour of a some of the individual executives in the Pre-Insulated Pipes Cartel, there was never any real prospect of their personal liability (criminal or otherwise) being established in the European context, whereas some of the individuals involved in the Marine Hose Cartel experienced the full rigour of the US criminal justice system, from handcuffed arrest to serving prison terms and much else in between.

This variability of outcome emerges as a central fact in the contemporary story of anti-cartel enforcement. It is a fact and feature of the process which should be borne in mind when reading statements such as that of DoJ official Scott Hammond in the title of one of his public presentations – 'from Hollywood to Hong Kong, criminal antitrust enforcement is coming to a city near you'.[6] As a description of the spread of cartel criminalisation across jurisdictions, that statement was accurate enough, but should not be understood literally as an inevitable result for all cartelists: criminalisation in the strict sense remains limited to certain jurisdictions, the probability of apprehension remains controversial but probably limited, and the imposition of criminal sanctions, especially imprisonment, remains variable and dependent on the happenstance of geography, jurisdiction, legal culture and leniency programmes. It would not be far-fetched to imagine an astute legal adviser saying in effect to a would-be cartelist: 'carve out the US, then bear in mind the possible right moment to apply for immunity under leniency programmes, and you should be quite safe'.

Desistance and recalcitrance

What is the evidence of cartel desistance – not engaging further in cartel activity – in the aftermath of enforcement, following an investigation, legal establishment of a cartel violation, and the imposition of sanctions? In one sense, examining the market in which such cartels had been operating, there is barely any evidence of

---

6   Scott D. Hammond, 'From Hollywood to Hong Kong: Criminal Antitrust Enforcement is Coming to a City near You', Address, 9 November 2001, Chicago.

a recurrence of cartel activity, so that would seem to be a positive enforcement outcome. It may be that companies do sometimes re-establish cartels in such markets and are able to keep the matter secret, but that is unlikely. In particular, such markets will be for some time 'under the radar' in that competition authorities and other market actors will be alert to signs of re-cartelisation. That is not to say that cartelist resilience and recalcitrance in that context should be dismissed entirely. It will be recalled for instance that in the Pre-Insulated Pipes Cartel, even after the Commission's investigation in June of 1995, the cartel operations continued to the end of that year.[7] In that instance, therefore, there was some evidence of determined recalcitrance, based on an awareness of the profit involved in continuing the cartel as long as possible, and that outweighing enforcement risks.

Overall, however, desistance in the immediate market is to be expected, and that appears to have happened in the cases reported in the biographies. Sometimes, companies leave the market altogether, as happened when Yokohama, apparently in contrition, announced that it would leave the marine hose market, and when ICI subsequently disposed of its interest in the soda ash market. Having said that, there may of course be other economic or business reasons for either not reviving a cartel or for leaving a market. One important question in this context is that of the 'dying' cartel and the possibility that enforcement takes place in relation to cartels which were already failing, or had come to an end some time before. It is clear from the biographies that sustaining a cartel may be difficult and few of the examples there involved arrangements which were stable and certain (perhaps with the exception of the Soda Ash Cartel). Bryan Allison stated later[8] that he thought that the Marine Hose Cartel would have ended in any case and that he was never fully secure about the commitment of the Asian partners. There were clear signs of fractiousness and dissension in some of the Cartels – for instance, in the case of LCD Panels and Pre-Insulated Pipes. Cartel instability is a well-established fact and it is received wisdom on the part of economists that many cartels will have a limited lifetime.[9] In such a context, it may not be warranted to assume that enforcement action will be the main determinant of cartel closure, and there is a worrying thought that enforcement efforts tend to engage with doomed cartels.

There is a complex and uncertain relationship between cartel termination and the operation of sanctions and leniency programmes. There are some basic facts of life: cartel instability, cartel proliferation in related markets, and the difficulty of legally proving cartel activity. The advent of leniency had an impact on instability,

---

7   In full awareness of the risks, as was evident from the note which advised destruction of evidence – 'EU case looks bad, Be careful for Christ's sake'. See the discussion in Chapter 5 above, at p. 150–51.

8   See the O'Kane interview, note 3 above, at p. 492.

9   Studies of cartel sustainability have suggested that the mean duration of discovered cartels is between five and eight years. See, for instance, Valerie Y. Suslow, 'Cartel Contract Duration: Empirical Evidence from Interwar International Cartels', 14 (2005) *Industrial and Corporate Change* 705.

but also raised a business opportunity – of reporting, and triggering investigation in related markets, so leading to the 'busting' of cartels in a number of jurisdictions, some of which may have been failing or even finished. In such a situation, it is less convincing to claim that it is the prospect of sanctions as such which leads to cartel termination, but rather a combination of economic circumstance and business exploitation of the sanctions. A study by Andreas Stephan concluded that a significant number of leniency cases in Europe related to cartels which had failed or were failing at the time of reporting.[10] He argues for instance, from an examination of the operation of the European Commission's 1996 leniency notice in the context of the chemicals industry that:

> There is also evidence that these infringements had largely failed before leniency applications were made, because of prevailing conditions in the market. Rather than inducing the self-reporting of successful cartels, the notice may have largely attracted leniency applications from firms seeking to put their competitors at a disadvantage following the failure of a cartel. Even in the United States, although some investigations (for example, Lysine and Auction Houses) were opened well before the cartels ceased operating, we know that in others (such as Methylgucamine and Sorbates) the investigation was opened after the cartel failed.[11]

And to take a more recent example: the Heat Stabilisers Cartel was dealt with by a Commission decision in November 2009,[12] and concerned cartel activity in two related markets, identified as having taken place between 1987 and 2000, and then investigated by the Commission in February 2003, following a report and immunity application by one of the participating companies, Chemtura. Such argument and circumstantial evidence casts doubt on the dissuasive impact of sanctions, either generally or via the medium of leniency. That is not to say, however, that there may be no justification in retributive or restorative terms for the application of sanctions in relation to dead cartels.

---

10   Andreas Stephan, 'An Empirical Assessment of the European Leniency Notice, 5 (2008) *Journal of Competition Law and Economics* 537. See also an earlier version of this paper: Andreas Stephan, 'An Empirical Assessment of the 1996 Leniency Notice', University of East Anglia Centre for Competition Policy Working Paper 05-10.

11   Stephan, 'An Empirical Assessment of the European Leniency Notice', note 10 above, at pp. 552–3. On the economic difficulties leading to cartel termination: 'A close examination of the Commission's decisions and industry literature reveals a number of difficulties that had largely undermined the chemicals cartels before self-reporting. These included new entry from China, arbitrage, decline, overcapacity and rising costs, barriers to entry, substitutability and distrust, the Asia crisis of the 1990s, and the effect of mergers and acquisitions.' Ibid., at p. 548.

12   Commission Press Release IP/09/1695, 11 November 2009. Yet again there was a strong admonition from Commissioner Neelie Kroes about repeat offenders, and companies 'learning the hard way'.

But there may be other and perhaps more significant indicators of either desistance or recalcitrance after the event of enforcement, if corporate conduct is examined in related and other markets. As noted already, many large businesses will operate in a number of markets, and again it is clear from the biographies that some companies are likely to cartelise in a number of markets, either contemporaneously or sequentially. Indeed, there is a well-attested enforcement pattern of investigation and cartel busting in one market leading to evidence and then similar action in relation to the same companies operating in related markets,[13] and indeed this is the basis of the US Department of Justice's 'amnesty plus' strategy.[14] From the biographies there is significant evidence of both related and repeated cartel behaviour across a number of markets after being the subject of enforcement action: for instance, in the case of Solvay, ICI, Asea Brown Boveri (ABB), and Samsung,[15] suggesting a habit which is not easily dissuaded by a single or even a number of instances of enforcement. There is also, in some of these cases, evidence of later involvement in what may be considered related illegal activity, especially of the kind covered by the US Foreign Corrupt Practices legislation, such as bribery of public officials – for instance, in the case of Trelleborg, Bridgestone and ABB.[16] Moreover, in the European context, a number of Commission decisions and statements by successive Commissioners for Competition refer to the established recidivism of some 'usual suspects' – Neelie Kroes for instance expressing her shock that 'companies like ICI and Arkema have been fined once again' and their managements needing a 'wake up call'.[17] As noted in the previous chapter, it is possible to argue about the definition of recidivist companies, but it is clear that a body like the European Commission has its own perception of continuing repeat offending and acts upon that in its fining practice, and the evidence does suggest at least that among a number of large companies there is a culture of unlawful business practice which is not easily susceptible to dissuasion through the application of legal sanctions.

Another category of suggestive evidence which emerges from a biographical survey concerns involvement in later anti-cartel proceedings and exploitation of appellate procedures and leniency programmes. For example, from the biographies, both ABB and Samsung were at a later date successful immunity applicants in relation to other cartel proceedings (ABB twice and Samsung once).[18] This suggest an intriguing possibility of related and repeated collusion, often with the same partners, but also serial desertion and betrayal, to gain the benefit (and

---

13   Again, see the discussion by Stephan, note 10 above.

14   That is, if already under investigation, report on a cartel in another market and then gain immunity there and some discount in relation to penalties imposed for involvement in the immediate cartel.

15   See Chapter 5 above, at pp. 118–19, pp. 150–51 and p. 184.

16   Ibid., at p. 136 and p. 154.

17   See Chapter 5 above, p. 123.

18   Ibid., at p. 152 and p. 186.

economic profit) of leniency. In the European context, many of the companies discussed in the biographies first cooperated with the Commission and then were involved in appeals to the EU Courts in order to obtain fine reductions, and with a fair degree of success.[19] Table 6.5 in Chapter 6[20] demonstrates an impressive record of serial cartel involvement accompanied by serial appeal and leniency applications, resulting in a considerable economic gain – no fines or reduced fines. In another notable example, Solvay engaged for 20 years in successive appeals to gain eventually the complete removal of its fine. At the least, this would indicate a resilient culture of cartel fight-back, whereby what is gained in the first place through the operation of the cartel may then be supplemented by gains from the enforcement process. In particular, a canny decision to join and stay with a cartel for the optimum period, coupled with a deft desertion and reporting of the arrangement and gain from immunity could prove to be profitable business all the way through.

Longer-term change in corporate culture and practice: Disappearing delinquents

There is, therefore, from the record, a good body of evidence to suggest an attitude of corporate recalcitrance – a defiance of official policy and legal sanctions, and a determination to cartelise repeatedly in different markets (not necessarily in the same market but across an economic sector). But a caveat has to be entered regarding that reading of the story, that it is history up to a point in time, and that there is a continuing story, which may cast some different light on the matter. In particular, if the European survey is taken beyond 2010, there is an interesting disappearance from the cartel enforcement arena of a number of usual suspect large companies: AkzoNobel, Bayer, Solvay, BASF, Degussa, Arkema (all broadly in the chemicals market), Pilkington Glass, Asahi Glass and Saint Gobain (in the glass market), ADM and Yokohama, have no longer been caught in the antitrust radar. Is this, after a number of years of repeated infringement and enforcement, evidence of eventual or 'long haul' desistance?

The case of AkzoNobel may be considered in more detail. As will be evident from the earlier discussion, AkzoNobel is a large multinational company with an impressive record of cartel activity coupled with leniency applications and appeals. This is clearly demonstrated in the record of legal process for the period 2001–2012 as laid out in Table 6.4. AkzoNobel's cartel activity also spread over

---

19   Another incentive to engage in the appellate process may be an advantage to be gained regarding any possible claims for damages. The latter cannot be dealt with by national courts until the infringement decision (including the imposition of fines) have been confirmed in the event of any appeal to the European Courts, and that may prompt earlier out-of-court settlement to the cartelists' advantage.

20   Chapter 6, at p. 208.

a number of related markets, often contemporaneously, and often with the same partners (what may be termed 'cartel cosying'). Figure 7.1 illustrates AkzoNobel's involvement in seven markets in the chemicals sector, most of them during the 1980s and 1990s and in each case also involving Degussa and Elf Aquitaine as regular partners.[21]

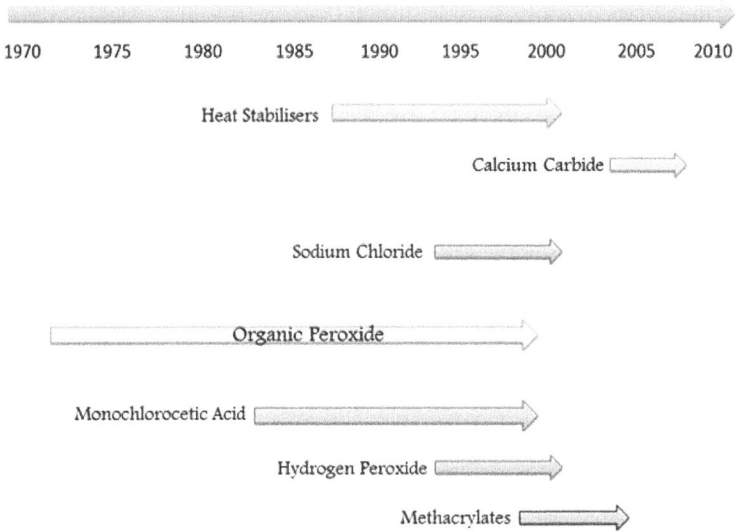

Figure 7.1   Cartel cosying in the chemicals sector

Akzo/Degussa/Elf Aquitaine

This, then, would seem to be evidence of a committed practice of cartelisation. But it should also be noted that most of this activity terminated by the turn of the century or early 2000s. There was a large amount of legal activity relating to these cartels after 2000, but that is partly a reflection of the typical duration of such proceedings, both the investigation and the appeals. Taking the nine cartels involving AkzoNobel in Table 6.5 in Chapter 6, most of these had terminated by the turn of the century:

---

21   See also Appendix One to this chapter for further examples of this 'cartel cosying' tendency in other economic sectors.

Table 7.1   End dates for AkzoNobel cartels

Cartel	End date
Heat Stabilisers	2000
Calcium Carbide	2007
Sodium Chlorate	2000
Hydrogen Peroxide	2000
Monochloroacetic Acid (MCAA)	1999
Choline Chloride	1998
Organic Peroxide	1999
Sodium Gluconate	1995
Acrylic Glass (ICI – inherited by AkzoNobel)	2002

The Calcium Carbide Cartel stands out as an exception, operating later, from 2004 until 2007. But, interestingly, it was reported to the Commission in 2006 by AkzoNobel, who then gained full immunity from what would otherwise have been one of the largest fines, notionally increased by 100 per cent on account of the company's strong recidivist record. One possible interpretation is that this was self-reporting on the part of a by then reformed company, although still beset by its earlier recidivist reputation and record, while some of the other participants were still determined cartelists – three of the other companies were inspired by the cartel to start another cartel in the related magnesium granulates market, actually adopting some of the mechanisms employed in the Calcium Carbide Cartel, such as a market sharing table referred to as the 'Bible'.[22]

There is one line of interpretation which views AkzoNobel as a reformed major cartelist. It appears to be absent from any cartel activity from the early 2000s, if Calcium Carbide is seen as a rogue involvement, reported by the company itself when it became aware of the participation. Significantly, at the start of the century the company proclaimed in strong terms a new compliance policy. In 2000 it introduced an internal Business Principles Program which offered to its employees and subsidiaries a 'one time amnesty' for breaches of business integrity, to be followed by a policy of zero tolerance. The company later stated that it was 'confident that [the programme] is well-established and implemented across the company's business'.[23] The company's *Competition Compliance Manual* also

---

22   Commission Press Release IP/09/1169, 22 July 2009.

23   Knottnerus, R., *AkzoNobel: Overview of Controversial Business Practices, 2008* (SOMO, 2009).

contains detailed advice on what kinds of communication and its content with trade rivals may or may not infringe competition rules.[24]

The apparent absence of AkzoNobel, and indeed also of other one-time usual suspects in the chemical sector from the cartel arena since about 2010, is therefore suggestive evidence of 'long haul' desistance, eventually coming one way or another to the view that 'enough is enough'. Against that interpretation should be set the possibility that the usual suspects are no longer on the scene because the scene, in the sense of the chemicals sector, has become tired or exhausted, both in terms of the possibilities of cartelisation and the scope for enforcement action. Or, another interpretation may be based on diversion of enforcement attention, in that competition authorities in both America and Europe have become interested in other sectors – for instance, automotive parts or information technology and communication – and turned their attention, and resources, to the possibility of rich enforcement pickings in those areas. In short, it is difficult to be categorical in seeking to explain the more recent indications in the chemicals sector and the apparent conduct of a significant player such as AkzoNobel. But, at the least, it would be worthwhile to maintain some observation of such usual suspect activity, to test the reality of these apparent recent trends of conduct.

Longer-term change: All in the past, but the song remains the same

This line of analysis, which considers some evidence of change in corporate business conduct and attitude towards regulatory norms alongside other evidence of continuing contest between regulators and corporate cartelists, may be taken a stage further, by briefly considering a hypothesis of systemic commitment to battle.

The basis of such a hypothesis would be, in the context of international and economically significant cartels, a conversion of top level management and parent companies to a more compliant culture in relation to competition governance and regulation (for instance, the surmise just above regarding AkzoNobel). If, for whatever reasons, that is happening to some extent, then how does that fit with an apparent continuing engagement on the legal battlefield. For instance, if in the case of Calcium Carbide, Akzo Nobel in a genuinely compliant manner voluntarily reported a rogue cartel activity from within its ranks, why was it necessary for the Commission to publicly castigate the company as a member of the cartel, and also significantly increase the amount of fine, which it would have had to pay if it had not gained immunity, on the ground of recidivist behaviour which was well in the past? Or again, if AkzoNobel had genuinely undergone a Damascene conversion at the turn of the century, why did the company continue to engage in the appeal procedure, challenging a number of aspects of the Commission's enforcement

---

24 http://www.akzonobel.com/system/images/AkzoNobel_Competition_Law_ Compliance_Manual.

procedure and fining decisions – in particular, its legally significant challenge[25] of the evolving EU doctrine on the liability of parent companies? And, thirdly, what was the motivation for AkzoNobel's reporting of the Calcium Carbide Cartel in 2006 – genuine contrition, or even revulsion towards the determined cartelism of the other partners, or on the other hand an opportunistic play for immunity and the economic and business gains which would flow from a successful immunity application – or perhaps a mix of both?

Once again, the evidence is ambivalent, and the difficulty in constructing a 'true' and fully informed narrative becomes apparent. But there may be then another narrative to present as a way of interpreting and making sense of the evidence – that, even if corporate actors change over time, they remain trapped in a system which has achieved its own momentum and established interests. It may be surmised, for instance, that regulators continue to chase even reformed cartelists because of the easier enforcement tally that may then be achieved, and also the large income which is generated by increasingly heavy fines. Equally, it may be surmised that companies continue to engage with leniency and the appellate process, not so much out of a disinterested commitment to clarification of law and policy, but because there may be further business gains in doing so, exploiting as it were the fruits of earlier and historical delinquency. And it may also be surmised that there is now a significant enterprise of corporate legal defence, so that for some law firms there are lucrative pickings from advising large companies of their rights in the context of competition governance and encouraging them to assert such rights. Such a narrative may appear cynical in its interpretation of events, but it would acknowledge the force of a systemic dynamic and of the complex of interests within that system. Such a narrative would deal in the concepts and theorisation of an 'anti-cartel enforcement *industry*' and 'business *capture* of regulation and enforcement'

Longer-term change: Crime followed by suicide,[26] aka cartel-bust followed by merger

There is another category of post-enforcement evidence which is worth some consideration, as an indicator of the impact of the anti-cartel enforcement process: the subsequent legal merger of corporate co-cartelists, or take-over of one by another, or transfer of part of a business from one to another. In the case of a merger this may be more dramatically and fancifully described as an instance of legal suicide in the wake of the enforcement action against illegal anti-competitive conduct, or another engaging metaphor is that of the former cartelist partners

---

25 Case C-97/08P, *AkzoNobel and others v Commission* (2009) ECR 1–8237.

26 The heading is inspired by the title of the classic criminological study by D.J. West, *Murder Followed by Suicide* (Harvard University Press, 1965). Homicide followed by suicide is a well-researched criminological phenomenon.

deciding to marry rather than 'sleep with the enemy'. Whatever, the description, it will be a significant outcome in terms of competition regulation, since it replaces the restriction of competition between actors who remain potential competitors with a complete removal of competition through the loss of that competing actor. Cartel strategies and mergers both aim to reduce horizontal competition, and although a merger does so more completely and finally, ironically in that perspective mergers have not attracted the kind of opprobrium now directed at cartels. Cartelisation and merger should be seen as possible alternative strategies, especially in the contexts of markets in economic difficulty, and the possibility that competing firms, having used a cartel and then suffered penalties for doing so, then decide to merge, is an important but under-investigated outcome. If it can be shown that the application of anti-cartel sanctions may lead to a merger, take-over, or transfer of business, and thereby a reduction of competition, then that is an outcome which should be taken on board in the design and application of such sanctions.

Mergers, take-overs and corporate restructuring have been particularly evident in the chemicals sector – notable examples involving cartelist usual suspects are the merger of Hoechst and Rhône-Poulenc in 1999 to form Aventis, the take-over of ICI by AkzoNobel in 2007, AkzoNobel's acquisition in 1999 of the European coatings business of BASF, and BASF's acquisition of Ciba in 2008. It is difficult to judge the relation between such corporate restructuring and any prior involvement in cartel activity, and the extent to which the latter experience of either collusion or sanctions relating to that collusion may steer companies towards merger and the like. But the possibility, and its implications for competition governance, are worth further investigation and reflection. There is also another kind of outcome, which has been discussed already in some of the earlier chapters – that subsequent changes in legal identity complicate the attribution of responsibility and the application of sanctions. A by now familiar example would be the attribution of ICI's cartel actions to its successor company AkzoNobel. On the one hand, changes in legal identity may be seen as a deft way of evading liability for proven illegal activity, while at the same time considerations of justice may be raised to argue against an easy transfer of liability to successor companies. In the context of international business and the operation of international cartels, corporate restructuring is a significant and frequent phenomenon, and a reminder that the kinds of action under investigation and the typical subject of sanctions are different from the typical acts and subjects of criminal law: in the domain of international cartels the assumptions of methodological individualism may not be easily warranted.

The individual as the target of sanctions: Facing the inferno, or business as usual?

It has become an established dogma of enforcement, especially in the context of leniency programmes, that individuals (being human) will be more susceptible to the deterrent impact of criminal law sanctions (especially serving a prison term) and for that reason should be targeted to ensure more effective enforcement.[27] It is argued that high-status and otherwise respectable business persons will genuinely fear the professional damage arising from large financial penalties and disqualification, the personal trauma of serving a prison sentence, and the damage to their careers following a criminal conviction. On first thoughts, these may seem fair assumptions, and there is now some opportunity to test such assumptions by examining the biographical record. But that particular record remains small, and by its nature tends to be anecdotal, and not easily accessible, and so does not encourage generalisation. Despite the increasing resort to criminalisation across jurisdictions, the actual prosecution of individuals and application of criminal law penalties, especially the severe option of actual imprisonment, remains limited.[28] In fact, from the biographical record presented here, the majority of the criminal law penalties experienced by individuals arise from the US criminal law system, whether the offenders are US nationals or come from elsewhere. The one notable instance of criminal sanctions in the UK (in the Marine Hose Cartel case) was 'piggy-backing' on enforcement in the US. And of course, as far as the EU enforcement is concerned, individuals are not the subject of sanctions and there is no direct enforcement of criminal law at that level. This part of the discussion is therefore very much a question of examining the impact of Sherman Act sanctions imposed on individual cartelists, and that is a relatively small sample.

But once again, the evidence suggests a narrative of variable impact, and it is certainly not a foregone conclusion that such a penal experience will be a traumatising, career-ending and life-changing experience ('the inferno'),[29] although undoubtedly in many respects an unpleasant experience, as may be clear from Michael O'Kane's interview of Bryan Allison.[30] Individual cartelists may face a range of sanctions, in particular: criminal conviction in itself (which may affect reputation and career opportunities), financial penalties, disqualification

---

27 See, for instance, Terry Calvani and Torello H. Calvani, 'Custodial Sanctions for Cartel Offences: An Appropriate Sanction in Australia?' 17 (2009) *Competition and Consumer Law Journal* 119 – 'Custodial sentences are the only sanction likely to provide sufficient deterrence' (at p. 135); Wouter P.J. Wils, 'Is Criminalization of EU Competition Law the Answer?', chapter 4 in Katalin J. Cseres, Maarten Pieter Schinkel and Floris O.W. Vogelaar (eds), *Criminalization of Competition Law Enforcement* (Edward Elgar, 2006): 'There is ample evidence, based in particular on the US experience, that imprisonment is a very effective deterrent for potential antitrust offenders' (at p. 83).

28 See Calvani and Calvani, note 26 above: the discussion there includes a brief survey of the experience of criminalisation and actual resort to criminal sanctions.

29 'To the businessman, however, prison is the inferno, and conventional risk-reward analysis breaks down when the risk is jail' – Arthur L. Liman, 'The Paper Label Sentences: Critique', 86 (1977) *Yale Law Journal* 619, at p. 630. 'Inferno' is also and more recently used by Gregory J. Werden, in 'Sanctioning Cartel Activity: Let the Punishment Fit the Crime', 5 (2009) *European Competition Journal* 19.

30 Note 3 above.

from certain business positions, and imprisonment. On the face of it, the personal impact of any of these will depend partly on individual circumstances such as social standing, financial resources and stage of career.

On the one hand, Diana Brooks' conventional career appeared to be over, she had to resign her Yale trustee position, and she endured a great deal of media attention, but on the other hand she avoided a prison term, and was able to retreat to the seclusion of a Florida mansion and was subsequently spotted bidding at New York auctions.[31] Ultimately, of course, reporting on these outcomes is a matter of description and interpretation, and writing in a newspaper article in 2001, Godfrey Barker stated:

> If she escapes jail – and orange trousers – there are still painful fines to be faced ...
> Brooks's standard of living has taken a tremendous tumble over the past year.
> The mansion in the Connecticut River valley has been sold and the Brooks family
> has decamped to Florida, where her husband, Michael, owns a house ... 'Get this
> clear', says a top Sotheby's man. 'Dian Brooks is now a convicted felon. She will
> never again hold a position of trust, in public life or in a private company. She will
> have to resign all her boards. She will not be able to vote'.[32]

How hard are such outcomes for a woman aged 51 with a successful career behind her? Would the missing autobiographical account provide some answer to that question?

The British Marine Hose cartelists faced the full force of US criminal law enforcement and the distinction of prison terms in the UK, yet Bryan Allison's interview transcript conveys an impression of thoughtful reflection rather than deep embitterment.[33] Alfred Taubman's published autobiographical account is defiant and far from repentant, and the very title of his self-justificatory and celebratory book, 'Threshold Resistance: The Extraordinary Career of a Luxury Retailing Pioneer', presumably happily agreed with his publishers, suggests the boastful self-satisfaction of an all-American hero. Indeed, any search for published summaries of Taubman's life and career will reveal accounts which make light of

---

31   See Chapter 5, above, at p. 176. There may be further interesting reflection on the role of Diana Brooks as a rare female cartelist in a senior corporate position (there appears to be only one other known example of a woman in a senior position in an international cartel: Maria Ullings, who, as senior vice-president of cargo sales and marketing at Martinair Cargo, was involved in the Air Cargo Cartel). Unlike Taubman, Brooks avoided a prison sentence, but this may be a reflection of her co-operation as much as her gender. Also note that the female cartelist, Fiona, in the ACCC film *The Marker*, avoids a prison term, but has to sell her house to pay the large fine.

32   Godfrey Barker, 'The Fall of Dede Brooks', *The Telegraph*, 6 January 2001.

33   Note 3 above.

or even do not mention his brush with the Sherman Act.[34] It is not clear that the outcome in Taubman's case corresponds with the perception of Bauer in 2004:

> The sight of A. Alfred Taubman, the extremely wealthy chairman of the board of Sotheby's, the world-famous auction house, convicted and sentenced, at the age of 78, to a one-year term of imprisonment and a substantial fine for participating in a price-fixing conspiracy, doubtless sent a message to other business executives about the risks and penalties for this kind of behaviour.[35]

The other celebrated and convicted American cartelist who has publicly discussed his penal experience is Mark Whitacre, the ADM whistle blower, but he is perhaps fairly categorised more as a maverick rather than typical as a cartelist. His born-again and reformed persona in later years[36] may not be a representative outcome, but does at least demonstrate that there can be much in life after serving a prison term as a cartelist, in terms of new career and even celebrity status.[37] Perhaps more representative would be the new career-path of Keith Packer, a British national who served a prison term in the US for his role in the Air Cargo Cartel, and later found himself very much in demand for advising at corporate compliance training sessions.[38] In fact, Packer's account of his own experience sheds some interesting light on some (good citizen) companies' efforts to inculcate awareness of and compliance with competition norms in their employees:

> Packer attended competition law training in October 2004 at a British Airways' auditorium, where he viewed Power-point presentations and various case studies. He said he had other business-related matters on his mind that day, and the fuel surcharge had already been in place since 2002 ... 'It's a very dry, boring subject for commercial people who have much higher priorities', he said. 'Looking back, I'm sure that if someone like me had stood up and brought it to life with real-life experience, then people like myself and others would have understood it better'.[39]

---

34   For instance, the present Wikipedia entry makes light of the Sherman Act conviction and sentence, and headlines the man as 'a real estate developer and philanthropist', while CBS News has headlined him as a 'legend in retailing'.

35   Joseph P. Bauer, 'Reflections on the Manifold Means of Enforcing the Antitrust Laws: Too Much, Too Little, or Just Right?', 16 (2004) *Loyola Consumer Law Review* 303, at p. 307.

36   See Chapter 5 above, at p. 165–6.

37   And perhaps some satisfaction in being played by actor Matt Damon in a Hollywood feature film.

38   Erik Larson, 'Ex-BA Executive Shares Prison Tales to Sway Violators', *Bloomberg*, 22 October 2010.

39   Ibid.

Again, the home social, business and legal culture of the sanctioned individual may be an important consideration. In the United States, it may be necessary to reinvent oneself, as in the case of Whitacre, or be able to fall back on other culturally favoured achievement, as in the case of Taubman. But in European and East Asian countries, the home culture may be more tolerant of the proven delinquency and even prove supportive of returning convicts from US prisons. As Harding and Joshua have commented:

> Anecdotal evidence that company executives fear imprisonment as an 'inferno' is balanced by different anecdotal evidence that such individuals may endure the experience in a robust fashion – in particular, there is significant evidence of this kind relating to the return of ex-cartelist prisoners to senior corporate roles and of the corporate support which may generally be given to such individuals who 'take the bullet for the team'.[40]

There is strong evidence especially of a supportive social and business culture in Japan. A recent account of individual experience is presented in the American publication *Automotive News*,[41] in the context of increasing anti-cartel enforcement in the automotive parts sector and the response of Japanese companies to such investigations in the US system:

> The story goes like this: 'I understand that you can always say no, but if you accept the request to go to jail, we'll support you 100 per cent', he said. 'If I fight and lose, I lose everything. But if I don't fight the company, the company will support me for the rest of my life'. Today Mr X has done his time and is back at work with his company.[42]

An antitrust defence lawyer in Tokyo is quoted as saying that the Japanese are lenient and want to take care of their employees; they often want to retain valuable employees, and there is a sense of solidarity arising from the Japanese cultural inclination towards lifetime employment.[43] At the same time, however, in addition to the pragmatic willingness to do a deal with the US authorities and sacrifice usually middle ranking executives, there is also a stubborn resolve on the part of senior executives to face out American enforcement as 'fugitives'. There are an increasing number of Japanese business persons retaining high-ranking

---

40   Christopher Harding and Julian Joshua, *Regulating Cartels in Europe* (2nd edn, Oxford University Press, 2010), at pp. 353–4. See also Dan Levine, 'You Went to Jail … But Howzabout Coming Back to Work for Us?', *The Recorder*, 12 April 2010.
41   Hans Gleimel, 'Confessions of a Price Fixer: Supplier Network Shelters Fugitives, Ex-cons', *Automotive News*, 16 November 2014.
42   Ibid.
43   Ibid.

and influential company positions, even though under indictment in the US,[44] presumably in the hope and expectation that extradition will not take place. Much of this evidence suggests a strong cultural tolerance of antitrust delinquency and a pragmatic acceptance of American enforcement as a business risk. In this regard there may be a significantly different impact and perception in the US compared to Japan, arising from differences in social and business culture. Baker reports on the comment of a senior American corporate executive:

> as long as you are only talking about money, the company can at the end of the day take care of me – but once you start talking about taking away my liberty, there is nothing that the company can do for me.[45]

Another instructive exercise would be to consider and assess the impact of the threat of sanctions on successful individual immunity applicants, although access to such data is naturally difficult. But, anecdotally, the fate of the two leading British players in the Art House Auctions Cartel is suggestive. Both Tennant and Davidge, along with Christie's as a company, benefited from immunity in dramatic contrast to their American counterparts, and although those two individuals had to leave Christie's, there is every indication that they continued to enjoy affluence and successful careers.[46] And therein perhaps lies the main lesson regarding individuals: the likes of Bryan Allison, Diana Brooks, Alfred Taubman and Japanese Mr X are like players in a game of musical chairs, who happen to be in the wrong place when the music suddenly stops. But that is a rare event, and for many individual cartelists there is a safe assumption of business as usual. This may not fit with the warning picture portrayed in some recent cartel cinema, such as *The Marker* and *Kom Forst*,[47] but the latter are depictions of the subject which are intended to support a particular message.

An enforcement minefield

Drawing upon the narratives of cartel activity and anti-cartel enforcement, and examining these narratives in terms of both corporate and individual agency and within both shorter and longer time frames, any conclusions suggest a rich diversity of outcome – both desistance and recalcitrance in different forms, complicated by a fluid state of corporate structuring and individual personal participation. This should perhaps be seen as both predictable and inevitable in an international and culturally diverse context. All this is well illustrated in the quotations at the start of

---

44   Ibid.
45   Donald I. Baker, 'The Use of Criminal Law Remedies to Deter and Punish Cartels and Bid-Rigging', 69 (2001) *George Washington Law Review* 693, at p. 705.
46   See Chapter 5 above, at p. 175.
47   See Appendix Three in Chapter 4.

this chapter, chosen to reveal the complexities of corporate structure and operation, of individual character, and of legal process. In short, the present assessment should be that this is an enforcement minefield, which should be navigated as such.

Appendix One: 'Cartel Cosying' in Different Economic Sectors

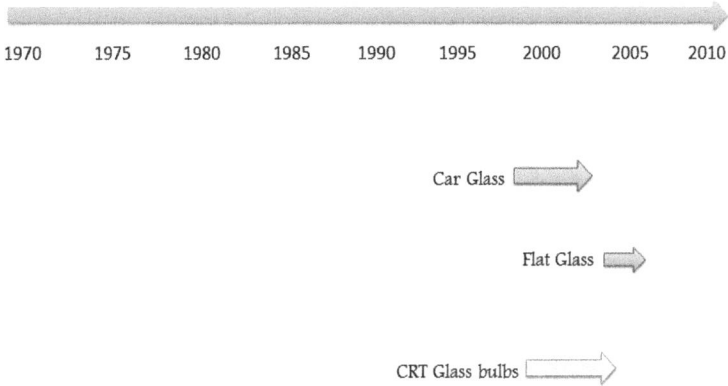

Figure 7.2(a) Pilkington Glass, Asahi Glass and St Gobain in the glass manufacturing sector

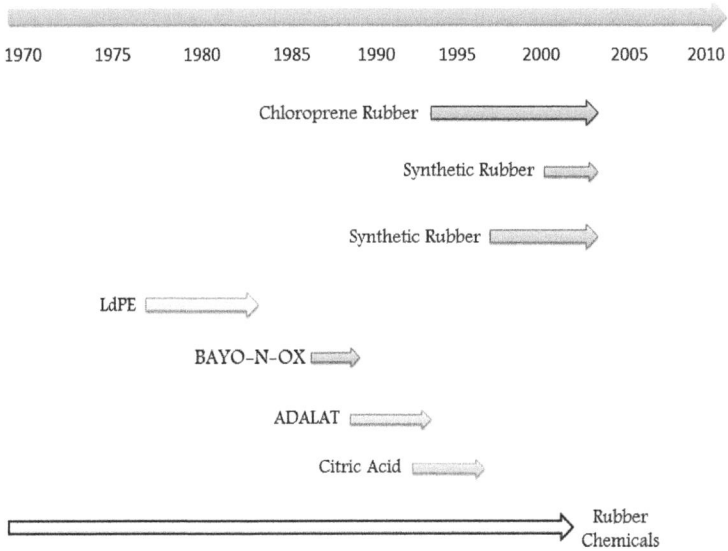

Figure 7.2(b) Bayer and Dow in the rubber products and chemicals sectors

Chapter 8
Tales of Cultural Diversity – How to Deal with the Dancing Giants?[1]

Lincoln County Road or Armageddon?

In drawing some final main conclusions from the discussion above, it is tempting to ask: what kind of battlefield, what kind of contest is this contemporary enterprise of regulation of business cartels and deployment of legal sanctions against such business actors? Is it a contest of fundamental beliefs, and a fight to the end, in the nature of an Armageddon, or is it a series of skirmishes involving particular economic interests, more in the nature of a nineteenth-century American frontier range war (such as the Lincoln County Range War in the late 1870s, which for purposes of analogy here,[2] involved warring economic groups on the New Mexico frontier, and brought in law enforcers, private 'regulators' and outlaw gangs)? The rhetoric of cartel regulation, as employed by politicians, policy makers and regulators, may suggest an Armageddon, but the verdict of history may see the contemporary regulatory battlefield as a range war kind of episode, and competition governance in the late twentieth and early twenty-first century as a zone akin to the south west American frontier in the late nineteenth century.[3]

---

1   'Dancing giant' was the metaphorical description used in relation to Asea Brown Boveri (ABB) in the work by Kevin Barham and Claudia Harmer, *ABB The Dancing Giant: Creating the Globally Interconnected Corporation* (Financial Times/Prentice Hall, 1998), but which may be appropriately applied to a number of the large transnational companies discussed in this study.

2   In Bob Dylan's *Señor (Tales of Yankee Power)* (1978), the question is posed: 'do you know where we're headin', Lincoln County Road or Armageddon?' Dylan's *Señor* is usually read as a reference to a search for direction in post-Vietnam War US, asking the way from the Third World (specifically, Mexico) – see Michael Gray, *Song and Dance Man III: The Art of Bob Dylan* (Cassell, 2000), at p. 216. Here, it may be used to convey the search for direction in anti-cartel regulation ('will there be any comfort there, señor?').

3   The metaphor and analogy with a late nineteenth-century range war may be appropriate in a number of ways. Like the subject of this study, such range wars as historical episodes have been subject to conflicting interpretation by historians, novelists and film-makers. There is also, in the case of the Lincoln County Range War, an earlier example of the American proclivity to plea bargaining and leniency in criminal justice. In 1879, New Mexico Governor Lew Wallace met with the outlaw William H. Bonney (aka Billy the Kid) and offered amnesty from criminal prosecution in return for testifying against other alleged offenders at a forthcoming trial. Bonney agreed to the deal and testified, but, according

The Lincoln County Range War involved a good deal of gunfire with uncertain outcomes, and it may be said that the verdict at present on the use of anti-cartel sanctions is much the same – sporadic bursts of gunfire, with a few immediate victims, but the final outcome is difficult to judge. In the previous chapter, the possibility was mooted that a major international company in the chemicals sector in recent years may have reformed, turned from being an antitrust recidivist into a compliant good citizen in the domain of competition governance. If that is so, it would still be uncertain how that had come about and what the more exact role of the application of different legal sanctions might have been in that transformation. The main lesson of this study is that the impact of such sanctions, especially at an international level, is variable, leading to what some may regard as an unsatisfactory or even evasive answer to the main research question. Sometimes, some sanctions may be effective and appropriate, sometimes some sanctions may not be so – it depends. Depends on what? The answer to that last question may be offered with more confidence: culture – and more exactly, social and political culture, business culture and enforcement culture. Hopefully, that argument and conclusion will be evident from what has been said in Chapter 6.

But, to make that point clearly, and to draw again on the narrative method employed in this study, some descriptions may be offered of the six narratives presented in Chapter 5, the main cartel biographies. The exercise will be to extract the salient narrative elements in those biographical accounts of cartels and present those elements in the form of media headlines[4] and summary narratives, a method which may be termed 'denouement analysis'.

Those six cartels may be regarded as similar in their basic form and employment of business strategies – suppliers in particular markets colluding through price fixing, market sharing, output control and bid rigging. Yet, it is clear from this presentation of denouements that the narrative of cartel activity and legal proceeding evolves in very different ways and with variable outcome. In short, cartel regulation at the international level does not follow in each case similar or parallel lines, and the happenstance of jurisdiction, market, and provenance of corporate and individual actors can have an important impact.

Arising from this observation and by way of a conclusion, four main points will be emphasised and briefly discussed:

- This is a field of activity bedevilled at present by major cultural differences, of the kind mentioned just above.
- There are major differences in enforcement process, in particular as between the US and Europe, in that in the former there is a preference for cutting a

---

to one account, the local district attorney then revoked the amnesty, according to another version, Governor Wallace refused to stand by the agreement (see Michael Wallis, *Billy the Kid: The Endless Ride* (W.W. Norton, 2007). Bonney escaped, to continue his outlaw career for a further two years.

4   As may be used, for instance, as the title of a leading newspaper article or report.

Table 8.1   The six biographies: Denouement analysis

Cartel	Headline and summary narrative
Soda Ash	CARTEL VETERAN FIGHTS ON! Belgian company Solvay, a long-standing and founding member of the Soda Ash Cartel, avoids a fine for its participation after 20 years of litigation in the European Courts.
Marine Hose	MARKETING MANAGERS PAY THE PRICE! After a classic international cartel was reported to American and European authorities by one of its members, fines and other sanctions, including prison terms, were imposed across a number of jurisdictions on those who negotiated and steered the operation.
Pre-Insulated Pipes	THE DANCING GIANT PROVOKES A SCANDI FIGHT-BACK! Bullying its way towards hegemony in the European district heating system market, an aggressive business is finally held to account.
Art House Auctions	TRANSATLANTIC EXECUTIVE FROLIC LEADS TO PERSONAL HUBRIS! A two-party elite cartel reveals the chances in the game for opportunistic turncoats and the risks for fallen heroes – whichever way these were bad apples at the top of the barrel.
Lysine	MAVERICK INSIDER BLOWS OPEN THE CARTEL! A crafty inside player comes unstuck and blows the whistle on a trans-Pacific business conspiracy, born of American intrusion into an East Asian dominated market, and the cartel is busted in a blaze of sanctions, revelations and celebration.
LCD Panels	FAR EASTERN CONSPIRACY IN THE DOCKS OF THE WESTERN COURTS! Heavy fines and prison terms are imposed on a group of self-aware Taiwanese and Korean producers who defy the open market ethos to maintain their role as market leaders.

deal (and keeping the story short) while in the latter there is a strong rights culture resulting in appellate sagas (and making the stories long).

- International cartel regulation is not a domain of methodological individualism but more one of complex corporate agency, wherein the challenge is to know how to deal with 'dancing giants'.
- Taking on board this picture of diversity and complexity, there are lessons here for any project of achieving compliance with policy, in that policy makers and law makers need to be sensitive to the normative understandings of the societies within which enforcement takes place.

It is too easy, in reductive economic and legal analysis, to see all business cartels as basically and generically the same and to argue as a matter of policy that they should be dealt with as such. Historical and empirical evidence, however, suggests that they are more idiosyncratic in their motivation and modes of operation, and this needs to be appreciated in deciding upon policy and in selecting strategies of legal control.

Cultural diversity

What has emerged strongly from the material collected in this biographical study of major international business cartels is a context of cultural diversity, in terms of business practice and attitudes, and also in terms of legal system, criminal justice and enforcement strategy. From the second half of the twentieth century, the policy against business cartels has been fuelled especially by the dominating trade liberalisation agenda and supported in particular by American policy and practice, while an established tradition of business collaboration has provided a site of resistance in Europe and elsewhere. Also, in the area of competition governance, American antitrust policy and its legal implementation have different origins and preoccupations compared to competition law elsewhere, and in Europe in particular. Finally, as a matter of legal implementation, there are significant differences between American and European approaches in criminal law and criminal justice – a strong tendency towards plea negotiation and trial avoidance in the US system, compared to a strong rights culture and resort to appellate process in Europe, and a ready resort to criminalisation in the US compared to an established preference in the regulatory sphere for 'administrative' penality in continental Europe.

On the particular question of anti-cartel sanctions enough has been said above to confirm the distinctive American legal and enforcement culture, both in terms of rhetoric, evident as far back as the seminal 'Roosevelt Letter' in 1944, and in terms of actual legal outcomes, which is strongly evident in the biographical studies above. What needs to be emphasised – as something which in some respects is less evident to the outside world – are the sites of resistance to such hard-hitting anti-cartel enforcement, whether in the form of European legal culture or Japanese business and social culture, as discussed at a number of points above. And to emphasise that point, a few more words may be said about the different traditions and legal preferences in the European context.

It is worth stressing the differing historical origins of antitrust in the US and *competition regulation* in Europe, and in particular the historical tolerance of and even support for cartelisation in Europe. It is worth recalling that a number of the prominent 'usual suspect' corporate cartelists in Europe have a long history of collusive business tradition. Table 8.2 below briefly illustrates the origin and heritage of a number of European companies as successors to the participants in the leading early twentieth-century *Interessengemeinschaft*, IG Farben.

Table 8.2   *Interessengemeinschaft* heritage

The successor companies of IG Farben, after it was dismantled in 1951, were to emerge as prolific European corporate cartelists. The four largest were quick to purchase the smaller ones, and presently Agfa, BASF, and Bayer remain. Hoechst demerged its industrial chemical operations to Celanese, then merged its life-sciences businesses with that of Rhône-Poulenc to form Aventis in 1999. A third part of Hoechst's operations was sold in 1997 to the Swiss Sandoz subsidiary, Clariant. Of these companies, all but Celanese and Agfa have been involved in European cartels within the last 30 years.

	Company name				
	BASF	**Hoechst**	**Aventis**	**Bayer**	**Clariant**
Peroxides					
Polypropylene	X	X			
PVC	X	X			
LdPE	X	X		X	
Heat Stabilisers	X				
Butadiene Rubber				X	
Nitrile Butadiene				X	
Chloroprene Rubber				X	
Rubber Chemicals				X	
Vitamins			X		
Monochloroacetic Acid					X

(CARTEL labels the rows LdPE through Butadiene Rubber)

Taking this narrative closer to the present time, there is the telling episode of the North Sea Shrimp Cartel. This was an arrangement originating in the Netherlands in the late 1990s, extending to Germany and Denmark, eventually covering the market in Belgium, France Germany and the Netherlands, involving wholesalers and a number of producer associations. The arrangement was dealt with first by the Dutch Competition Authority in 2003 in respect of its operation between 1998 and 2000, and administrative fines totalling €13.8 million were imposed.[5]

5   Netherlands Competition Authority (NMa) posting, 14 January 2003, www.acm.nl.

However, following appeals through the Dutch courts, these fines were eventually reduced by the Dutch Trade and Industry Appeal Tribunal to €4.4 million in 2011, one of the grounds for reduction being the fact that the shrimp traders had some understanding that the Dutch Government was not averse, in the context of the former EU agricultural exemption in relation to competition enforcement, to measures taken to limit the supply of shrimps. But following the imposition of the fines and the during the time the appeals were being dealt with, many of the same companies continued the cartel operation, and this continuation cartel, in action from 2000 until 2009, was then dealt with by the European Commission in a decision of November 2013. The Commission imposed a total of Euro 18 million in fines and expressed astonishment at the determined and detailed operation of the Cartel, even following the clear warning given to the companies by the earlier decision of the Dutch authority.[6] This case expresses nicely a sense of recalcitrance and some ambivalence in the European context.[7]

In the European context there is an ongoing debate relating to the need for and desirability of criminal law sanctions in relation to cartel infringements. Part of this arises from the well-established alternative model of administrative penalty in continental European jurisdictions, well exemplified now in the EU system of competition regulation. Theoretically, there is now the possibility that Article 83(2) of the Treaty on the Functioning of the European Union (TFEU) could be used as the legal basis for an EU directive requiring the use of criminal law at the Member State level in relation to cartel activity, as something which would be necessary for proper implementation of EU policy.[8] But there is scant indication of such a legal move, and it should be anticipated that European reserve on this question will to a large extent be maintained.

Enforcement proclivities: What is the sheriff's preference?

Arising from these cultural differences, there is the crucial dichotomy in legal enforcement: on the one hand, a readiness to use criminal law and in a very pragmatic fashion not to waste time in doing so, and thus to negotiate an outcome

---

6   Commission decision, 27 November 2013, Press Release IP/13/1175.

7   See also the discussion by Pieter Kalbfleisch, Director-General of the Netherlands Competition Authority, explaining a preference for administrative over criminal law sanctions in this context: 'Criminal competition sanctions in the Netherlands', chapter 8 in Katalin J. Cseres et al. (eds), *Criminalization of Competition Law Enforcement* (Edward Elgar, 2006).

8   See, for instance Jacob Òberg, 'Union Regulatory Criminal Law Competence after the Lisbon Treaty', 19 (2011) *European Journal of Crime, Criminal Law and Criminal Justice* 289; Aaron Khan, 'Rethinking Sanctions for Breaching EU Competition Law: Is Director Disqualification the Answer?' 35 (2012) *World Competition 77*. Both authors express doubt as to whether the criteria for action under Article 83(2) would be satisfied.

and not go to full trial; on the other hand, to be reserved on the use of criminal law, but be transparent and give the defence the fullest opportunity to present its case in the legal process. In the context of the present study and its methodology, this has led to another significant outcome. The first approach involves a shorter and more hidden story, a foreclosure of the narrative, or at least the public telling of the tale. The cartelist may not have his or her day in court and a full political and normative examination and evaluation of the subject is side-stepped. The second approach involves a longer, fuller and more transparent story, evidenced in both formal legal decisions and court proceedings, sometimes even to the extent of an enforcement and legal saga (20 years or more talking about soda ash!) In that context, the cartelist is better able to tell the inside story to the rest of the world.

These differing enforcement proclivities result in sometimes different outcomes and often a very different experience in particular cases. But more generally, there is an important and different result in a systemic sense, one which affects not only the potential for research into the matter (the experience here) but also the opportunity for a critical and continuing examination and assessment of policy and its legal implementation. The possibility that certain narratives may be lost or missed, especially the inside account by the cartelist, is an important issue for healthy policy and legal development.

The complexities of corporate agency

There may a great deal of difference in dealing with a local cartel of taxi drivers, or businesses comprising single or a small group of people, and dealing with a cartel comprising large transnational companies operating in a context of international trade. The focus of this study, and underlying it of efforts of legal regulation, has been the latter, for fairly obvious reasons. But the international context has its own challenges and complexities, not the least of which is the problem of dealing, as a matter of both policy and law, with large corporate actors, whose reach across markets is widespread and economically significant (recall the metaphor of the octopus so loved by political cartoonists attacking the original American trusts)[9] and whose economic and legal structures are very complex. This is the problem of responding to the activities of the 'dancing giants'.

Again there is considerable evidence from the biographical accounts of this special challenge to enforcement efforts, and a lesson regarding the deployment of criminal law and criminal law sanctions in this context of grand scale competition governance. Criminal law, in its conventional (Western) model, is rooted in an ideology of methodological individualism – the assumption that the relevant actor and agent, the subject of the allocation of responsibility and the imposition of

---

9   See the illustrations in Chapter 2.

sanctions, is the single human individual.[10] The domain of the dancing giant is a much less penetrable area of activity and conduct, comprising a mix of human and collective action which may be difficult to disentangle, to prove and to understand. This again stands as an important lesson for policy makers, economist and lawyers, and those involved in the design and the implementation of any kind of normative provision and accompanying sanctions.

Models of compliance

A final lesson to be urged at this point brings together these conclusions regarding cultural diversity, enforcement preferences, and complexities of agency. Much of this discussion has been concerned essentially with ensuring compliance with certain norms and how certain methods of enforcement may be used for that purpose. Enforcement and compliance are related concepts and phenomena: enforcement may be seen as aiming at compliance (in the future), yet at the same time compliance (in the present) should determine the need for and nature of enforcement. Most importantly, it should be remembered that compliance in fact precedes enforcement and perhaps does so most of the time. Much normative compliance occurs automatically and naturally and without effort; in practice, it is only when compliance does not take place that there is any real need to talk about enforcement. One way of expressing this point is to say that much compliance with norms is 'bottom-up', coming from below as an expression of a strong and established sense of values and desired behaviour (in which case criminal and other prescriptive law serves as an expression of such values), while a certain (and probably lesser amount) of compliance is 'top-down', when it is necessary to enforce adherence to such values from above, and this is achieved through the mechanism of criminal or other prescriptive law.

This observation becomes more easily evident by taking up the valuable analysis offered by the criminologist Anthony Bottoms in his 'typology' of legal compliance mechanisms.[11] Bottoms identifies four main types of compliance:[12]

- Instrumental or prudential compliance, inspired by a rational calculation of self-interest.
- Constraint-based compliance (there are natural and circumstantial obstacles to non-compliant conduct).

---

10   See the discussion for instance in Christopher Harding, *Criminal Enterprise: Individuals, Organisations and Criminal Responsibility* (Willan Publishing, 2007).

11   A.E. Bottoms, 'Morality, Crime, Compliance and Public Policy', in A.E. Bottoms and M. Tonry (eds), *Ideology, Crime and Criminal Justice: A Symposium in Honour of Sir Leon Radzinowicz* (Willan Publishing, 2002), at p. 23.

12   Ibid., p. 42 *et seq.*

- Normative compliance, as a response to principles or standards which reflect people's expectations of behaviour and serves to regulate action and judgment.
- Compliance based on habit or routine, which is almost automatic in nature.

Or, the four types may be expressed more colloquially as:

- 'I comply because I fear otherwise the application of a sanction.'
- 'I comply because circumstances do not allow me to do otherwise.'
- 'I comply because that is the right thing to do.'
- 'I comply because to do so has been inculcated in my nature.'

From this typology, it might be argued that the third kind of compliance, normative compliance, is the most healthy, in that is based on a critical and thought-out acceptance of the norm or standard, and that may be the optimal state of compliance to aim for in a healthily functioning society or polity. Indeed, a strong need for instrumental compliance, on the other hand, may be a measure of a society or polity that is not functioning well. Bottoms goes on to argue that, to ensure compliance, any enforcement policy should be sufficiently informed about and sensitive to the normative understandings of the society in which compliance of whatever kind is sought and enforcement may be required.[13]

Applying this analysis and reasoning to the regulation of cartel activity, especially in an international context, there is a clear lesson. Whatever the political or economic force underlying a policy, if the intention is to give effect to that policy globally, then its likely reception in different places and within different cultures needs to be considered and understood. If the evidence suggests that the reception may not be the same in the US, in the Netherlands, and in Japan, then that evidence should be examined and the differing outcomes appreciated and understood. And, to return to the line of enquiry raised in the first part of the book – the subjects of regulation need to be convinced by the pathology and mythology of the subject presented by the regulators.

Also, it may be argued, those who construct and contribute to the pathology and mythology should be aware of their own role as actors on this stage. A worthwhile historical question is the following: when did the term 'cartel' become a dirty word, something much more pejorative than 'das Kartellproblem' – when did 'cartel' acquire derogatory equivalence with the American 'trust' (as in antitrust)? This is an important and useful question for a criminological enquiry, even if it has been skated over in much of the economic and legal analysis. One possible answer, in the European context, and for those who like their history neat, is – at the turn of the 1960s and 1970s. The subject can be viewed in that light.

To finally illustrate these points of argument, perhaps the last word should be that of a cartelist, speaking from experience. Keith Packer, one-time executive

---

13   Ibid., at p. 43.

with British Airways and convicted and sentenced to a prison term in the US for his role in the Air Cargo Cartel, had the following to say as a former member of the professional community in which it was sought to promote compliance with anti-cartel norms: he asserted that competition compliance

> is a very dry, boring subject for commercial people who have much higher priorities.[14]

If that indeed is the culture of reception, then the kind of legal outcome described in the narratives above should come as no surprise.

---

14   As quoted in Eric Larson, 'Ex-BA Executive Shares Prison Tales to Sway Violators', *Bloomberg*, 22 October, 2010.

Postscript

Having relied so determinedly on the narrative method in this research, and stated in the Preface to the book that what is said here will certainly not provide the end of the story or the last word on the subject, it would be appropriate to add this short postscript on the absence of finality in the present discussion, and hopefully provide a link between the present and the future.

The point has been made forcefully enough that the present operation of anti-cartel sanctions appears uncertain, and much less straightforward and less understood than the more confident comments and assertions of a number of policy-makers, regulators, lawyers and economists would suggest. Taking a close and critical view of how the whole process of legal control of business cartels has developed over the last half-century, it may finally be asked whether it will be easy to address this situation of complexity and uncertainty. And one reason for having some doubt on that score might lie in the dynamic and the set of interests which now appear to be well established in the international context of anti-cartel enforcement. More specifically any argument which urges some kind of reverse in the present process – to ease up, to become softer or more consensual – is unlikely to command much support in the near future. First of all, such a course would not accord with the presently dominant imperative of the open or free market, especially at the international level. But there may now be also some significant vested interest – in particular of enforcement agencies collecting huge fines, whether in the form of criminal law or administrative penalties, of lawyers in advising powerful corporate clients, and of large businesses exploiting or gaming the enforcement system for profit. In that sense, the ongoing battle, especially if characterised as a range war as above, may be in itself an attractive prospect for many of its participants.

This last observation, it is suggested, gives an idea of how the story may continue – or, rather, what may emerge as a significant narrative among a number of possible narratives – and therefore what might be worthy of a future agenda of research.

Bibliography

This bibliography lists books, articles and reports which have been referred to in the discussion and have been used as major sources in secondary literature to inform the discussion and argument.

Anwar, S.T., 'ASEA Brown Boveri (ABB): What Went Wrong?', entry in H. Deresky, *International Management: Managing across Borders and Cultures* (5th edn, Pearson Education International, 2006), at pp. 304–7.

Ashenfelter, O. and Graddy, K., 'Anatomy of the Rise and Fall of a Price-Fixing Conspiracy: Auctions at Sotheby's and Christie's', 1 (2005) *Journal of Competition Law and Economics* 3.

Ashraf, N., Camerer, C.F. and Loewenstein, G., 'Adam Smith: Behavioral Economist', 19 (2005) *Journal of Economic Perspectives* 131.

Austin, A., 'A Price-Fixer's Memoir: Exculpation and Revenge while Confronting the Antitrust Abyss: An Essay on *Threshold Resistance* by Alfred Taubman', *The Antitrust Source*, October 2008.

Baker, D.I., 'The Use of Criminal Law Remedies to Deter and Punish Cartels and Bid-Rigging', 69 (2001) *George Washington Law Review* 693.

Bal, M., *Travelling Concepts in the Humanities: A Rough Guide* (University of Toronto Press, 2002).

Bal, M., *Narratology: Introduction to the Theory of Narrative* (3rd edn, University of Toronto Press, 2009).

Barham, K. and Heimer, C., *ABB The Dancing Giant: Creating the Globally Interconnected Corporation* (Financial Times/Prentice Hall, 1998).

Barker, G., 'The Fall of Dede Brooks', *The Telegraph*, 6 January 2001.

Bauer, J.P., 'Reflections on the Manifold Means of Enforcing the Antitrust Laws: Too Much, Too Little, or Just Right?', 16 (2004) *Loyola Consumer Law Review* 303.

Beaton-Wells, C. and Ezrachi, A. (eds), *Criminalising Cartels: A Critical Interdisciplinary Study of an International Regulatory Movement* (Hart Publishing, 2011).

Beaton-Wells, C., Edwards, J. and Harding, C., 'Leniency and Criminal Sanctions in Anti-Cartel Enforcement: Happily Married or Uneasy Bedfellows?', in C. Beaton-Wells (ed.), *The Leniency Religion: Anti-Cartel Enforcement in a Contemporary Age* (Hart Publishing, 2015).

Bottoms, A.E., 'Morality, Crime, Compliance and Public Policy', chapter 2 in A.E. Bottoms and M. Tonry (eds), *Ideology, Crime and Criminal Justice: A Symposium in Honour of Sir Leon Radzinowicz* (Willan Publishing, 2002).

Budzinski, O. 'Monoculture versus Diversity in Competition Economics', 32 (2008) *Cambridge Journal of Economics* 295.

Calvani, T. and Calvani, T.H., 'Custodial Sanctions for Cartel Offences: An Appropriate Sanction in Australia?', 17 (2009) *Competition and Consumer Law Journal* 119.

Chandler, A.D., *Scale and Scope: The Dynamics of Industrial Capitalism* (Harvard University Press, 1994).

Cheffins, B.R., 'Corporations', chapter 23 in P. Cane and M. Tushnett (eds), *The Oxford Handbook of Legal Studies* (Oxford University Press, 2003).

Clarke, J.L. and Evenett, S.J., 'The Deterrent Effects of National Antitrust Laws: Evidence from the International Vitamins Cartel', 48 (2003) *The Antitrust Bulletin* 689.

Combe, E. and Monnier, C., 'Fines against Hard Core Cartels in Europe: The Myth of Over Enforcement', 56 (2011) *The Antitrust Bulletin* 235.

Coffee Jnr, J., '"No Soul to Damn; No Body to Kick": An Unscandalized Inquiry into the Problem of Corporate Punishment', 79 (1981) *Michigan Law Review* 386.

Conley, J.M. and O'Barr, W.M., 'Crime and Custom in Corporate Society: A Cultural Perspective on Corporate Misconduct', 60 (1997) *Law and Contemporary Problems* 5.

Connor, J.M., 'What Can We Learn from the ADM Global Price Conspiracies?', Staff Paper #98–14, August 1998, Department of Agricultural Economics, Purdue University.

Connor, J.M., 'Recidivism Revealed: Private International Cartels 1990–2009', (2010) *Competition Policy International* 101.

Cox, H., 'The Anglo-American Tobacco War of 1901–02: A Clash of Business Cultures and Strategies', unpublished paper, Business History Conference, 21–23 March 2013, Columbus, Ohio.

Cseres, K.J., Schinkel, M.P. and Vogelaar, F.O.W. (eds), *Criminalization of Competition Law Enforcement: Economic and Legal Implications for the EU Member States* (Edward Elgar, 2006).

Davies, S. and Ormosi, P., 'A Comparative Assessment of Methodologies Used to Evaluate Competition Policy', 8 (2012) *Journal of Competition Law and Economics* 765.

Davies, P. and Garcés, E., *Quantitative Techniques for Competition and Antitrust Analysis* (Princeton University Press, 2009).

Deloitte and Touche for the Office of Fair Trading, 'The Deterrent Effect of Competition Enforcement by the OFT', Office of Fair Trading, OFT 962, 2007.

Dicey, A.V., *Law and Public Opinion in England* (2nd edn, 1914).

Drabble, M., *The Sea Lady* (Penguin Books, 2006).

Eichenwald, K., *The Informer* (Broadway Books, 2000).

Eichenwald, K., *The Informant: A True Story of Greed, Conspiracy and Whistleblowing* (Portobello Books, 2009).

European Commission, *Guidelines on the Method for Setting Fines* (2006) OJ C210/2.

European Commission, Communication: 'Towards and EU Criminal Policy: Ensuring the Effective Implementation of EU Policies through Criminal Law', COM (2011) 573 final.

Fear, J., 'Cartels and Competition: Neither Markets nor Hierarchies', Harvard University Working Papers, October 2006.

Fletcher, G.P., *Basic Concepts of Criminal Law* (Oxford University Press, 1998).

Garfield, S., *Mauve* (Faber and Faber, 2000).

Garnett, N.S., 'Relocating Disorder', 91 (2005) *Virginia Law Review* 1075.

Gerber, D.J., *Law and Competition in Twentieth Century Europe: Protecting Prometheus* (Oxford University Press, 1998, 2001).

Gleimel, H., 'Confessions of a Price Fixer: Supplier Network Shelters Fugitives, Ex-Cons', *Automotive News*, 16 November 2014.

Goyder, D.G., Goyder, J. and Albors-Llorens, A., *Goyder's EC Competition Law* (5th edn, Oxford University Press, 2009).

Grout, P.A. and Sonderegger, S., 'Predicting Cartels: Discussion Paper', Office of Fair Trading, OFT 773, March 2005.

Hammond, S.D., 'From Hollywood to Hong Kong: Criminal Antitrust Enforcement is Coming to a City near You', Address, 9 November 2001, Chicago. Available at: Department of Justice, http://www.justice.gov/atr.

Harding, C., 'Vingt ans après: Rainbow Warrior, Legal Ordering, and Legal Complexity', 10 (2006) *Singapore Yearbook of International Law* 99.

Harding, C., *Criminal Enterprise: Individuals, Organisations and Criminal Responsibility* (Willan Publishing, 2007).

Harding, C., 'Cartel Deterrence: The Search for Evidence and Argument', 56 (2011) *The Antitrust Bulletin* 345.

Harding, C., 'The Interplay of Criminal and Administrative Law in the Context of Market Regulation: The Case of Serious Competition Infringements', chapter 9 in V. Mitsilegas, P. Alldridge and L. Cheliotis (eds), *Globalisation, Criminal Law and Criminal Justice: Theoretical, Comparative and Transnational Perspectives* (Hart Publishing, 2015).

Harding, C., 'The Relationship between EU Criminal Law and Competition Law', in V. Mitsilegas, M. Bergstrom and T. Konstadinides (eds), *Research Handbook on EU Criminal Law* (Edward Elgar, forthcoming, 2016).

Harding, C. and Edwards, J., *Project: Explaining and Understanding Cartel Collusion*, Leverhulme Trust funded project (2015), website at: http://www.aber.ac.uk/en/law-criminology/research/research-clusters/global-commerce/cartel-collusion.

Harding, C. and Gibbs, A., 'Why Go to Court in Europe? An Analysis of Cartel Appeals, 1995–2004', 30 (2005) *European Law Review* 349.

Harding, C. and Joshua, J., *Regulating Cartels in Europe* (2nd edn, Oxford University Press, 2010).

Hayes, P., 'Carl Bosch and Carl Klauch: Chemistry and the Political Economy of Germany, 1925–1945', 47 (1987) *The Journal of Economic History* 353.

Hayes, P., *Industry and Ideology: IG Farben in the Nazi Era* (2nd edn, Cambridge University Press, 2000).

Herman, D. (ed.), *Cambridge Introduction to Narrative* (Cambridge University Press, 1997).

Hexner, E., *International Cartels* (Pitman, 1946).

Imperial Tobacco, *The Imperial Story 1901–2001: Celebrating One Hundred Years* (Imperial Tobacco, 2001).

Jamieson, K.M., *The Organization of Corporate Crime: Dynamics of Antitrust Violation* (Sage Publications, 1994).

Jensen-Eriksen, N., 'Disband or Go Underground? The Nordic Pulp and Paper Export Cartels and European Competition Policies, 1970–1995', unpublished paper, 11th Annual Conference of the European Business History Association, September 2007, Geneva.

Joliet, R., *The Rule of Reason in Antitrust Law: American, German and Common Market Law in Comparative Perspective* (Martinus Nijhoff, 1967).

Jones, F.D., 'Historical Development of the Law of Business Competition', 35 (1926) *Yale Law Journal* 905.

Joshua, J.M., 'Attitudes to Antitrust Enforcement in the EU and the United States: Dodging the Traffic Warden or Respecting the Law?', 1995 *Fordham Corporate Law Institute* 101.

Kahneman, D., *Thinking Fast and Slow* (Penguin Books, 2011).

Kalbfleisch, P., 'Criminal Competition Sanctions in the Netherlands', chapter 18 in K.J. Cseres et al. (eds), *Criminalization of Competition Law Enforcement* (Edward Elgar, 2006).

Karlson, B., 'Cartels in the Swedish Forest Industry in the Interwar Period', chapter 13 in S.-O. Olsson (ed.), *Managing Crises and Deglobalisation* (Routledge, 2010).

Khan, A., 'Rethinking Sanctions for Breaching EU Competition Law: Is Director Disqualification the Answer?', 35 (2012) *World Competition* 77.

Klein, J.I., 'The War against International Cartels: Lessons from the Battlefront', *Fordham Corporate Law Institute*, 26th Annual Conference, International Antitrust Law and Policy, 14 October 1999, New York.

Knottnerus, R., *AkzoNobel: Overview of Controversial Business Practices, 2008* (SOMO, 2009).

Korah, V., *Monopolies and Restrictive Practices* (Penguin Books, 1968).

Kotsiris, L.E., 'An Antitrust Case in Ancient Greek Law', 22 (1988) *International Law* 451.

Kozul-Wright, R. and Rayment, P., *The Resistible Rise of Market Fundamentalism: Rethinking Development Policy in an Unbalanced World* (Zed Books, 2007).

Landes, D.S., *The Unbound Prometheus: Technological Change and Industrial Development in Western Europe from 1750 to the Present* (Cambridge University Press, 1969).

Lantschner, P., 'Justice Contested and Affirmed: Jurisdiction and Conflict in Late Medieval Italian Cities', chapter 3 in Fernanda Pirie and Judith Scheele (eds), *Legalism: Community and Justice* (Oxford University Press, 2014).

Larson, E., 'Ex-BA Executive Shares Prison Tales to Sway Violators', *Bloomberg*, 22 October, 2010.

Leibowitz, J., 'The Good, the Bad and the Ugly: Trade Associations and Antitrust', American Bar Association, Antitrust Spring Meeting, 30 March 2005, Washington DC. Available at: https://www.ftc.gov.

Lee, H., *Biography: A Very Short Introduction* (Oxford University Press, 2009).

Levi-Faur, D., 'Regulatory Capitalism and the Reassertion of the Public Interest', 27 (2009) *Policy and Society* 181.

Lieber, J., *Rats in the Grain: The Dirty Tricks and Trials of Archer Daniels Midland, the Supermarket to the World* (Basic Books, 2002).

Liman, A.L., 'The Paper Label Sentences: Critique', 86 (1977) *Yale Law Journal* 619.

London Economics, 'The Impact of Competition Interventions on Compliance and Deterrence – Final Report', OFT 1391, December 2011.

McGowan, L., *The Antitrust Revolution in Europe: Exploring the European Commission's Cartel Policy* (Edward Elgar, 2010).

Mann, F.A., 'The Dyestuffs Case in the Court of Justice of the European Communities', 22 (1973) *International and Comparative Law Quarterly* 35.

Marx, L.M., Mezzetti, C. and Marshall, R.C., 'Antitrust Leniency with Multi-Product Colluders', (2014) *American Economic Journal* 1.

Mason, C., *The Art of the Steal: Inside the Sotheby's – Christie's Auction House Scandal* (Putnam Publishing, 2004).

Monti, G., *EC Competition Law* (Cambridge University Press, 2007).

Monti, M., 'Fighting Cartels – Why and How?', Opening Address at the Third Nordic Competition Policy Conference, 11 September 2000, Stockholm. Available at: http://www.konkurrensverket/se.

Nesmith, M., *Total Control* (from the album *The Newer Stuff* (Rhino, 1989)).

Neyrinck, N., 'Granting Incentives, Deterring Collusion: The Leniency Policy', Working Paper 2/2009, Institut d'Etudes Juridiques Européennes (IEJE), p. 15.

Öberg, J., 'Union Regulatory Criminal Law Competence after the Lisbon Treaty', 19 (2011) *European Journal of Crime, Criminal Law and Criminal Justice* 289.

OECD, *Sanctions against Individuals*, Roundtable discussion paper (OECD, 2005).

OECD, *Collusion and Corruption in Public Procurement*, Roundtable discussion paper, 15 October 2010, DAF/COMP/GF (2010) 6.

O'Kane, M., 'Does Prison Work for Cartelists?: The View from behind Bars', 56 (2011) *The Antitrust Bulletin* 483.

Oxera, 'Flat Screens, Raised Prices: Pursuing the Global LCD Cartel', *Agenda*, March 2013.

Packer, K., 'A Cautionary Tale: How a Competition Law Breach Led to a Jail Term for One BA Exec', *Legal Week*, 22 September 2011.

Parlast, G., 'How a Few Little Piggies Tried to Rig the Market', *The Guardian*, 25 October 1998.

Parker, C., 'The Compliance Trap: The Moral Message in Regulatory Enforcement', 40 (2006) *Law and Society Review* 591.

Pasano, M.S., Calli, P.A. and Descalzo, M., 'An Antitrust Case History'. Available at: http://apps.americanbar.org.

Peers, A., 'Five Years Après le Sotheby's vs. Christie's Scandale', *New York Magazine* 2007.

Piotrowski, R., *Cartels and Trust: Their Origin and Historical Development from the Economic and Legal Aspects* (George Allen & Unwin, 1933).

Polletta, F., 'Contending Stories: Narrative in Social Movements', 21 (1998) *Qualitative Sociology* 419.

Riley, A., 'The Consequences of the European Cartel-Busting Revolution', 12 (2005) *Irish Journal of European Law* 3.

Rodensky, L., *The Crime in Mind: Criminal Responsibility and the Victorian Novel* (Oxford University Press, 2003).

Schröter, H.G., 'Competition and Cooperation or Why Japan Was Not Included into the International Dyestuffs Cartel 1929–1939: A New Explanation Based on Communication', 50th Congress of Business History Society of Japan (2014). Available at: http://bhs.ssoj.info.

Sokol, D., 'Cartels, Corporate Compliance, and What Practitioners Really Think about Enforcement', 78 (2012) *Antitrust Law Journal* 201, p. 212.

Spar, D., *The Cooperative Edge: The Internal Politics of International Cartels* (Cornell University Press, 1994).

Spivack, G.B., *Comparative Aspects of Anti-Trust Law* (BIICL, 1963).

Starbuck, W.H., 'The Origins of Organization Theory', chapter 5 in Haridimos Tsoukas and Christian Knudsen (eds), *The Oxford Handbook of Organization Theory* (Oxford University Press, 2003).

Stewart, J.B., 'Bidding War: How an Antitrust Investigation into Christie's and Sotheby's Became a Race to See Who Could Betray Whom', *The New Yorker*, 15 October 2001, 158.

Stephan, A., 'An Empirical Assessment of the European Leniency Notice', 5 (2008) *Journal of Competition Law and Economics* 537.

Stocking, G.W. and Watkins, M.W., *Cartels in Action: Case Studies in International Business Diplomacy* (The Twentieth Century World Fund, 1946).

Stucke, M.E., 'Behavioral Economists at the Gate: Antitrust in the 21st Century', 38 (2007) *Loyola University Chicago Law Journal* 513.

Stucke, M.E., 'Am I a Price Fixer? A Behavioural Economics Analysis of Cartels', chapter 12 in C. Beaton-Wells and A. Ezrachi (eds), *Criminalising Cartels: A Critical Interdisciplinary Study of an International Regulatory Movement* (Hart Publishing, 2011).

Sullivan, E.T. (ed.), *The Political Economy of the Sherman Act* (Oxford University Press, 1991).

Suslow, V.Y., 'Cartel Contract Duration: Empirical Evidence from Interwar International Cartels', 14 (2005) *Industrial and Corporate Change* 705.

Tarbell, I.M., *The History of the Standard Oil Company* (McClure, Phillips & Co, 1904).

Taubman, A., *Threshold Resistance: The Extraordinary Career of a Luxury Retailer Pioneer* (Harper Business, 2007).

Teubner, G. (ed.), *Juridification of Social Spheres* (de Gruyter, 1987).

Tuckett, D., *Minding the Markets* (Palgrave Macmillan, 2011).

Van Gerven, G. and Navarro Varona, E. 'The *Wood Pulp* Case and the Future of Concerted Practices', 31 (1994) *Common Market Law Review* 575.

Veljanovski, C., 'A Statistical Analysis of UK Antitrust Enforcement', 10 (2014) *Journal of Competition Law and Economics* 1.

Wardaugh, B., *Cartels, Markets and Crime: A Normative Justification for the Criminalisation of Economic Collusion* (Cambridge University Press, 2014).

Warin, F.J., Burns, D.P. and Chesley, J.W.F., 'To Plead or Not to Plead? Reviewing a Decade of Criminal Antitrust Trials', *The Antitrust Source*, July 2006, 5.

Wells, C., *Corporations and Criminal Responsibility* (2nd edn, Oxford University Press, 2001).

Wells, C., 'Corporate Crime: Opening the Eyes of the Sentry', 30 (2010) *Legal Studies* 370.

Werden, G.J., in 'Sanctioning Cartel Activity: Let the Punishment Fit the Crime', 5 (2009) *European Competition Journal* 19.

Werden, G.J., Hammond, Scott D. and Barnett, B.A. 'Recidivism Eliminated: Cartel Enforcement in the United States since 1999' (US Department of Justice, September 2011).

Whelan, P., *The Criminalization of European Cartel Enforcement: Theoretical, Legal and Practical Challenges* (Oxford University Press, 2014).

Wigger, A., 'Towards a Market-Based Approach: The Privatization and Micro-Economization of EU Antitrust Law Enforcement', in H. Overbeek et al. (eds), *The Transnational Politics of Corporate Governance Regulation* (Routledge, 2007), at p. 98.

Wilks, S., 'Cartel Criminalisation as Juridification: Political and Regulatory Dangers', chapter 15 in C. Beaton-Wells and A. Ezrachi (eds), *Criminalising Cartels: Critical Studies of an International Regulatory Movement* (Hart Publishing, 2011), at pp. 350–51.

Wils, W.P.J., 'Is Criminalization of EU Competition Law the Answer?' 28 (2005) *World Competition* 148.

Wils, W.P.J., 'Is Criminalization of EU Competition Law the Answer?', chapter 4 in K.J. Cseres, M.P. Schinkel and F.O.W Vogelaar (eds), *Criminalization of Competition Law Enforcement* (Edward Elgar, 2006).

Wils, W.P.J., *Efficiency and Justice in European Antitrust Enforcement* (Hart Publishing, 2008).

Wils, W.P.J. 'Recidivism in EU Antitrust Enforcement: A Legal and Economic Analysis', 35 (2012) *World Competition* 5.

Wilson, C., *The History of Unilever* (Cassell, 1954).

Wilson, J.F., *British Business History, 1720–1994* (Manchester University Press, 1995).

Yamazaki, H. and Miyamoto M. (eds), *Trade Associations in Business History: The International Conference on Business History 14* (University of Tokyo Press, 1988).

Name Index

Subject Index